Secularists, Religion and Government
in Nineteenth-Century America

Timothy Verhoeven

Secularists, Religion and Government in Nineteenth-Century America

palgrave
macmillan

Timothy Verhoeven
Monash University
Clayton, VIC, Australia

ISBN 978-3-030-02876-3   ISBN 978-3-030-02877-0 (eBook)
https://doi.org/10.1007/978-3-030-02877-0

Library of Congress Control Number: 2018959736

© The Editor(s) (if applicable) and The Author(s) 2019
This work is subject to copyright. All rights are solely and exclusively licensed by the Publisher, whether the whole or part of the material is concerned, specifically the rights of translation, reprinting, reuse of illustrations, recitation, broadcasting, reproduction on microfilms or in any other physical way, and transmission or information storage and retrieval, electronic adaptation, computer software, or by similar or dissimilar methodology now known or hereafter developed.
The use of general descriptive names, registered names, trademarks, service marks, etc. in this publication does not imply, even in the absence of a specific statement, that such names are exempt from the relevant protective laws and regulations and therefore free for general use.
The publisher, the authors, and the editors are safe to assume that the advice and information in this book are believed to be true and accurate at the date of publication. Neither the publisher nor the authors or the editors give a warranty, express or implied, with respect to the material contained herein or for any errors or omissions that may have been made. The publisher remains neutral with regard to jurisdictional claims in published maps and institutional affiliations.

Cover illustration: George Barnard, 1862. Trinity Episcopal Church, 3rd & Ind. Ave.; unfinished Capitol in the background. From Library of Congress: Brady-Handy Collection
Cover design: Fatima Jamadar

This Palgrave Macmillan imprint is published by the registered company Springer Nature Switzerland AG
The registered company address is: Gewerbestrasse 11, 6330 Cham, Switzerland

ACKNOWLEDGEMENTS

Many people have contributed to this book from its earliest inception. David Goodman at the University of Melbourne helped to shape the initial postdoctoral research proposal that marked the beginning of the project. Since my arrival in 2010, the history program at Monash University has provided a wonderfully supportive atmosphere, and thanks go to the many colleagues who have listened to papers, read drafts and generally encouraged me to persist. I would particularly like to thank David Garrioch, who read a full draft of the manuscript and made a number of incisive comments, as well as Bain Attwood, who has been a great mentor and friend. As a research assistant, Nicholas Ferns had many thankless tasks, but carried them out with immense diligence and also creativity.

I would also like to record my gratitude to the Australian Research Council (ARC) which generously funded this project through its early career researcher fellowship program. Writing books about the United States from far away Australia has become easier in the digital age. But rifling through boxes of petitions in the archives requires an enormous investment in time and in money and would simply have been impossible without the ARC's support.

A number of archivists shared their expertise with me. For a while I haunted the National Archives in Washington, DC, and I would like to thank the legislative records staff there. Bill Davis and Rod Ross in particular showed a great interest in my research and pointed me to a number of valuable sources. Richard McCulley gave me a warm welcome and a personal tour of the stacks. Two other institutions provided generous support. The Library Company of Philadelphia granted me a short-term fellowship which accelerated the project at a critical period. In the final stages, a month as visiting scholar at the American Antiquarian Society sharpened my thinking and opened up a wealth of resources. In no particular order, I also received wonderful assistance from staff at the State Archives of Massachusetts, Harvard University archives, Harvard Divinity School, Pennsylvania State Archives, Huntington Library, Massachusetts Historical Society, Boston City Archives, New York Public Library, New York Historical Society, and the manuscripts division of the Library of Congress. I would also like to thank Sally Barringer Gordon. Not only has her work been a great inspiration, but she and her family welcomed me twice to Thanksgiving celebrations in their home, which was a marvelous experience for me.

My love and gratitude go to Jana, not least for giving up her holiday time to whip the manuscript into shape. Lastly, a dedication to Mark and Luise, who have grown into such fine young people over the course of this project.

Contents

1 Introduction   1

2 "Stepping Stone to an Establishment": The 1785 Campaign Against the Religious Tax in Virginia   19

3 "Prostrating Our Rights on the Altar of Superstition and Bigotry": The Sunday Mail Controversy in the Early Republic   33

4 "Exposing Priestcraft and All Its Cognate -isms": Chaplains, Temperance and Sunday Travel   63

5 "God's Vice-Regents": Political Preachers and the Crisis Over Slavery   93

6 How Christian Were the Founders? God and the Constitution After the Civil War   121

7 The Bible Wars: Religion, Morality, and Schools in an International Age   151

8 "Sunday Clubs for Wealthy People": Taxing the Churches   181

9	"A Professedly National Secular Show": The Chicago World's Fair and the American Sabbath	207
10	Conclusion	241
	Appendices	253
	Select Bibliography	259
	Index	277

List of Figures

Fig. 3.1 James Akin, *"The Holy Alliance," or, Satan's Legion at Sabbath Pranks* (1830) (Courtesy of American Antiquarian Society)   54
Fig. 4.1 *"Hypocrisy and Rum"*, John L. McGee (1852) (Courtesy of American Antiquarian Society)   73
Fig. 4.2 *A Remarkable Difference 'Twixt Tweedledum and Tweedledee* (1859) (Courtesy of New York Public Library)   80
Fig. 4.3 *Beauties of the Sunday Law* (1855) (Courtesy of Library Company, Philadelphia)   84
Fig. 6.1 *The Prayer at Valley Forge*. From the original painting by Henry Brueckner (1889) (Courtesy of Library Company, Philadelphia)   133
Fig. 9.1 *An Unholy Alliance*, Puck (August 24, 1892) (Courtesy of New York Public Library)   222
Fig. 9.2 *It Will Be Open!* Puck (December 14, 1892) (Courtesy of New York Public Library)   233

CHAPTER 1

Introduction

On May 31, 1892, Charles W. Smouse addressed a petition to Congress on the subject of the World's Columbian Exposition in Chicago. Set to open the following year, the World's Fair promised to be a dazzling showcase of American prowess for a domestic and international audience. But Smouse, along with thirty-seven fellow residents of Mount Pleasant, Iowa, worried that the much-anticipated Fair might become instead a vehicle for clerical ambition. At the urging of evangelicals, lawmakers were poised to pass a measure that would force the Fair directors to shut the gates on the Sunday Sabbath. Were it to impose Sunday-closing, Smouse warned, Congress would be embarking on a dangerous path of "Religious Legislation," and as such violating both the First Amendment to the federal Constitution as well as the wishes of the founders of the Republic. Now more than ever, Smouse declared, it was imperative to keep "Religion and the State Separate."[1]

This book is a history of men and women like Charles W. Smouse who, across a range of church-state battles from the early Republic to the Progressive era, campaigned for a greater separation between religion and government. Smouse was not a prominent jurist, politician, or cleric, and he lived far from the economic and intellectual centers of American life. But his protest over Sunday-closing is a fitting point of departure for three reasons. First, Smouse's petition captures the core demand of the group that I refer to as secularists. The terms "secularism" and "secularist" first entered American parlance in the antebellum era, though they only became common after the Civil War. From the outset, their meaning was contested. Protestant evangelicals dismissed them as a mere dressing up of an old foe, atheism. But another understanding, which I follow in this book, also took hold. A secularist, as a Protestant minister who embraced the label explained, wanted "an absolute and unqualified divorce of the State from things spiritual."[2] Opponents understood the term in the same way. Secularists, the Congregationalist Josiah Strong explained, believed in a distancing of religious and government institutions.[3] To his dismay, their ranks included many Christians as well as Jews and agnostics.

This points to a second revealing feature of Smouse's petition, its balance of religious and non-religious voices. Smouse, along with several of his fellow petitioners, was a member of a religious minority, the Seventh-Day Adventists. But others signed simply as citizens, eschewing any affiliation with the Adventists or other churches. Nineteenth-century secularists were a diverse group, and their diversity extended to religious belief. The call for a secular state won support across the spectrum of belief, from those whose faith was fierce to merely tepid or even nonexistent. Some secularists cited Scripture, others preferred Thomas Jefferson, and many saw no contradiction in drawing on both. The third reason to begin with Charles W. Smouse and his obscure fellow petitioners from their small town in Iowa is to signal the grassroots dimension to this story. The lettered elite will play a significant role. But in analyzing a series of church-state controversies, I have tried to incorporate popular attitudes and protests. Without opinion polls or mass surveys, the best way to do this is through collective petitions, which feature heavily in the pages that follow. In sum, this is a history of secularist mobilization as much as ideology.

Placing a figure like Charles W. Smouse at center-stage runs against the grain of two interrelated approaches to church-state relations in nineteenth-century America. The first sees most Americans as instinctive non-preferentialists, a modern term which denotes an acceptance of state support for faith so long as it is distributed equally among all (Protestant) denominations. In his *Commentaries on the Constitution of the United States*, Supreme Court Justice Joseph Story famously argued that the free exercise and establishment clauses of the First Amendment had a clear and limited goal: to "prevent any national ecclesiastical establishment." The national government was barred from levying taxes in support of one church, or using its powers to enforce a specific creed. But indirect and indiscriminate aid to religion was entirely appropriate.

Since Protestant values provided the solid foundations of republican government, the majority expected their faith to, in Story's terms, "receive encouragement from the state."[4] Story was writing in the midst of the explosion of evangelical energy known as the Second Great Awakening, and historians have long seen a connection between the model of disestablishment that he outlined and the religious vitality of the era. In one account, the demise of direct state support infused religion with a new democratic fervor. The rising Methodist and Baptist churches appealed directly to previously marginal groups, developing new techniques of persuasion that would enable them to prosper in an open marketplace of religion.[5] Other scholars paint a darker picture. Evangelical churches in this view relied more on fear than on hope, binding Americans to their faith by stoking fears about the alarming spread of irreligion and immorality.[6] But whether their vision was sunny or gloomy, evangelical churches profited from the absence of a state church to construct a vast network of reform and voluntary associations, in the process winning a privileged public position for their faith.

The result, for many historians, was a swift march to social control. A second line of interpretation, then, emphasizes religious power. Nineteenth-century Americans, as William R. Hutchison notes, liked nothing better than to congratulate themselves for casting off the state churches that disfigured the Old World. But they soon developed a "very effective religious establishment of their own."[7] Whether through Sabbath restrictions, temperance laws or censorship regimes, evangelicals built an informal establishment. Along with other historians, Mark A. Noll sees its highpoint in the antebellum era when a "republican calculus" brought together the forces of faith and democracy in a mutually beneficial embrace.[8] But many see a more enduring reign. In David Sehat's account, the regime of Protestant coercion, or what he terms the "moral establishment," was at its most imposing near the end of the century, as the various groups who felt its lash—Catholics, Mormons, freethinkers, and others—could attest. "For much of its history," as Sehat concludes, "the United States was controlled by Protestant Christians who sponsored a moral regime that was both coercive and exclusionary."[9]

In this narrative, a figure like Smouse plays a marginal role, the forlorn protester whose crushing at the hands of the moral establishment serves only to underline its ascendancy. However, if we understand secularists as a category to extend beyond the irreligious to encompass all those who rallied to a strict separation of church and state, a different narrative emerges. Evangelicals remain an imposing force. But their energy spurred an equally impressive secularist mobilization that managed to defeat or at least hold in check the push for a tighter fit between religion and government. The result was not a sweeping secularist victory. Smouse's vision of a clean break between religion and state was never achieved. But far from succumbing to an evangelical juggernaut, nineteenth-century secularists proved remarkably effective in rallying support for their contention that the United States was not, in political or constitutional terms, a Christian nation.

In making this case, my analysis builds on the work of other scholars who have challenged the depiction of the nineteenth-century as the golden age of the informal Protestant establishment. Steven K. Green has argued most forcefully that this era witnessed a second disestablishment which, extending the gains made in the Revolutionary era, introduced secularist principles to law and public education. By the century's end, he argues, the majority of Protestants had "reconciled with the idea that, while the culture retained Christian influences, the nation's civic institutions were secular."[10] The view that the Second Great Awakening produced a united evangelical front which swept all before it has also come under scrutiny. The competitive marketplace of religion, which is often seen as spurring evangelical growth, also had the effect of pitting preacher against preacher in the endless race for converts taking place in communities across the nation. As much as they celebrated the advance of religion as a whole, church leaders worried about losing ground to their rivals.[11] Nor, as Frank Lambert suggests, was there necessarily unanimity amongst Protestants in regard to political questions. On questions such as Sunday mail delivery, he argues, "Protestant unity in the public square was more illusory than real."[12] Perhaps the most striking challenge to the story of evangelical dominance is the tolerance, albeit often grudging, granted to atheists. As Leigh Eric Schmidt shows, though often ostracized and regularly subjected to legal persecution, freethinkers carved out a prominent place in cities and small towns across the nation.[13] A handful even achieved great public renown. To the dismay of evangelicals, the notorious freethinker Robert Green Ingersoll dazzled large audiences with his biting attacks on moralizing clerics and their blind faith in dogma.[14]

This book goes beyond a focus on freethinkers to encompass the diverse impulses which came together to make the case for a secular state. Without discounting the influence of figures such as Ingersoll, we need to look further than irreligion if we are to make sense of the vitality of secularist mobilization.[15] Some of the most prominent advocates of a secular state in nineteenth-century America were men and women of faith. It was a poor religion, they argued, that relied on government props to keep it upright. True faith had need of nothing more than the enduring power of its creed. But the social and cultural forces animating political secularism did not end there. Class animosity was a further powerful factor. In many church-state contests, labor activists denounced a Protestant clergy that seemed more interested in currying favor with the wealthy elite than uplifting the lives of the poor.

Nor can we ignore the element of race. The argument for a strict separation of church and state served multiple purposes in nineteenth-century America. In the hands of white southerners, it became a tool to uphold racial privilege. This became clear when northern evangelicals attacked the Kansas-Nebraska Act of 1854, which opened the door to the extension of slavery into the territories. The response of white southerners was furious. By using their pulpit as a political soapbox, they charged, these abolitionist preachers were overstepping the boundary between faith and government. The call for a secular state served, in this case, to silence critics of slavery. The defeat of the Confederacy only hardened opposition to what southerners saw as the politicized religion which ruled over northern society.

In short, secularist campaigns brought together an odd group of bedfellows: religious skeptics, liberal theologians, minority faiths, white supremacists, labor reformers, German radicals, and more. These alliances were largely informal, often sporadic, and occasionally uncomfortable. For example, liberal Protestants held their noses when siding with radicals who gave off in their view a strong whiff of atheism. But they found common ground in the proposition that only a secular state could keep religion free from government control, and just as importantly, government safe from clerical ambition. Politics and religion were a combustible and dangerous mix, they agreed, and both would suffer from their combination.

These alliances were found at the grassroots as much as the elite level of society. Much of the literature on secularization has a top-down bias. In *The Secular Revolution: Power, Interests and Conflict in the Secularization of American Public Life*, Christian Smith and other contributors explore the manner in which secular models of knowledge and authority displaced religious understandings. Breaking with theories that posit secularization as the inevitable outgrowth of modernization, Smith argues that conflict drove this development. The secularization of public life was the "outcome of a power struggle between contending groups with conflicting interests and ideologies."[16] This emphasis on struggle and contest as critical to advancing the secularist cause is important. But whereas Smith and his contributors limit their analysis to elite producers of knowledge such as sociologists, journalists, and educators, my book introduces a bottom-up dimension. Through examining petition campaigns, we begin to see how mass meetings and popular mobilization, often taking place far from the political, economic, and cultural centers of American life and drawing in thousands of largely anonymous figures, played a vital role as well.

A further ambition of this study is to pay attention to the international dimension of American secularism. For decades now, historians have been investigating the cross-border connections and exchanges which shaped the American past. In the case of nineteenth-century reformers, these international ties were particularly vibrant. As they campaigned to abolish slavery or to win the vote for women, American activists reached across the Atlantic, forging networks with like-minded fellows and absorbing lessons that might be applied at home.[17] Studies of secularist movements, in contrast, have tended to remain fixed in a national frame. Yet nineteenth-century secularists were highly conscious of developments abroad, seizing on key events both to make the case for a secular state and to discredit the claims of their opponents. To demonstrate the perils of bringing sectarianism into the classroom, for example, or leaving church property untaxed, secularists routinely pointed to the Old World, where a series of national governments seemed desperate to unwind the close ties between church and state that had crippled civil and religious liberty. Another major theme of the book, anti-Catholicism, shows the same outward-looking perspective. Hostility to the church was no doubt stoked by domestic pressures and circumstances. But we should not overlook the impact of international controversies, notably the First Vatican Council of 1869–1870, in sharpening animosity toward Rome. Particularly in the second half of the century, international events played an ever-increasing role in driving and directing the contest over the proper relationship between religion and government.

True Versus False Religion

At first glance, Charles W. Smouse's plea for religion and state to be kept apart seems beguilingly simple. Yet if we look harder, we begin to see another powerful element in the secularist case, an effort to enshrine a vision of true as opposed to false religion. In his influential study, Charles Taylor argues that in a secular age, religion does not disappear but is instead reconfigured.[18] Scholars in the field of secularist studies have made a persuasive case that political secularism's core demand—that the modern state remain aloof from clerical claims and theological quarrels—carried a series of hidden injunctions about what counts as true religion.[19] Good religion is deemed to be private, rational and grounded in belief rather than coercion. Bad religion, in contrast, is emotional, authoritarian and perhaps most damningly of all, politically ambitious.[20] Read in this way, the First Amendment takes on a different light. It held out the promise of religious liberty and state non-interference to all faiths. But it worked to privilege certain expressions of religiosity while demonizing others.

In the American context, historians have identified evangelical Protestantism as the beneficiary of secularism's discursive power. The endless process of sorting good from bad religions which the First Amendment unleashed provides a key, in this argument, to the creation of the informal Protestant establishment. Evangelicals skillfully wielded the specter of Catholicism—cast as an alien and authoritarian faith which allegedly made no secret of its thirst for raw political power—to make their own claims to public authority seem palatable. Tracy Fessenden has described how this dynamic unfolded in the context of the fierce debates over the reading of the Protestant Bible in public schools. Protestants made two apparently contradictory claims. The first was that the nation's common schools must be nonsectarian in character. The second was that their Bible, the King James, be read every day to students of all faiths and backgrounds, including Catholics, who used a different version, the Douai-Rheims Bible, and Jews. They were able to reconcile these two claims because to their mind the public school was itself a creation of the Protestant ethos. Only Protestantism, with its stress on unmediated contact between the faithful and Scripture, could have created a mass education system. Since the common school was an outgrowth of their faith, the presence of their Bible escaped the censure of sectarianism. The Catholic Bible, in contrast, could only be an intruder.[21] The principle of church-state separation, then, offered a fiction of state neutrality, a fiction which in fact served to smooth the path to Protestant dominance.

The problem with this account is that it limits conflict to a broad Catholic-Protestant divide. Fessenden refers to a "nonspecific Protestantism" dominating American public life, but even a casual glance at the religious landscape of the nineteenth century reveals a Protestant world riven with internal conflicts and rivalries. The same criticism might be applied to John Lardas Modern's *Secularism in Antebellum America*. Modern sets out the processes through which an evangelical social imaginary set the terms for what it meant to be religious in antebellum America. Evangelical Protestantism in his account was an "imperial discourse" that enabled a "broad Protestant majority... to convince themselves that they were religious."[22] In Modern's account, this majority is capacious, encompassing not just conservative evangelicals but liberal Protestants, spiritualists, and even freethinkers. But as Michal Warner argues, even if we accept that these ostensibly rival groups all operated within the same broad formation of secularism, "they certainly put competing spins on its political implications."[23] This was clear in the Bible Wars. Those who argued for the reading of the King James Bible may have insisted that, in a republic founded on Protestant values, there was nothing sectarian about such a practice. But it was not just Catholics who realized how untenable this position was. Liberal Protestants, Jews, freethinkers, and many others saw very clearly that the reading of the King James Bible was as intrusive as the reading of the Douai Bible, and that both had to be excluded.

The true/false religion dichotomy was indeed powerful, but we need to see how it worked *against* evangelical claims to authority. No issue demonstrates this more clearly than anti-Catholicism. Scholars often contend that support for a strict separation of church and state has its roots in anti-Catholic bigotry.[24] The argument runs as follows. Nineteenth-century Protestants were convinced that the Vatican thirsted after political as much as spiritual authority. To beat back the threat, they embraced the principle of church-state separation, a measure which they regarded as an antidote to Catholic ambition specifically. Again, though, secularism worked to enshrine Protestant influence. For at the same time as they denounced Catholic aggression and proclaimed the virtue of separation, these same Protestants were urging the state to enact and enforce laws to stamp out drunkenness, blasphemy, and Sabbath-breaking.

The purportedly watertight principle of separation, in this argument, allowed Protestant claims to public authority to pass unhindered.

This interpretation ignores, however, the manner in which anti-Catholicism rebounded against evangelicals themselves. Secularists were as forthright as anybody else in nineteenth-century America in denouncing Catholicism as a politicized, hierarchical, and intolerant faith. But again and again, they skillfully directed this prejudice against the Protestant clergy. By seeking political privileges for their faith, evangelicals were guilty, they argued, of mimicking the sinister papists they professed to oppose. In a culture saturated with anti-Catholicism, tarring the Protestant clergy with the spirit of Romanism proved a powerful weapon. In the never-ending effort to sort good from bad religions, in short, the proponents of the Christian nation thesis could end up on the wrong side of the ledger. By the end of the century, advocates of strict Sabbath laws or state-backed Prohibition were coming to be seen by more and more Americans as curious relics of a discarded age of zealotry. Secularists were a diverse group. Some were deeply hostile to religion. But most sought to circumscribe religious activism within what they regarded as fitting limits in an era of progress and of democracy. And in determining these limits, they held up certain faiths as foils—Puritans, Mormons, and Catholics, but also conservative evangelicals who now bore in their eyes the same fatal mark of the fanatic.[25]

THE ROLE OF PETITIONING

In order to understand the nature and depth of secularist mobilization in nineteenth-century America, this book draws on a neglected historical source, collective petitions to Congress. The right to petition government is guaranteed by the First Amendment to the Constitution, the same amendment which contains the religion clauses. But in stark contrast to the mountainous literature on the latter, studies of mass petitioning in American history are rare. The few that exist chart a crucial shift from the colonial to the national eras. On matters of public controversy, colonial-era petitioners aimed directly at reshaping policy and laws.[26] By the early Republic, the goal had expanded to the more diffuse aims of mass politicking: generating publicity for a cause, bringing new members into civic associations, and binding them together ever more firmly in a shared cause. Petitioning became enveloped in what Johann N. Neem has called the "massive release of civic energy" during the Jacksonian era and took on the hallmarks of mass mobilization.[27] The masters of this new style of petitioning were antislavery activists, who from the mid-1830s bombarded Congress with protests signed by thousands of men and women. As they understood, petitioning was becoming a numbers game. Congress, as the abolitionist *Liberator* reminded its readers, "is more powerfully moved by large numbers than by strong arguments."[28]

This book begins in the Jacksonian era, when it was not uncommon for petitions to be handwritten, and ends in the Progressive age, when pages and pages of names followed a printed, uniform and often terse text. But though changing in format, the petition remains a rich source of information. Even as it became shorter over time, the claim at the head of the document offers a window onto secularist arguments. Studying petitions allows us to plot the regional strengths of secularist feeling, and how this evolved over the course of the century. In addition, as Daniel P. Carpenter argues, the process of collecting signatures brings to light the shape of local organizational networks.[29] Sometimes these networks sprang into life in response to a particular issue before fading away; others proved to be more enduring. But in preserving the names of organizers, including all those tasked with distributing sheets and collecting names, petitions allow us to grasp the outlines of networks which otherwise would be almost impossible to trace.

Most of all, petitions offer the chance to take the temper of popular opinion. Admittedly, it would be naive to see petitioning as an entirely grassroots phenomenon. Petitions were often drafted, printed, and distributed by small groups of men and women, who then enrolled local notables to fan out and to solicit signatures. "It is not so much the signatory who seeks the petition," in Carpenter's neat description of the process, "but the petition that seeks the signatory."[30] Yet nor was this a purely top-down process. In certain eras, local meetings of townspeople either drafted their own petition texts or amended standard forms to better convey their opinion. In some cases, signers added notes and comments to make their views clear. Even signing one's name was a significant and public act. In short, petitions take us as close as we can get to ideological battles on the ground.

In studying these petitions, I have privileged those that went to Congress rather than to state legislatures. This book thus leans toward national rather than state-level controversies. Studies of church-state relations in the nineteenth-century have often taken the opposite perspective.[31] As a matter of law, the religious clauses of the First Amendment were not yet binding on individual states. On many church-state issues, state and local laws reigned supreme, and protestors were as likely to direct their anger at town or city authorities as national legislators. Yet there are good reasons to opt for a broader perspective. Even when welling up from the local level, church-state controversies tended to balloon quickly into questions of national import. This is notably true for the issue of Bible-reading in schools, where the decision of one School Board in the city of Cincinnati in 1869 touched off a nationwide debate. Furthermore, many of the issues that vexed both evangelicals and their opponents, from Sunday mails to legislative chaplains to the wording of the nation's founding text, revolved around federal power and responsibility. But more than this, even if the First Amendment did not formally hold sway over state constitutions, Americans looked on it as a decisive reference point nonetheless. Petitioners sometimes quoted a state Constitution or even a local ordinance, but most privileged the First Amendment because they understood it to set the course for the entire nation.

The story begins with a Revolutionary-era petition campaign that in many ways set a template for those that followed: James Madison's successful effort to defeat a proposed religious tax in Virginia in 1785. Decades later, some of the key arguments made by Madison would reappear in a very different context. Chapter 3 examines the Sunday mail controversy of the early Republic. When evangelicals launched a campaign to stop the delivery and transportation of mail on Sundays, a furious national debate ensued. Scholarship on this controversy focuses on the Sabbatarian movement, a coalition of evangelical churches which petitioned against Sunday mails. My focus is the petition campaign in their favor. This chapter explores the major themes, arguments, and social identity of these petitioners who defended Sunday mails and who rejected what they saw as a clerical attempt to harness the power of the state for the benefit of their faith.

The two chapters that follow explore the secularist impulse in the antebellum era, when evangelical control is often seen to be at its most imposing. But as Chapter 4 shows, contest rather than consensus remained the rule, and faith itself often provided the spark. In the late 1840s, a small church known as the Primitive Baptists launched a determined effort to overturn what seemed a settled institution, legislative chaplains to Congress. This effort failed, but resistance to other expressions of religious control proved more successful. Temperance was one flashpoint. Sabbath controversy returned, this time around the question of Sunday travel. In Philadelphia in 1859, uproar ensued when Mayor Alexander Henry banned the city's streetcars from running on the Sabbath. The antebellum era also brought to a head an issue which had long divided Americans, the political role of the pulpit. The trigger, as demonstrated in Chapter 5, was slavery. When a group of clergymen from New England publicly urged Congress to rescind the controversial Fugitive Slave law, a furious backlash ensued against what was known as "political preaching." This episode reveals the manner in which the argument for separating religion and politics drew its energy from southern resentment of abolitionist preachers, a resentment that would obstruct clerical-led reform for much of the century.

The Civil War brought the controversy over slavery to an end, but inaugurated a new round of church-state battles. Energized by their belief that a nation cleansed of the sin of slavery could at last bask in Divine favor, northern evangelicals embarked on an ambitious program of government-backed moral reform. The decade after 1865 saw three great contests. Chapter 6 examines the resistance to the campaign to acknowledge God and Jesus Christ in the preamble of the federal Constitution. Though sometimes dismissed as a foolhardy and eccentric venture, the drive to amend the Constitution triggered a nationwide debate as well as a great petition campaign. This chapter examines the question which to some degree inflected all church-state battles of the nineteenth-century: How Christian were the Founders? Through biographies, sermons, and prints, evangelicals portrayed the Founders as devout Christians intent on forging a Godly republic. But secularists resisted this campaign, depicting the Founders as Enlightenment deists who had constructed a Republic in which faith was a private and not a public concern.

The focus of Chapter 7 is the place of religion in public schools. When, in 1869, the School Board in Cincinnati, Ohio voted to end the practice of Bible-reading, the upshot was a fierce national controversy known as the "Bible War." Historians have studied this contest in some detail. But a key element—the international dimension—remains largely untold. As supporters and opponents of Bible-reading made their case, overseas models were a vital point of reference. Leading educational reformers went abroad, and particularly to Europe, to study the role of religion in schools and drew on their experiences to guide the debate at home. Chapter 8 investigates a secularist campaign that ultimately failed.

In the aftermath of the Civil War, calls to tax church property were heard in state constitutional conventions and legislatures, tax commissions, the secular press, and even in some pulpits. The issue was important because it crystallized a deep-seated resentment that religion was losing its popular mission. As opulent churches sprang up in Gilded Age cities, more and more Americans feared that houses of worship were turning into exclusive clubs for the wealthy. The final chapter returns to the question of Sabbath laws through the clash over the Sunday opening of the World's Fair at Chicago. As Gaines M. Foster has shown, far from subsiding in a wave of secularization, reformers set about with renewed vigor and purpose from the 1880s to enact their vision of a Christian nation.[32] For the leaders of this drive, the nation had the opportunity to affirm its commitment to the Lord's Day by shutting the gates of the Fair on Sunday. But their push for Sunday-closing sparked an immense backlash. Thousands of Americans petitioned Congress to ensure that the Fair remained open on every day of the week, setting forth their view not just of the meaning of Sunday, but more fundamentally, the proper relationship between government and religion in a nation which was increasingly diverse and now emerging as a global force.

The protagonists in these contests saw a clear-cut divide. The General Secretary of the national association lobbying for a Christian amendment to the Constitution, David McAllister, identified two antagonistic theories of the relationship between government and religion. The first, held by many evangelical churches, rejected a state church in the mold of the Church of England but maintained nevertheless "that civil government has a proper and necessary connection with religion." The opposing doctrine "excludes all matters of religion from the true sphere of civil government. It separates not only the church, but all religion from the state."[33] Such polarized depictions were common, but do not do justice to the complexity of the debate. Some petitioners proclaimed their desire for a thoroughgoing secularization of public life. But many might be better characterized as situational, objecting vehemently to certain expressions of clerical authority while remaining sanguine about others. The attempt to enforce Sabbath laws produced great outpourings of opposition. The saying of prayers in faraway Congress moved fewer citizens to protest. Furthermore, there are reasons to be skeptical of McAllister's winner-takes-all approach. As legal scholars now increasingly argue, apparently blunt concepts such as establishment and disestablishment mask a much more fluid and dynamic set of relationships.[34]

The key question becomes not if religion and government are connected but rather the nature of their entanglement. My aim, then, is not to replace a narrative of evangelical hegemony with one of secularist triumph. At the end of the century, religion and public policy continued to intersect in many ways. Yet McAllister was not entirely wrong either to see a deep-seated disagreement about the legacy of the Revolution, the origin of state authority and the shape of religion in a democratic republic. Through a series of popular mobilizations, a loose alliance of activists and their supporters articulated a powerful vision of a secular state, in the process branding their opponents as threats both to democratic liberties as well as true religion. Showing how this came about is the goal of this book.

Notes

1. Rec. June 6, 1892. SEN 52A-J27.1 (National Archives, Washington, DC). Emphasis in original. In researching this book, I have examined petitions held in archives. The alternative is to analyze lists of petitions received that appear in Congressional journals. Each approach has its pros and cons. The major disadvantage of my approach is that many relevant petitions have no doubt been lost or discarded and therefore do not appear in the archives. However, as I hope will become clear, taking the time to study physical documents opens up rich and indispensable lines of analysis.
2. Samuel T. Spear, *Religion and the State, or, the Bible and the Public Schools* (New York: Dodd, Mead & Co, 1876), 38. Emphasis in original.
3. Josiah Strong, *Our Country: Its Possible Future and Its Present Crisis* (New York: Baker and Taylor, 1891), 99–100.
4. Joseph Story, *Commentaries on the Constitution of the United States: With a Preliminary Review of the Constitutional History of the Colonies and States, Before the Adoption of the Constitution*, vol. 3 (Boston: Hilliard, Gray, 1833), 726, 728. For more recent iterations, Robert Cord, *Separation of Church and State: Historical Fact and Current Fiction* (New York: Lambeth Press, 1982), 15. See also Richard John Neuhaus, *The Naked Public Square: Religion and Democracy in America* (Grand Rapids, MI: Eerdmans, 1984); John Witte jnr., "Review: That Serpentine Wall of Separation," *Michigan Law Review* 101 (2003): 1869–1905.
5. Nathan O. Hatch, *The Democratization of American Christianity* (New Haven: Yale University Press, 1989).
6. Amanda Porterfield, *Conceived in Doubt: Religion and Politics in the New American Nation* (Chicago: University of Chicago Press, 2012).

7. William R. Hutchison, *Religious Pluralism in America: The Contentious History of a Founding Ideal* (New Haven: Yale University Press, 2003), 59. Daniel Walker Howe also argues that "the evangelical movement in the antebellum United States was in many respects the functional equivalent of an established church." See his "The Evangelical Movement and the Political Culture of the Second Party System," *Journal of American History* 77 (1991): 1222.
8. "By the early nineteenth-century, evangelicalism was the unofficially established religion in a nation that had forsworn religious establishments." Mark A. Noll, *America's God: From Jonathan Edwards to Abraham Lincoln* (New York: Oxford University Press, 2002), 208. See also Richard J. Carwardine, *Evangelicals and Politics in Antebellum America* (New Haven: Yale University Press, 1993); James S. Kabala refers to a "non-sectarian Protestant consensus" in his *Church-state Relations in the Early American Republic, 1787–1846* (Brookfield, VT: Pickering & Chatto, 2013).
9. David Sehat, *The Myth of American Religious Freedom* (Oxford: Oxford University Press, 2011), 8. Catherine L. Albanese charts the ongoing power of "public Protestantism" after the Civil War in her *America, Religions and Religion*, 5th ed. (Belmont, CA: Cengage, 2013), 276. Robert T. Handy, though sensitive to the level of dissent and challenge, nonetheless concludes that at the end of the century "an unofficial, diversified establishment of religion continued to operate effectively in the society." *Undermined Establishment: Church-State Relations in America, 1820–1920* (Princeton: Princeton University Press, 1991), 126. In Jon Butler's analysis, American Protestantism was as avid in its "pursuit of coercive authority and power" as in its commitment to individualism. *Awash in a Sea of Faith: Christianizing the American People* (Cambridge: Harvard University Press, 1990), 287.
10. Steven K. Green, *The Second Disestablishment: Church and State in Nineteenth-Century America* (New York: Oxford University Press, 2010), 385. Mark McGarvie has argued that "non-sectarian liberals" managed to impose, albeit briefly, a secularist vision of the Revolution and its legacy in the period of the early Republic. Mark McGarvie, *One Nation Under Law: America's Early National Struggle to Separate Church and State* (DeKalb: Northern Illinois University Press, 2004). For an earlier separationist reading of the First Amendment, Leonard W. Levy, *Constitutional Opinions: Aspects of the Bill of Rights* (New York: Oxford University Press, 1986).
11. Sam Haselby argues for a broad fissure between what he terms "frontier revivalism" and "national evangelism" within Protestantism in the early Republic. See his *The Origins of American Religious Nationalism* (New

York: Oxford University Press, 2015). See also Mitchell Snay, *Gospel of Disunion: Religion and Separatism in the Antebellum South* (New York: Cambridge University Press, 1993). Denominational competition is explored in Paul K. Conkin, *The Uneasy Center: Reformed Christianity in Antebellum America* (Chapel Hill: University of North Carolina Press, 1995), 130–37.

12. Frank Lambert, *Religion in American Politics: A Short History* (Princeton: Princeton University Press, 2008), 44.
13. Leigh Eric Schmidt, *Village Atheists: How America's Unbelievers Made Their Way in a Godly Nation* (Princeton: Princeton University Press, 2016).
14. Susan Jacoby, *The Great Agnostic: Robert Ingersoll and American Freethought* (New Haven: Yale University Press, 2013). For other secularist leaders, see her *Freethinkers: A History of American Secularism* (New York: H. Holt, 2004).
15. Noah Feldman, *Divided By God: America's Church-State Problem—and What We Should Do About It* (New York: Macmillan, 2005), examines the push for a strict separation of church and state after the Civil War, but limits the scope to organized secularists. For an analysis which also takes a capacious view, Eric R. Schlereth, *An Age of Infidels: The Politics of Religious Controversy in the Early United States* (Philadelphia: University of Pennsylvania Press, 2013). Schlereth examines a series of what he calls "infidel controversies" in the early republic which pitted the proponents of the Christian nation thesis against a loose coalition of Deists, freethinkers, and non-evangelical Protestants.
16. Christian Smith, "Secularizing American Higher Education: The Case of Early American Sociology," in *The Secular Revolution: Power, Interests, and Conflict in the Secularization of American Public Life*, ed. Christian Smith (Berkeley: University of California Press, 2003), 153.
17. Ian Tyrrell, *Woman's World/Woman's Empire: The Woman's Christian Temperance Union in International Perspective, 1880–1930* (Chapel Hill: University of North Carolina Press, 1991); Daniel T. Rodgers, *Atlantic Crossings: Social Politics in a Progressive Age* (Cambridge, MA: Belknap, 1998); Margaret McFadden, *Golden Cables of Sympathy: The Transatlantic Sources of Nineteenth-Century Feminism* (Lexington: University Press of Kentucky, 1999); and Kathryn Kish Sklar and James Brewer Stewart, eds., *Women's Rights and Transatlantic Antislavery in the Era of Emancipation* (New Haven: Yale University Press, 2007).
18. Charles Taylor, *A Secular Age* (Cambridge, MA: Belknap Press, 2007).
19. Key works are Talal Asad, *Formations of the Secular: Christianity, Islam, Modernity* (Stanford: Stanford University Press, 2003); Gil Anidjar, "Secularism," *Critical Inquiry* 33, no. 1 (2006): 52–77; Joan Wallach

Scott, *The Politics of the Veil* (Princeton: Princeton University Press, 2007); Saba Mahmood, *Religious Difference in a Secular Age: A Minority Report* (Princeton: Princeton University Press, 2016); and Jonathon S. Kahn and Vincent W. Lloyd, eds., *Race and Secularism in America* (New York: Columbia University Press, 2016).
20. Robert A. Orsi, *Between Heaven and Earth: The Religious Worlds People Make and the Scholars Who Study Them* (Princeton: Princeton University Press, 2004), esp. 177–204; Winnifred Fallers Sullivan argues that the "precondition for political participation by religion increasingly became cooperation with liberal theories and forms of governance." *The Impossibility of Religious Freedom* (Princeton: Princeton University Press, 2005), 7.
21. Tracy Fessenden, *Culture and Redemption: Religion, the Secular, and American Literature* (Princeton: Princeton University Press, 2007), Chapter 3.
22. John Lardas Modern, *Secularism in Antebellum America* (Chicago: University of Chicago Press, 2015), 114.
23. Michael Warner, "Was Antebellum America Secular?" available at: http://blogs.ssrc.org/tif/2012/10/02/was-antebellum-america-secular/.
24. The longest exposition of this argument is Philip Hamburger, *Separation of Church and State* (Cambridge: Harvard University Press, 2002). For a critique, see Mark McGarvie's comments at: http://www.h-net.org/reviews/showrev.php?id=7329.
25. Several scholars have studied the ways in which Americans came to see Mormonism as a theocratic, illiberal and therefore illegitimate faith. See J. Spencer Fluhman, *A Peculiar People: Anti-mormonism and the Making of Religion in Nineteenth-Century America* (Chapel Hill: University of North Carolina Press, 2012); Sarah Barringer Gordon, *The Mormon Question: Polygamy and Constitutional Conflict in Nineteenth-Century America* (Chapel Hill: University of North Carolina Press, 2002).
26. For the colonial era, Raymond C. Bailey, *Popular Influence Upon Public Policy: Petitioning in Eighteenth-Century Virginia* (Westport, CN: Greenwood Press, 1979).
27. Johann N. Neem, *Creating a Nation of Joiners: Democracy and Civil Society in Early National Massachusetts* (Cambridge: Harvard University Press, 2008), 113, 167–68.
28. *Liberator*, June 23, 1837.
29. Daniel P. Carpenter, "Recruitment by Petition: American Antislavery, French Protestantism, English Suppression," *Perspectives on Politics* 14, no. 3 (2016): 700–23.
30. Ibid., 701.

31. For interpretations of the First Amendment which emphasize its delineation of federal versus state responsibility, see Daniel L. Dreisbach, *Thomas Jefferson and the Wall of Separation Between Church and State* (New York: New York University Press, 2002), 59–62; Donald L. Drakeman, *Church, State and Original Intent* (Cambridge: Cambridge University Press, 2010), 74–76.
32. Gaines M. Foster, *Moral Reconstruction: Christian Lobbyists and the Federal Legislation of Morality, 1865–1920* (Chapel Hill: University of North Carolina Press, 2002).
33. *Proceedings of the national convention to secure the religious amendment of the Constitution of the United States Held in Pittsburg, February 4, 5, 1874* (Philadelphia: Christian Statesman Association, 1874), 1.
34. See Lori G. Beaman, "Beyond Establishment," in *Politics of Religious Freedom*, eds. Winnifred Fallers Sullivan, Elizabeth Shakman Hurd, Saba Mahmood and Peter G. Danchin (Chicago: University of Chicago Press, 2015), 207–19; Winnifred Fallers Sullivan and Lori G. Beaman, eds., *Varieties of Religious Establishment* (London: Ashgate, 2013).

CHAPTER 2

"Stepping Stone to an Establishment": The 1785 Campaign Against the Religious Tax in Virginia

Across the nineteenth century, petitions and counter-petitions were a feature of many church-state battles. But the most famous single petition setting out the proper role of religion in the republic dated from the Revolutionary era. In 1785, James Madison rallied public opposition to a proposed religious tax in Virginia. His "Memorial and Remonstrance against Religious Assessments," though designed to defeat a specific bill, took on a more enduring status, providing a template for secularists in the decades ahead. The campaign in 1785 looked forward in another sense too. By bringing together Deists and religious dissenters, it prefigured the uneasy, albeit effective alliances that would remain a hallmark of secularist mobilization in the following century.

THE ANGLICAN ESTABLISHMENT IN VIRGINIA

In the colonial era, taxpayer support for established churches was common. In Massachusetts, New Hampshire and Connecticut, towns were obliged to select and support through taxes an orthodox, which in these parts denoted Congregational, minister. In the South, the Anglican Church reigned. Like the Carolinas, Georgia, and Maryland, colonial Virginia established the Church of England and taxed all residents for its support. This was far from a rigorous establishment, at least in relation to Protestants. In 1699, the legislature recognized the British Parliament's Toleration Act, and as a result non-Anglicans, or dissenters as they were known, were exempted from the requirement to attend Anglican services, and allowed to build and maintain their own houses of worship. Still, while enjoying a measure of toleration, dissenters could rightly complain of being second-class citizens. In order to preach, ministers required a license which was often difficult to obtain. Furthermore, dissenters, like all parish residents, were obliged to pay the annual levy which supported the Anglican Church and its activities.[1]

Events before the American Revolution would show the narrow limits of toleration in Virginia. The backdrop was the spread of a new and, from the perspective of the Anglican gentry, unsettling brand of dissent. From the 1730s, a religious revival known as the First Great Awakening swept the colonies. More than doctrinal innovation, the Awakening was significant for enshrining a brand of worship that emphasized the truth of experience. Denouncing orthodox ministers for their obsession with ritual and form, itinerant preachers traversed the colonies exhorting the faithful to cast aside their dry adherence to doctrine and to open their hearts to Christ. The main beneficiaries of this surge in religious enthusiasm were the Presbyterian and Baptist churches, which spread into the south. Within Virginia, these rising faiths were strongest in the west, but soon began winning over followers in the east of the state.

The expansion of Separate Baptists posed the greatest challenge to the Anglican establishment. Separate Baptist preachers made no secret of their scorn for state-backed creeds. Convinced that their authority came from God alone, and deeply hostile to any form of state control, they refused to apply for preaching licenses. Just as troubling was their defiance of social hierarchy. The Baptists' zeal for conversion and their conviction that redemption was accessible to all, regardless of race, gender or class, clashed with the model of rank and deference so dear to the gentry. A striking example of their willingness to upend convention was their approach to selecting preachers. For the Anglican parson, social rank was a reward for years of education. A Baptist preacher, in contrast, only needed to convince his audience that he possessed an authentic spiritual gift. For the Anglican gentry, these Baptists seemed a disruptive element, and their potential to create disorder was only magnified when large numbers of slaves began to embrace their message of individual salvation. From the 1760s, county officials launched a crackdown. In 1768, sheriffs and magistrates in several counties began to imprison Baptist preachers for disturbing the peace. Over the next six years, at least thirty would be jailed.[2]

James Madison and Religious Liberty

Such measures revolted the young James Madison. A fierce aversion to state compulsion on matters of faith as well as a sincere attachment to the principle of liberty of conscience seem to have marked Madison from an early age. In 1774, the twenty-three-year-old denounced the jailing of ministers in a letter to his friend William Bradford. Here, he wrote, was the "diabolical, Hell conceived principle of persecution" at work.[3] Two years later, as a delegate to the Virginia Convention, Madison ensured that the Declaration of Rights contained an expansive understanding of religious liberty that went well beyond the colonial-era concession of toleration. The initial draft of Article 16 provided for only the "fullest toleration." As Madison understood, this phrasing suggested an ongoing role for the state in setting the limits of dissent. The final version drafted by Madison guaranteed instead "the free exercise of religion," thereby enshrining a much greater liberty of religious belief and practice. The logic of this formulation was that diverse religious views would now be placed on an equal footing.[4] When his friend Thomas Jefferson proposed his bill for establishing religious freedom in 1779, Madison was an enthusiastic supporter. This bill failed to pass. But one victory had already been achieved. Conscious of the need for unity in a time of war, the legislature on December 9, 1776 eliminated the religious tax on dissenters and suspended it for Anglicans. Virginia began an experiment in a voluntary system of church support.

Would the experiment work? In 1784, prominent members of the House of Delegates, supported by popular petitions, began to complain that the Anglican Church was starved of funds. Petitioners from Dinwiddie County bemoaned the ministry's "precarious Dependence of annual Subscriptions" which had proven to be "very inadequate."[5] But if the increasingly moribund state of the Anglican Church preoccupied many petitioners, others made a broader case about the role of Protestant Christianity as a foundation of the political and social order. State support for religion, petitioners from Surry County argued, was an appropriate response to the novel conditions of a newly formed republic. The fortunes of a republic hinged on the virtue of its citizenry to a degree that had no parallel in the aristocratic societies of Europe. As it navigated the challenges ahead, the commonwealth would need religion more than ever to keep public officials honest and unruly citizens in order. It was therefore in the interests of all citizens of Virginia, dissenters or not, for the government to "encourage the progress and diffuse the influence" of Christianity. It was only fair that the cost be borne equally, and the best way to achieve this was to institute a tax.[6]

Acting on such sentiment, the famed orator Patrick Henry moved for a bill which would levy a tax of three pence to support "Teachers of the Christian Religion." For Henry and the bill's supporters, the General Assessment bill was a sensible and progressive measure which would put religion on a solid financial footing while avoiding a return to the former Anglican establishment. As they repeatedly stressed, all Protestant denominations would benefit, for the bill empowered those who paid the tax to determine which denomination would receive the funds. In its scrupulous effort to avoid the appearance of preferential treatment, the bill even stipulated that Quakers and Mennonites, denominations which lacked clearly identifiable ministers, could use the funds as they saw fit. The feeling that this was a common sense response to declining ministerial salaries was captured by George Washington. As he wrote to his friend George Mason, there was no doubt that coercion in spiritual affairs was abhorrent. But it was questionable if the proposed religious assessment amounted to a spiritual tyranny. To his mind, it seemed reasonable to make "People pay towards the support of that which they profess."[7] Henry and other supporters had strong grounds to believe that this would prove to be the majority view.

From the outset, however, James Madison rejected the proposed religious assessment as an infringement of religious liberty and an attempt to revive an ecclesiastical establishment. As he wrote to Jefferson, it was "obnoxious on account of its dishonorable principle and dangerous tendency."[8] Stopping it from passing was another matter. In a letter to James Monroe, Madison informed him that the Committee of the Whole House had voted forty-seven to thirty-two in favor. "A trial," he thought, "will be made of the practicability of the project."[9] When the ensuing bill passed its second reading by only two votes, however, and its ablest proponent, Patrick Henry, left the legislature to take up the position of Governor, Madison saw a chance to slow proceedings down. In part at his urging, on December 24 delegates voted to postpone any consideration of the proposed assessment until the next session, at the same time asking Virginians to "signify their opinion respecting the adoption of such a Bill."

The way to do this was through petitioning. As Raymond C. Bailey has argued, in eighteenth-century Virginia petitions played a vital role in transmitting public sentiment to the legislature. By the Revolutionary era, techniques for devising and circulating petitions were well-established, and a broad cross section of society participated in the process. Furthermore, there is much evidence that the legislature considered and acted upon petitions. There was no gag rule to block their reception or reading, and it was not uncommon for laws to come about as a direct result of campaigns.[10] This was true of religious controversies. In 1776, petitions calling for disestablishment began flooding into the legislature, including the famous "ten thousand name petition." This pressure was not enough to overcome establishment resistance to Jefferson's 1779 religious freedom law. But dissenter petitions did help to win a series of concessions, notably the legal right for their ministers to perform the marriage ceremony.

With the bill stalled, Madison's friend, George Nicholas, urged him to write a petition for circulation. This was the only way, he argued, that legislators could be made aware of public opinion on the question. There was clearly a majority against the religious tax, Nicholas assured Madison, but since pro-assessment petitions had to that point been most prominent, the House of Delegates might not be alive to the fact. It was therefore necessary to petition. "If," he wrote, "this majority should not appear by petition the fact will be denied."[11] In response, Madison wrote the text of his famous memorial.[12]

Madison's Memorial

In terms of galvanizing public support and influencing later secularist campaigns, three features of the memorial stand out. The first is its delicate balancing act between civil and religious liberty, allied to a careful argument about the nature of true religion. Religious liberty was so fundamental that, in Madison's account, it stood outside the social contract. In relation to the state, religion was, he argued, "wholly exempt from its cognizance."[13] He then made a powerful case about the nature of true faith. A legitimate religion shunned government aid, and instead relied on nothing more than the purity and power of its precepts. The resort to compulsion was the mark of a decaying faith. No faith demonstrated this more clearly than Protestantism which, alone among the major religions, had shown a capacity to thrive in the absence of state patronage. "Every page of it," Madison argued, "disavows a dependence on the powers of this world."[14] A measure like the assessment bill, which was purportedly designed to bolster religion, would therefore have the perverse effect of tarnishing one of its great virtues. He then turned from religious to civil liberty. History showed that political despotism worked hand in hand with clerical ambition. Aspiring dictators always saw the clergy as "convenient auxiliaries," and the clergy in turn would find the lure of worldly power and reward hard to resist.[15] Bringing religion and government together, then, threatened to bring out the worst instincts in both.

The second striking feature of the Memorial is the way that it takes a relatively innocuous measure—a small tax which would bolster all Christian sects—and constructs a nightmarish scenario of escalating persecution leading to utter tyranny. Church-state battles were only ever partly shaped by the issue at hand. As the nineteenth century would show, much of their energy came from the way in which protagonists looked beyond the immediate controversy and tried to discern longer term patterns. For Madison, this was the lesson of the American Revolution. The significance of apparently isolated infringements on liberties only became clear when fitted into a deeper and far more disturbing chain of events. The British justified their various tax measures as reasonable fixes to the problem of financing colonial government. But the Revolutionaries saw at once where such measures would lead. As Madison wrote, they "did not wait till usurped power had strengthened itself by exercise, and entangled the question in precedents." They had the foresight to discern "the consequences in the principle," and their "prudent jealousy" was a model for all to emulate.[16] A bill in favor of all sects could easily lead to the establishment of a particular sect; the concession of a small tax might turn into a far more onerous form of proscription. To show what was on the horizon, Madison cited the event which more than any other distilled the excesses of fanaticism, the Inquisition. The proposed assessment, Madison admitted, seemed a long way short of instituting an Inquisition on American soil. But he insisted that it "differs from it only in degree."[17]

The final element of the Memorial that would resonate so strongly then and afterwards was its deployment of national exceptionalism. Across the nineteenth century, advocates of strict separation would accuse their opponents of seeking to enmesh the New World in the violence and corruption of the Old. In 1785, Madison made the same case. European governments justified state creeds as a means of calming sectarian rivalries and imposing religious peace. But establishments had entirely the opposite effect, inflaming hostility between faiths and unleashing "torrents of blood." The assessment bill was taking the young American nation down the same path of proscription and discord, and at the same time robbing it of one of its most signal achievements, the freedom it offered to all newcomers to worship freely and without fear of discrimination. Were the assessment bill to pass, the republic would lose the "lustre" it now boasted as "an Asylum to the persecuted and oppressed of every Nation and Religion."[18]

Having drafted the text, Madison relied on his friends, George Mason and George Nicholas, to circulate it. The arguments of a petition were only valuable, after all, if they visibly captured public support. Together Mason and Nicholas printed and mailed the memorial to at least six counties, attracting large numbers of signers. In July, Nicholas reported with satisfaction to Madison that no less than "One hundred and fifty of our most respectable freeholders signed it in a day."[19] Just as important was their status. In October, Mason wrote to George Washington, enclosing a copy of the petition and asking for his support. Sensitive perhaps to the air of controversy around it, Mason stressed that the text was dispassionate in tone and reasonable in its contentions. Clearly, the support of a man as well-known and distinguished as Washington was prized; as Mason wrote, "your Signature will both give the Remonstrance weight, and do it Honour."[20] Washington, who saw no reason to be alarmed about the proposed tax, declined to sign. But other notables were willing to participate, and in the end Nicholas and Mason could be satisfied. Eventually, more than thirteen copies of the Remonstrance with over fifteen hundred signatures reached the House of Delegates.

Two other features of the circulation of the petition are noteworthy. Firstly, Madison chose to hide his authorship. This might have been an attempt to avoid alienating conservative members of the House of Delegates. But it was more likely to have stemmed from a desire to reinforce the memorial's character as an expression of community feeling. Adding his name would give the document an elitist cast, and thereby dilute its impact. For a petition to cut through, it needed to be seen as welling up from below, the product of community feeling rather than elite direction. Secondly, the campaign showed that significant church-state controversies in one state soon attracted attention in others. Newspapers in Baltimore and in Boston re-printed Madison's petition, and in 1786 the printer Isaiah Thomas published a copy in Worcester, Massachusetts, a state with a religious tax of its own.

The text was commended to Thomas by a correspondent as one that every "sober man" might properly consider. Though likely to attract the hostility of the local Congregational ministry, arguments such as Madison's that "have swayed the legislature of a neighbouring government would be thought to deserve some consideration." After all, as the correspondent argued, "Truth is uniformly the same in all places."[21] The hoped for debate did not materialize, however, and the religious tax in Massachusetts would remain in force for several more decades.

THE DISSENTER PETITION CAMPAIGN

As influential as it was, Madison's petition was only one element in the anti-assessment campaign. Most of the grassroots energy required to defeat the bill came not from Nicholas' influential freeholders but from dissenting communities who placed religious liberty at the forefront of their claim. The convention of ministers and laity of the Presbyterian Church issued a petition declaring that the legislature should have no interest in religious matters apart from protecting the right of conscience. A state-supported religion was no religion at all; to their mind, a church could only ever rely on "internal conviction" and "voluntary choice" to win and retain followers.[22] Quakers, too, protested a measure which would "materially oppress tender consciences."[23] These petitions showed the same fear of a looming establishment that animated Madison's text, but expressed it in even more graphic terms. Two petitions from Amelia and Accomack Counties accused the legislature of seeking to dictate who could preach and on what subjects, decrying the bill as a "stepping stone to an Establishment." They then raised the specter of Catholic persecution. It was clear, they argued, that the ultimate aim of the backers of the bill was to establish a tribunal to judge heresy, thereby "kindling Smithfield's fires in America," a reference to the martyrdom of hundreds of Protestants during the reign of the Catholic Queen Mary (1553–58).[24]

The distinctive tenor of dissenter petitions was most apparent among Baptists. Scarred by their experience of persecution, Baptists threw themselves into the anti-assessment campaign, issuing a stream of petitions that, while referring to civil liberty, put Gospel truth front and center. The petition of the General Association began by reminding legislators of the "original genius and simplicity of the Christian Church." This was a faith that had required nothing more for its success than "the spiritual weapons of grace and mercy."[25] The most common and widely circulated Baptist petition similarly drew on the lessons of history to show that state patronage was both redundant and harmful. The Roman Emperor Constantine granted the church official shelter from persecution for the first time in its history. But the result, the petitioners argued, was a descent into clerical corruption and immorality. The lesson was clear. State emoluments tempted unscrupulous men into the ministry and had the perverse effect of boosting skepticism more than faith. By triggering an influx of "hirelings" motivated more by worldly than spiritual reward, the religious tax was likely to tarnish the reputation of the clergy, and thereby foster the spread of irreligion. If, as the petition argued, "Deism, with its baneful influence," was infiltrating the commonwealth, the remedy was not to entangle faith in the machinery of government but instead to encourage an infusion of true spiritual vitality into the ministry. The proof lay in nearby Pennsylvania. Its founder, the Quaker William Penn, made religious toleration the watchword of his colony. Under the 1682 Frame of Government, all those who professed their belief in God were free to worship as they pleased and could not be forced to support any church. For the Virginia petitioners, Pennsylvania, with its thriving economy and vibrant religious landscape, showed conclusively the benefits of a voluntary system.[26]

Aside from their greater emphasis on matters of the spirit, the Baptist petitions differed from Madison's as documents. When Nicholas was urging Madison to write his petition, he emphasized the need for uniformity. "Would it not add greatly to the weight of the petitions," he wrote, "if they all hold the same language?"[27] For Nicholas, variations to the text would dilute its impact; for this reason, the majority of Madison's petitions were printed. Even versions that were written out by hand followed faithfully the original text. The Baptist effort was organized on a different model of petitioning which, while working within a shared framework, allowed greater scope for amendment and variation. All are handwritten rather than printed, and many use a series of stylistic devices to impart emotion. Petitions from Surry and Buckingham County balance their stately presentation—the text filling one page in elegant script—with a frequent recourse to capitals, highlighted terms and underlining. Much more than Madison's petition, these documents hum with energy and feeling. To some degree, this is the difference between the lawyer and the preacher. As Rhys Isaac argues, Madison's petition, with its point by point structure and its formal language, was designed to appeal to the eye more than the ear. The Baptist petitions in contrast have the urgent cadence of the preacher, using emphasis to hammer home key points, and building through a series of cascading questions to a rousing climax. If the tone of Madison's petition was persuasion, that of the Baptist petitions was closer to exhortation.[28]

THE DEFEAT OF THE RELIGIOUS TAX

Together these various anti-assessment petitions won a large victory. From October 27, 1785, some eighty petitions opposed to the General Assessment bill reached the legislature, compared to only eleven in favor. As Madison wrote with satisfaction to Jefferson, "The steps taken throughout the Country to defeat the Genl. Assessment, had produced all the effect that could have been wished. The table was loaded with petitions & remonstrances from all parts against the interposition of the Legislature in matters of Religion."[29] The majority came from counties where dissenters were most numerous, particularly in the Shenandoah Valley and Northern Neck. Overall close to eleven thousand Virginians signed anti-assessment petitions, but less than one-fifth of these appeared on the Madison memorial. Just as striking as the strength of dissenter opposition was the tepid level of support for the bill. Petitions in favor came from just ten counties, and in all but one of these opposition was also expressed. Even in areas where Anglicanism was traditionally strong, the level of support was low.[30] If even the Anglican laity refused to support openly the proposal, the House of Delegates could hardly countenance it. The assessment bill, which had seemed so sure to pass in late 1784, never reappeared before the legislature.

Nor was this the final word. Buoyed by success, Madison now pushed for the passage of Jefferson's Bill for the Establishment of Religious Freedom, which was at last enacted in January 1786. The statute settled the question of the religious tax by declaring that no citizen could be forced to support financially any church; it further removed all legal disabilities related to faith. A measure designed to bring about a multiple Protestant establishment had ended instead in a decisive shift toward disestablishment. The question then moved to the federal level. As a representative from Virginia to the first Congress, Madison introduced, on June 8, 1789, the initial draft of what would become the Bill of Rights. From that point, he played a key role in maintaining the first amendment's prohibition on religious establishment against various attempts to dilute its language. The final version did not, as Madison had hoped, extend the ban on establishment to the states. But under the impulse of the federal Constitution, disestablishment at state level accelerated. Between 1789 and 1792, Delaware, South Carolina, and Georgia abolished religious tests for office. By 1800, only three states maintained active assessment regimes, and these would soon come under attack. First Connecticut (1818) and then New Hampshire (1819) abolished religious taxes. Only Massachusetts still resisted the advent of the voluntary principle.

The 1785 campaign against the religious assessment bill was a significant moment in the history not just of Virginia but the new nation as a whole. Its influence over subsequent secularist campaigns would be just as telling. Madison's memorial provided a storehouse of arguments and rhetorical strategies, from the corruption of true faith to the overthrow of civil liberties and the vision of grand and sinister plans lurking beneath seemingly innocuous measures. By turning the tables on a proposal that initially seemed sure to succeed, the campaign provided a lesson in the power of petitioning that activists would heed in the decades ahead. Finally, by bringing together Deists and Dissenters in a common battle against ecclesiastical power, the anti-assessment push prefigured the alliances of convenience that would emerge in the next century.

However, there were already signs that this particular alliance was unlikely to endure. Madison argued that the state should have as little to do with religion as possible. But the Baptists, while just as opposed to formal mechanisms of support, were already signaling their willingness to countenance more informal forms of cooperation between Church and State.[31] The same General Association petition that denounced compulsory religious taxes went on to argue that government should nevertheless work "in favour of Christianity" by making "adequate provision ... for supporting those Laws of Morality, which are necessary for private and public happiness."[32] The more common Baptist petition similarly called on legislators to pass laws that "punish the vices & immoralities [sic] of the times."[33] Their opposition to a religious tax in no way extended, the petitioners were keen to stress, to measures intended to punish sinful behavior, whether drunkenness, fornication or blasphemy.

The battle, then, was set to move to new and more vexed questions concerning the public role of religion, and the old coalitions were set to fracture. Did, for example, laws protecting the Christian Sabbath constitute a form of establishment? Many of the Virginia Baptists seemed to think not. After all, the state of Pennsylvania, held up by the Baptist petitioners as a bastion of religious liberty, had a long history of state-backed Sabbath observance. As early as 1682, a law called on its people to "abstain from their usual and common toil and labor" on the Lord's Day.[34] In 1784, Virginia itself passed a statute punishing any person who worked on Sundays. Sabbath laws were common across the states. But the question as to whether they amounted to a form of establishment, left unresolved in Virginia in 1785, would only come to the fore in the period of the early Republic when evangelicals, including many Baptists, launched a campaign against Sunday mails.

Notes

1. Thomas J. Curry, *The First Freedoms: Church and State in America to the Passage of the First Amendment* (New York: Oxford University Press, 1986), 135–36.
2. On the harassment of Baptist preachers, Thomas E. Buckley, *Establishing Religious Freedom: Jefferson's Statute in Virginia* (Richmond: University of Virginia Press, 2013). On the Baptists in Virginia, Monica Najar, *Evangelizing the South: A Social History of Church and State in Early America* (New York: Oxford University Press, 2008); Reuben E. Alley, *A History of Baptists in Virginia* (Richmond: Virginia Baptist General Board, 1973). On the Baptist challenge to the Anglican establishment and the power of the gentry, see Rhys Isaac, *The Transformation of Virginia: 1740–1790* (Chapel Hill: University of North Carolina Press, 1982), 161–77.
3. Madison to Bradford, January 24, 1774. Reprinted in *The Papers of James Madison*, vol. 1, eds. William T. Hutchinson and William M.E. Rachal (Chicago: University of Chicago Press, 1962), 106.
4. On Madison's opposition to church establishments, Ralph Ketcham, "James Madison, Thomas Jefferson, and the Meaning of 'Establishment of Religion' in Eighteenth-Century Virginia," in *No Establishment of Religion: America's Original Contribution to Religious Liberty*, eds. T. Jeremy Gunn and John Witte (Oxford: Oxford University Press, 2012), 158–79.
5. Rec. December 1, 1784. The petitions cited in this chapter are collected in the Virginia State Library, and are available on-line at: http://www.virginiamemory.com/collections/petitions.
6. Rec. December 1, 1784.

2 "STEPPING STONE TO AN ESTABLISHMENT": THE 1785 CAMPAIGN ...   31

7. Washington to Mason, October 3, 1785. Reprinted in *The Papers of George Mason*, Robert A. Rutland, ed., vol. 2 (Chapel Hill: University of North Carolina Press, 1970), 832.
8. Madison to Jefferson, January 9, 1785. Reprinted in *The Papers of James Madison*, vol. 8, eds. Robert A. Rutland et al. (Chicago: University of Chicago Press, 1973), 229.
9. Madison to Monroe, November 14, 1784. Reprinted in ibid., 136–37.
10. Bailey, *Popular Influence upon Public Policy*.
11. Nicholas to Madison, April 22, 1785. Reprinted in *The Papers of James Madison*, vol. 8, 264.
12. On Madison's Memorial, Vincent Phillip Muñoz, *God and the Founders Madison, Washington, and Jefferson* (Cambridge: Cambridge University Press, 2009), 15–31; Green, *Second Disestablishment*, 40–41; Lance Banning, "James Madison, the Statute for Religious Freedom, and the Crisis of Republican Convictions," in *The Virginia Statute for Religious Freedom: Its Evolution and Consequences in American History*, eds. Merrill D. Peterson and Robert C. Vaughan (Cambridge: Cambridge University Press, 1988), 109–38; Curry, *First Freedoms*, 142–44.
13. James Madison, "Memorial and Remonstrance Against Religious Assessments", June 20, 1785. Reprinted in *The Papers of James Madison*, vol. 8, 299.
14. Ibid., 301.
15. Ibid., 302.
16. Ibid., 300.
17. Ibid., 302.
18. Ibid.
19. Nicholas to Madison, July 7, 1785. Reprinted in ibid., 316.
20. Mason to Washington, October 2, 1785. Reprinted in *The Papers of George Mason*, vol. 2, 831.
21. *A Memorial and Remonstrance, Presented to the General Assembly of the State of Virginia, at Their Session in 1785* (1786). For newspaper references, *Maryland Journal* (Baltimore), November 11, 1785; *American Recorder* (Boston), March 7, 1786.
22. Signed August 13, 1785. A stream of further petitions declared their approval of the Presbyterian convention resolution.
23. Rec. November 14, 1785.
24. Rec. October 28, 1785; December 9, 1785.
25. Rec. November 3, 1785.
26. The text cited here is that of Surry County, Rec. October 26, 1785.
27. Nicholas to Madison, April 22, 1785. Reprinted in *The Papers of James Madison*, vol. 8, 264.

28. Rhys Isaac, "'The Rage of Malice of the Old Serpent Devil': The Dissenters and the Making and Remaking of the Virginia Statute for Religious Freedom," in *Virginia Statute for Religious Freedom*, 154–55.
29. Madison to Jefferson, January 22, 1786. Reprinted in *Papers of James Madison*, vol. 8, 473. A useful analysis of the petition campaign appears in the same volume, 295–98.
30. For a geographic breakdown of petitions for and against, see Bailey, *Popular Influence Upon Public Policy*, 155–58.
31. Sehat, *Myth of Religious Freedom*, 36–37.
32. Rec. November 3, 1785.
33. Nansemond county. Rec. October 27, 1785.
34. Boris I. Bittker, Scott C. Idleman, and Frank S. Ravitch, *Religion and the State in American Law* (Cambridge: Cambridge University Press, 2015), 26.

CHAPTER 3

"Prostrating Our Rights on the Altar of Superstition and Bigotry": The Sunday Mail Controversy in the Early Republic

In January 1829, James Madison's memorial made another public appearance. Reprinting the text in full on its front page, the *Hartford Times* praised "one of the ablest productions of that great statesman" which deserved to be widely circulated. Other papers were just as fulsome.[1] The timing of this resurgence in interest was not accidental. At that moment, the nation was engaged in a fierce debate over the public role of religion and the meaning of true faith. That debate was triggered by the delivery and transportation of mail by the federal postal service on the Sunday Sabbath.

Madison's arguments entered a vastly different religious and social landscape in 1829. In the decades since 1785, the nation had witnessed a development that few anticipated, the surge in evangelicalism known as the Second Great Awakening. Far from subsiding, religious commitment accelerated. By 1850, some 34% of the population was directly affiliated to a church, a doubling since the Revolutionary era.[2] Much of this growth occurred in the evangelical faiths, particularly the Methodists and Baptists. The abolition of religious taxes, a process which had occurred everywhere by 1829 save Massachusetts, proved a boon rather than a blow to their fortunes. Forced to rely on the voluntary support of congregations, evangelical churches developed a charismatic and emotional brand of faith that had mass appeal. They offered a form of spiritual egalitarianism that matched the democratic tenor of the nation, promising salvation to all adults who were willing to experience Christ's redeeming power, recruiting their preachers from the common people, and launching mass revivals which extended their reach across the nation.

As the Virginia Baptists had signaled as early as 1785, these evangelicals, while vociferously opposed to formal establishment, were nevertheless intent on imprinting a Protestant ethos on the institutions of government. Their opportunity came with the Sunday mail controversy. The postal service was an ideal site for a contest over church-state relations. In an era of small government, the postal department employed more workers and touched directly the lives of more citizens than any other federal agency. As the physical boundaries of the nation expanded, the postal service emerged as a vital artery of communication and trade. To avoid any disruption, its elaborate distribution and delivery system ran seven days a week. On Sundays, mail was transported on the major interstate routes—from Washington, DC up to Augusta, Maine in the North and down to Savannah, Georgia in the South, and from New York across to Youngstown, Ohio. Twenty-seven states and territories were crisscrossed by a web of Sunday mail routes.[3]

With mail coming in, local post offices opened on Sundays too. Under an 1825 regulation, postmasters were obliged to open their offices "on every day on which a mail shall arrive," and to deliver this mail to its recipients "on every day of the week."[4] In order to spare religious sensibilities, most opened outside of the hours usually dedicated to worship. In Hagerstown, Maryland, for example, the post office opened from 12.30 to 1.30 in the afternoon; in New Bern, North Carolina, 9.30–11.00 in the evening.[5] Nevertheless, for that time, and on an otherwise sleepy day, the post office bustled with activity as townspeople flocked to collect letters, read the news, and swap gossip.

For evangelicals, this was an appalling intrusion of worldly matters into the Lord's Day. Lyman Beecher was a theologian, educator, and preacher who would emerge as a leader of the movement, known as Sabbatarianism, to uphold the Sunday Sabbath. Beecher was typical of the evangelical approach to church-state relations. After some initial hesitation, he threw his support behind the campaign to abolish the religious tax in his home state of Connecticut. But he was adamant that institutional disestablishment did not entail a separation of religion and government. To begin with, Beecher drew a direct line between the Reformation, with its assertion of individual conscience and revolt against ecclesiastical authority, and the thirst for freedom exhibited by the Revolutionaries. Only Protestantism could nurture a democratic society like the United States. "Daylight," he argued, "is not more uniformly found in the track of the sun, than civil liberty is found in the track of Christianity." For Beecher, faith and democracy were even more tightly entwined through popular morals. Despots backed by draconian laws and standing armies might not care if their citizens were pious or not. But a republic rested ultimately on public virtue, and religion was therefore its indispensable stabilizing element. Shorn of the guiding hand of faith, Beecher warned, "our destruction does not slumber."[6] But many signs—drunkenness, dueling, even a growing atheism—indicated to Beecher that public virtue was slipping. His response was typically energetic. Through the agency of the Connecticut Society for the Reformation of Morals, Beecher, along with fellow evangelicals, mobilized to boost the public virtue which was the bedrock of the Republic.

THE SABBATARIAN MOVEMENT

But it was the defense of the Sabbath, that great fulcrum of the nation's devotion to God, that preoccupied evangelicals in the late 1820s. To end the practice of Sunday mail delivery, they turned to the favored tool of activists. Beginning in 1827, petitions flowed to Congress demanding a law "prohibiting the transportation of the Mail and the opening of Post offices on the Sabbath." Coordinating the campaign was the General Union for Promoting the Observance of the Christian Sabbath (GUPOCS), which met for the first time in May 1828 and which, together with a network of local auxiliaries, printed and distributed hundreds of blank petitions. The membership of GUPOCS included several wealthy merchants, including the New York brothers Arthur and Lewis Tappan. But its backbone was the clergy, with the Presbyterian and Congregationalist churches particularly prominent. Through Beecher's initiative, the General Assembly of the Presbyterian Church resolved to "earnestly recommend the formation of auxiliary societies throughout our congregations."[7] The result was a flood of petitions. As John G. West has calculated, Sabbatarians sent no less than 868 petitions to the House of Representatives in the period 1827–1830.[8]

Sabbatarians employed a diverse set of arguments. One was the benefit to body and mind of a day of rest. By maintaining the Sabbath, as Philadelphia petitioners argued, "*the comfort and health of man are promoted.*"[9] But the overall tenor of the petitions was much more religious. Their beginning point was the theological grounding of the Sunday Sabbath. Sabbatarians believed, firstly, that God had set apart one day in seven as sacred when He rested after the sixth day of creation and secondly, that the resurrection of Christ transferred the sacred day from the seventh to the first. Both beliefs were controversial in theological terms. Right through the nineteenth century, some Christians argued that no time should be held more sacred than any other. God should be venerated on every day, not just one. Minority churches, first the Seventh-Day Baptists and then the Seventh-Day Adventists, insisted that Scripture anointed the Jewish Sabbath and that the transferal to Sunday was a later ecclesiastical innovation. Observing the Saturday Sabbath became, to their mind, an act of cleansing true faith from the corruptions wrought by the papacy. But Sabbatarians were dismissive of such arguments. As the president of Yale Timothy Dwight argued, the day on which Christ rose from the dead established the only perpetual and divinely inspired Sabbath, which would remain binding on Christians until the end of time. "There is now, there has always been," Dwight declared, "but one such day," and that was the first day.[10]

As Dwight went on to argue, there was also only one way to keep that day, as a "holy, heavenly rest from every sinful, and every secular concern."[11] Sunday mails, though, disrupted its holiness. Some might be tempted away from prayer and churchgoing by the arrival of a letter from a loved one or a long-awaited parcel. Even the faithful who steered clear of the post-office were likely to be distracted by the hubbub of the crowds gathering there. As Wethersfield, Connecticut petitioners lamented, Sunday mails resulted in "the attention of large portions of the community [being] withdrawn from a becoming reverence of the day."[12] But for those postal employees who were obliged to work on the Sabbath, the difficulties were even greater. In an argument that is familiar today, Sabbatarians invoked an overriding right of individual religious freedom. By obliging postmasters to labor on Sunday, the federal government was forcing them to break the fourth commandment. Petitioners from Bedford, New York, argued that religious freedom was "secured by the Constitution to every citizen," but that it was violated when the government "exacts from postmasters and others services forbidden by the religion which most of them profess."[13] Christian employees were unfairly caught between their duties as government employees and their religious obligations.

Most pressing for Sabbatarians was the question of national survival. A holy and respected Sabbath was the bedrock of public virtue, keeping the eyes of citizens and public officials turned toward God's redeeming power, and holding the forces of skepticism at bay. Using language that was repeated in many petitions, Virginia Sabbatarians likened Sabbath desecration to "opening the floodgates of impiety, immorality, disorder, and all the long catalog of crimes."[14] Even more alarmingly, it was an invitation to Divine wrath. In an argument that would be repeated through the century, evangelicals voiced their conviction that the Almighty had blessed their nation above all others. If America was prosperous and free, it was largely thanks to this special covenant with God. But the flipside of this covenant was that His anger at being spurned would be all the greater. "We have been peculiarly favored as a people," petitioners from Washington County, Maryland, warned, "but we have no right to presume on the continued smiles of Providence."[15] One of the surest triggers for an outburst of Divine displeasure would be the desecration of the day set aside for worship and prayer.

As such references to the peculiar favors enjoyed by the United States suggest, the Sabbatarian petitioners expressed an unshakeable belief in their nation's exceptionalism. In contrast to continental Europe, so filled with immorality and skepticism, America shone as a stronghold of Christian piety. No institution better exemplified this trans-Atlantic gulf than the Sabbath. Foreign visitors, particularly those from Catholic nations, tended to agree. During his visit in 1831–1832, Alexis de Tocqueville was flabbergasted at the sight of busy cities coming to a halt on Sunday. All the familiar sounds of urban life—the "movements of industry," the "accents of joy," the "confused murmur" of a vibrant city—were replaced with an eerie stillness. Long chains were stretched across streets to prevent carriages disrupting religious services, men and women spent the day clustering in shuttered houses, and the great thoroughfares emptied, the void only occasionally broken by the odd lonely figure.[16] The next day, those same streets burst into life once more. Nothing, the Frenchman concluded, was as remarkable for the foreign observer as the American Sabbath.

While Tocqueville's words might have comforted evangelicals, there were other signs that America was slipping down the international table of Sabbath observance. The holy day, as one group of petitioners in Franklin, New Hampshire lamented, was more and more being "secularized," a term which denoted a preoccupation with worldly rather than spiritual concerns.[17] Admittedly, such concerns are hard to fathom given

Tocqueville's picture of deserted and silent streets. But visitors from Protestant rather than Catholic nations were much less impressed by the American Sabbath. The Scottish businessman Peter Neilson lived in the United States from 1822 to 1828. While there, he observed a very different Sabbath to that seen by Tocqueville. At a fair on the banks of the Schuylkill in Philadelphia, he saw well-dressed men and women indulging in amusements "without much regard to decorum or quietness." He was particularly shocked by the sight of such people spinning around on what he called a "whirligig," a primitive form of carousel. Such "open bare-faced Sabbath breaking," Neilson sniffed, would be confined to the vulgar classes in his native Scotland.[18]

THE ANTI-SABBATARIAN PETITION CAMPAIGN

Historians of the Sunday mail controversy have focused on the Sabbatarian crusade.[19] But what is significant about the clash is that for the first time it brought to the fore a powerful anti-Sabbatarian movement.[20] In December 1828, petitions demanding that the mail "be carried seven times each week as heretofore" began arriving in Congress. Initially, the result was meager. The records of the House Committee on Post Offices and Roads contain only 32 pro-Sunday mail petitions with 3275 signers from December 1828 to May 1829. But the campaign soon picked up pace. In the following session of Congress, 224 petitions carrying 25,863 signatures conveyed a strong message of popular support for Sunday mails. These petitioners went well beyond a call to retain a cherished service. The demise of Sunday mails, they argued to Congress, would be the first step in the overthrow of the civil and religious liberties that had made their country the envy of the civilized world. In making this case, these anti-Sabbatarian petitioners articulated their understanding of the boundaries of religious activism and the extent to which Christianity was woven into the constitutional structure of the nation, putting forth a series of arguments which would reverberate through the rest of the century.

The first point to make about this petition campaign is that it showed a mix of central coordination and local mobilization. Anti-Sabbatarians could not match the organizational sophistication of their opponents. But the Democratic Party, which had come to power with the election of President Andrew Jackson in 1828, provided a framework. In New York, the Tammany Hall machine which dominated Democratic politics in the city held a series of public meetings and established a coordinating committee. Leading figures in the party also played a prominent role in another hotbed of petitioning, Philadelphia, where agents were appointed to circulate petitions throughout the city. On January 14, 1829, the *United States Gazette* reported that "a paper styled a Remonstrance against the petition to stop the passage of the mail on the first day of the week has been left at our office." A similar petition had been left at a nearby coffee house.[21] In smaller towns and villages, the postmaster acted as a crucial local agent, particularly where he was a Jacksonian appointment. Notes attached to several petitions implore him to fill the columns with as many names as possible before sending the document to Congress.

Alongside such central direction was a spontaneous mobilization on the part of aggrieved townspeople. The spur to petition was often their fear that Congress would mistake the views of the local community. Philadelphia anti-Sabbatarians began by referring to a Sabbatarian protest which, they worried, might "be thought to speak the voice of the freemen of this district."[22] The citizens of Bloomfield New York regretted that an opposing petition "conveys the idea that a majority of the people in this state do not wish the mail to be carried on Sunday," an idea which was "highly erroneous."[23] The importance of local initiative is clear as well in the nature of these documents. Identical printed forms circulated in specific areas—Brown County, Ohio, for example, or Bucks County, Pennsylvania. But in contrast to the mass campaigns later in the century, where short identical texts dominated, there was still much scope for local inflection. Overall the wording varied greatly, hand-writing was the rule and, as in the eighteenth-century petitions, underlining and bold letters conveyed a palpable emotion.

One area in which the anti-Sabbatarian petitions were highly uniform was in their exclusion of women. There was a long tradition of individual women petitioning legislatures for redress. But mass petition drives aiming to shift public policy were a different matter.[24] For both evangelicals and their opponents, the arguments which barred women from voting and holding office applied with as much force to the act of signing a petition. These arguments rested largely on biology. Only men were endowed with the intellectual rigor and physical strength to thrive in the rough and tumble world of politics and business. Women, in contrast, were deemed too frail and sensitive to survive in any setting but the protected space of the home. Their role was to act as the moral custodians of the family and in this way to exert an uplifting influence over society as a whole. In this regard, women's possibilities had diminished rather than expanded with the advent of mass democracy. In the eighteenth century, when suffrage was commonly reserved to property holders, women of sufficient means were, in a small number of jurisdictions, able to vote. With the abolition of property restrictions and the shift to universal white suffrage in the early republic, voting became the biological birthright of men. What is interesting is that a similar narrowing of female possibilities had occurred with petitioning. In the eighteenth century, some women joined mass petition campaigns on religious questions. In 1785, eleven women signed a Baptist petition against the religious tax in Virginia.[25] This was admittedly a tiny minority of the total number of signers. But it was a contrast nonetheless with the exclusively male character of the pro-Sunday mail petitions.

The ban on female political petitioning was coming under challenge. As the Sunday mail controversy raged, Lyman Beecher's daughter Catharine set about organizing the first national female petition campaign in American history to protest against Indian removal. As Alisse Portnoy notes, Beecher was careful to frame such activism as conforming to rather than challenging the accepted norms of female behavior. Unlike most other areas of government policy, the Indian question involved weighty moral considerations. As such, Beecher argued, women, who were acknowledged by all to be the guardians of virtue, might exceptionally intervene in such a public manner.[26] But for anti-Sabbatarians, there was evidently no justification for female petitioning. The proof is in one pro-mail petition from Kentucky. Somehow, three women managed to add their names to those of 113 men. By the time it arrived in Congress, however, an anonymous hand had drawn a line through all three names.[27]

In terms of social background, anti-Sabbatarians were a mixed bunch. Merchants were a prominent voice, particularly in the first phase of 1828–1829. The initial burst of petitions came from a cluster of towns along the recently opened Erie Canal—Rochester, Buffalo, Perryville, Canandaigua, Lewiston, and others—which were all linked by Sunday mail routes and which were enjoying an economic boom driven largely by a regular and unimpeded flow of goods and commercial information to and from New York City. In these towns, businessmen took the lead in protesting against any disruption to the networks on which their prosperity hinged. A petition from Buffalo portrayed a business community almost unanimously opposed to the Sabbatarian crusade. Any attempt to stop the mails, it declared, "will meet with strenuous opposition from seven-eighths of the business community."[28]

To prove their personal investment in the issue, petitioners listed the amount of postage paid. In Rochester, 183 petitioners together had paid $6808.07 in postage the preceding year.[29] In Canandaigua, one signatory, Henry B. Gibson, a leading banker and businessman, claimed to have accrued no less than $324 in postal fees.[30] These men were fearful of losing access to the most up-to-date information about markets and prices. Such information, as Rochester petitioners warned, "is indispensable, and without it their business would be far more hazardous."[31] A second anxiety centered on the prospect of unfair competition as private companies moved to fill the gap left by the shutting down of the federal postal service. "If the mails," Canandaigua petitioners declared, "were statedly suspended for one day in each week, intelligence would in many instances be transmitted at great expense by interested individuals in anticipation of the regular mail."[32] The only fair approach was to ensure that the postal system, the great "arterial system of the Union," remained open and accessible to all on equal terms.[33]

Was it all, then, about money? Some Sabbatarians thought so, casting the push for Sunday mails as a familiar tale of greed trumping morality. But this was far from the case. To begin with, wealth alone was a poor predictor of an individual's position. Some of the wealthiest merchants in the nation bankrolled the Sabbatarian campaign. In addition to Arthur Tappan, leading merchants such as Peter Hoffman Jr. in Baltimore and Samuel Appleton in Boston signed petitions against Sunday mails. Nor were they alone. The Sabbatarian petitions are dotted with the names of presidents of banks, insurance companies, and law firms.[34] Conversely, pro-mail petitions from the Erie Canal towns are signed by a broad cross section of occupations. In the case of Rochester, this includes several mechanics, an innkeeper, a butcher, a plow-maker, a sword instructor, and the editor of the *Rochester Telegraph*.[35] More fundamentally, the towns along the Erie Canal provided only a fraction of the anti-Sabbatarian petitions. The records of the 20th and 21st Congresses show that the Atlantic states provided two-thirds of the petitions (see Appendix A). But while New York was an important center, Pennsylvania dominated all others, sending 46% of the petitions and an even higher percentage of the signatures. The northwest, and particularly Ohio, was also well represented. In contrast, New England as well as the southern states accounted for less than 10% of petitions, respectively.

In the case of the Baptists, the Sunday mail clash showed the shift that had occurred since 1785. A small number joined the anti-Sabbatarian side. The famed Baptist preacher John Leland was a vocal critic both of Sabbath laws and their enforcement by State agencies. Less prominent Baptists added their names to petitions in favor of Sunday mails. Among the signers of the Philadelphia petitions was Thomas J. Kitts, pastor of the Second Baptist church, and Elisha Cushman of the New Market Street church. In Cincinnati, the Enon Baptist church hosted a pro-mail meeting. The narrative of persecution through which so many Baptists understood their history once again came to the fore. In 1831, the Alabama Baptist Association wrote to Congress, warning that the nation was on the verge of reverting to the spirit of intolerance that had marked the colonial era. We have not forgotten, the Association wrote, "our whipping Posts, Poisons, Fines, Lawsuits, and Costs that we suffered in the State of Virginia and Massachusetts."[36]

Yet Baptists by and large joined the Sabbatarian coalition. Already in 1785, as we have seen, Baptists expressed their support for Sabbath laws. As William G. McLoughlin argued, by the early Republic the New England Baptists were well on the way to shedding their historical character as dissenters and becoming a mainstay of the evangelical establishment. This included a wholehearted support for the anti-Sunday mail crusade.[37] The *American Baptist* magazine acclaimed the formation of the GUPOCS as sure to "inspire peculiar joy in every pious and benevolent breast," and urged its readers to join as auxiliaries.[38] The names of Baptist pastors are sprinkled throughout the Sabbatarian petitions: two appear on a petition from New Brunswick, New Jersey, for example.[39] This is in many ways not surprising. Baptists had a long and proud tradition of opposing formal establishments. But in the same manner as other evangelical churches, they regarded more informal measures in favor of their faith as not only legitimate but indispensable to the fortunes of the republic.

One of the factors that may have driven Baptists to join the anti-mail side was the presence of so many freethinkers in the opposing camp. Though embracing an eclectic set of views, freethinkers shared a commitment to human improvement through rational inquiry, a devotion to a strict separation of church and state, and a fierce hostility to clerical authority. As the mail controversy escalated, freethought societies sprang into life. Formed in January 1827 in New York, the "Free Press Association" aimed to spread freethought principles by funding a newspaper, the *Correspondent*, and by holding public lectures on Sundays. The next year, a "Society of Free Enquirers" further augmented the ranks of New York's freethinkers. In their view, the push to ban Sunday mails was part of a broader assertion of clerical authority that, if left unchallenged, would stifle individual freedoms and inaugurate a dark era of intolerance. The Englishwoman Frances Wright was the most prominent freethought lecturer and activist in the nation. In speeches in New York and in Philadelphia, she denounced the fanatical clergy who were at that moment showering Congress with their "Sabbath law petitions." Their ambitions, she warned, were far larger. If not firmly checked, clerical intolerance would infect all the institutions of the land, from schools to courts and legislatures, blanketing the nation with its "reason-confounding, heart-distorting creeds."[40] Dogma would displace science, superstition would trump instruction, and persecution rather than freedom would become the ruling principle of the once great American nation.

Freethinkers were a natural constituency for the pro-mail campaign. Yet the extent of their participation in the petition drive is difficult to assess. Though some may have signed, none of the petitions show an obvious freethought affiliation. Furthermore, while animated by the same fear of clerical power, no petition text contains anything resembling Wright's call for Americans to make nature their Bible and to transform their churches into halls of science. Petitions were public documents designed to sway legislators. As such, they could not admit arguments that smacked of a doctrine as controversial and in many quarters reviled as atheism. Many petitioners were in fact keen to distance themselves from even the slightest hint of irreligion. We claim, as petitioners in Russia, New York, wrote, "as high a reverence for the laws of God, and as strict an observance of religious duties," as anyone else.[41]

A more identifiable group, which had strong anticlerical leanings, was urban artisans. A primary reason that Philadelphia was such a hotbed of anti-Sabbatarian petitioning was its active, politically articulate and sizeable working class. One of its leading figures was the cordwainer William Heighton. A determined advocate of the surplus theory of labor, which held that working people should benefit from the wealth that they produced, Heighton played a pivotal role in uniting the city's journeymen societies into the first organized political workingmen's party. In 1829, Heighton's party achieved its greatest result, polling 2400 votes in the city and country of Philadelphia, and electing sixteen candidates.[42] Heighton was also founder and editor of the country's first working-class newspaper, the *Mechanics' Free Press*. Although his name is not identifiable on any of the extant petitions, Heighton left no doubt about his position on the Sunday mail issue. On December 5, 1828, the *Mechanics' Free Press* alerted its readers to the threat posed by the national Sabbatarian campaign; on December 27, it reported that an anti-Sunday mail petition was now circulating in the city. Heighton's reaction was unequivocal. He angrily denounced "another attempt at prostrating our rights on the altar of superstition and bigotry," and urged his readers to launch a counter-petition campaign. "A counter-memorial ought immediately to be circulated for signatures," he wrote, "and every part of the city and county searched for names to the remonstrance."[43]

Across the nineteenth century, religion and class interacted in complex ways. As a number of social historians have made clear, religion played an important role in the lives and reforming visions of workers.[44] In the case of Heighton, the promise of salvation for all at the heart of Universalism was immensely appealing. Rejecting Calvinism and its doctrine of predestination, Universalists stressed a positive faith in humanity and its capacity for rational self-improvement. Just as importantly for Heighton, Universalists eschewed ecclesiastical authority and rigid doctrine in favor of a loose alliance of like-minded fellows. This kind of rational Christianity was very congenial to Heighton, who gave speeches in Philadelphia's two Universalist churches.[45] Reform-minded evangelicalism, however, was a different matter. Evangelical churches had long sought to win over Philadelphia's artisans. In the Northern Liberties district, Presbyterians were represented from 1814 by the energetic minister of the First Church, James Patterson. Ronald Schultz suggests that some workers were attracted to their promise of communal support and personal redemption.[46] But the positives were outweighed by resentment at clerical moralizing about gambling and drinking, which many working people saw as harmless forms of recreation.

The Sunday mail controversy showed the depth of this working-class hostility to clerical ambition. One moment in particular stood out. In May 1829, the city's press reported that a mail car traveling from New York to Philadelphia had been forcibly stopped by Sabbatarian activists in Princeton, New Jersey. Outraged, the *Mechanics' Free Press* denounced the perpetrators as an "arrogant, crafty and designing priesthood" intent on crushing the liberties of freemen. "Shall we allow," the paper demanded of its readers, "the saddle of priestly domination to be thrown on our necks?"[47] As Sabbatarians circulated through working-class districts seeking names to add to their petitions, the reaction of artisans was often fierce. The *Mechanics' Press* reported one such confrontation. When several Sabbatarians, described as "long-visaged disciples," visited a workshop with their petition, a printer told them brusquely to clear off, adding that he would never lend his name "to such a ministerial humbug."[48]

THE ARGUMENTS FOR SUNDAY MAILS

Turning from the petitioners to their arguments, we see a similar level of diversity. A constant preoccupation was the nature of true faith. As we have seen, many of the petitioners were keen to stress their piety. Far from attacking religion, they outlined a vision of a faith which relied on nothing more than its core truths to prosper. Again and again, petitioners argued that a true faith did not require state protection or endorsement and would prosper if left to its own resources. "All it asks from the government," one petition from Columbia County, Pennsylvania argued, "is to be let alone, to make its own way."[49] A memorial of the General Assembly of the state of Indiana echoed Madison's memorial in arguing that this desire to stand alone had elevated Christianity over all other faiths. "All legislative interference in matters of religion," the memorialists declared, "is contrary to the genius of Christianity ... there are no doctrines or observances inculcated by the Christian religion which requires the arm of civil power either to enforce or sustain them."[50] More than unnecessary, state sponsorship would deform true faith. The greatest threat to religion, according to a series of printed petitions that circulated throughout Pennsylvania, was not the spread of infidelity, but "the corrupting hand of secular power."[51] Once it relied on government enforcement to survive, faith became a mere "engine of state policy."[52]

The result would be not only a debasement of true faith, however. More saliently, the petitioners feared the consequences for civil liberty when a zealous clergy armed itself with the powers of secular government. If ever, one group of petitioners warned, the government were to fall into the "iron grasp of the church," the results would be disastrous. History was proof of the cruelties, suffering, and abuses which would ensue.[53] A public meeting held in July 1829 in Philadelphia emphasized the point. Evangelicals had a plan to "subject Civil Liberty to religious

Intolerance"; in response, it was time for all freemen to rally to protect "our civil rights and privileges untrammeled by ecclesiastical influence."[54] This concern with civil liberty, a phrase repeated again and again in the petitions, drove much of the desire to maintain a strict separation of church and state. "The maintenance of our Constitutional lines of demarcation between the affairs of Church and State," as protesters in Poughkeepsie, New York warned, "is essential to the preservation of our civil freedom."[55]

These were freedoms that had been bequeathed by the Revolutionary generation, and the desire to defend their legacy weighed heavily in the minds of anti-Sabbatarian petitioners. In this respect, their campaign was part of a broader cultural impulse. The decade from 1820 to 1830 was, as Michael Kammen argues, a "sharp point of demarcation" in the practice of commemorating the Revolution. Histories of the Revolution appeared in multiple editions. An outpouring of memoirs and reminiscences by war veterans, and the national grief which followed the deaths of Thomas Jefferson and John Adams in 1826, provided more raw material for a burgeoning tradition of Revolutionary commemoration.[56] As the nation celebrated the Revolutionary achievement with a newfound vigor, anti-Sabbatarians staked their claim to be the custodians of a cherished inheritance. References to the "wise framers" abound in their petitions. Speakers at town meetings sought to link the Sunday mail clash to the Revolutionary battles of the past. One petition bore the mark of a man identified as a Revolutionary soldier.[57] At an Ohio town meeting, pride of place was given to a veteran of the Revolutionary wars.[58] Rather than innovators on the question of church-state relations, anti-Sabbatarians saw themselves as faithful to the guiding principles laid down by the Founding Fathers.

Their understanding of these principles derived from the document which more than any other captured the Founders' vision for the nation, the federal Constitution. In the minds of anti-Sabbatarians, this document took precedence over state or local law, and they drew from it their conviction that any mingling of religion and politics was unlawful. The Constitution, as Pennsylvania petitioners argued, had forever barred "anything which tends to unite religion and politics."[59] Again and again, anti-Sabbatarian petitioners denounced the campaign of their opponents as "contrary to the spirit and letter of the Constitution," "derogatory to the spirit of the Constitution," and a violation of "our great national Compact, the Constitution." The great authors of that document, they confidently asserted, would be horrified by any attempt to enforce religious doctrine through law or public policy. As petitioners from Poughkeepsie explained, those men, scarred by their experience of colonial establishments, and highly conscious of the evils produced by church-state alliances in continental Europe, carefully designed the Constitution to avoid such an outcome. Their fear of the "baneful influence" produced by the "unnatural union" of religion and state inspired the nation's ruling text.[60]

To guard against such a union, the Founders devised the first amendment. Anti-Sabbatarian petitioners often quoted its religion clauses and were in no doubt as to their meaning. To begin with, the first amendment banned a national church along the lines of the Catholic Church in France or the Anglican Church in England. This was not a controversial argument; evangelicals, too, vociferously opposed formal establishments. But where the two sides diverged was in their definition of establishment. Sabbatarians listed the features of national churches in Europe: state salaries for clergy, for example, or legal penalties for dissenters. Anti-Sabbatarians, in contrast, saw a religious establishment forming whenever churches appealed to state enforcement rather than moral persuasion and whenever the government began taking sides in theological disputes. The only sure way to block such an establishment was to maintain the government as wholly secular, a term which in the minds of petitioners denoted not a hostility to religion, but simply an aloofness from all questions of dogma or doctrine. The "very letter of our Constitution," Erie County (Pennsylvania) petitioners reminded Congress, guaranteed that "our government was a civil compact totally unconnected with the church."[61] "That one great and leading object in the adoption of the Constitution of the United States," as the citizens of Poughkeepsie argued, "was to exclude or separate religion from the affairs of state."[62] In their understanding, the Founders, through the agency of the first amendment, constructed a government which treated questions of faith as outside its cognizance.

From this principle, anti-Sabbatarians drew the conclusion that a law to enforce the Sunday Sabbath was unconstitutional. If Congress were to ban Sunday mails, it would be intervening in a theological dispute, taking on the role of religious arbiter, and thereby straying from its secular mission. The key to this argument was religious disagreement over, firstly, whether it was right to elevate one day above others. "There is no small diversity of opinion among mankind," petitioners from Chester

County, Pennsylvania reminded Congress, "regarding the propriety of keeping one day in seven holy."[63] There was also disagreement about which day to keep. Some petitioners referred to Christian churches that regarded Saturday as the true Sabbath, others to Jews, Muslims, Turks, even pagans and heathens. Since the question was far from settled, government should stay out. The Sabbatarian campaign was an attempt "to obtain indirectly the decision of the highest tribunal of the land in settling a religious controversy," and as such a violation of the first amendment and the civil character of the national government.[64]

The Fear of Conspiracy

Statements of constitutional principle provide only one key, however, to the anti-Sabbatarian campaign. If so many citizens interpreted a campaign to end Sunday mails as a fateful step toward clerical despotism, it was because of a pervasive fear of conspiracy. This was a fear that had deep roots in republican political culture. But the advent of mass democracy gave it an even sharper edge. The 1828 victory of Andrew Jackson, the orphan from the western frontier who rose to prominence through his military exploits, over John Quincy Adams, Harvard-educated son of a former President, signaled a major shift in power. For his supporters, Jackson was the "people's President" who would smash the old financial and political elites and bring about a new era of the common worker. But alongside this optimistic vision was a nagging fear that powerful and hostile elites were scheming to subvert the public will.

This was exactly how anti-Sabbatarians interpreted the drive to end Sunday mails. When they looked at GUPOCS and the web of churches and local auxiliaries sending petitions across the nation, they did not see a legitimate effort to shape public opinion in an emerging mass democracy. Instead, they saw a sinister and undemocratic plot with a far-reaching goal. An observant citizen could now detect, as one polemic argued, the "many strings and wires which were set in motion to accomplish this design," which was not just an end to Sunday mails but "an unnatural union of clerical and secular governments."[65] Faced with such shadowy maneuvers, Philadelphia freemen declared themselves to be "fearful and suspicious, alarmed and apprehensive."[66] To their mind, a vast conspiracy had now come to light.

This style of thinking infused the anti-Sabbatarian petitions. In a similar manner to Madison in 1785, they made a leap from a specific if objectionable proposal to a far more disturbing pattern of events. The Sunday mail crusade was but the opening gambit in a vast clerico-political plot. All the elements of a conspiracy were present. The enemy, though small in number, boasts daunting financial and intellectual resources. The resolutions adopted by an anti-Sabbatarian meeting in Salina, New York are typical. Their opponents, characterized as "crafty and ambitious men," wield formidable weapons, from their "scientific and literary acquirements" to "the vast funds which are at their disposal."[67] They work to a clear and predetermined plan, methodically filling public offices with their allies and surreptitiously molding public opinion. Petitioners from Perryville New York detected a scheme "to coerce and subject the public mind to sectarian views, and to fill every important station with Officers of congenial views."[68] Within this conception of the enemy, no battle could be regarded as insignificant. The passage of a law to ban Sunday mails would, in a much-repeated phrase, be the "entering wedge" in a more thorough plan of clerical despotism.

In response, Sabbatarians professed themselves bewildered. The proposal to stop the post office operating on Sunday would merely bring one department of government into line with the rest. Congress did not deliberate on Sunday, and other branches of government were shut as well. How could anti-Sabbatarians seriously claim that their nation was faced with the nightmare prospect of a union of church and state? Editorialists who were sympathetic to the Sabbatarian cause expressed their puzzlement. The *Connecticut Courant* dismissed as "senseless clamor" the charge that Sabbatarians wished to unite church and state.[69] This was clearly not their goal. As petitioners in Erie County, New York declared, they were among the "warmest and most strenuous opposers" of any "Church-State combination."[70]

Their opponents, however, insisted that such statements masked a deeper intent which, though cleverly hidden, occasionally drifted into view. The petitions refer again and again to one such moment. In 1827, the Presbyterian Ezra Stiles Ely gave a sermon in which he called for the formation of a "Christian party in politics."[71] Ely apparently envisaged a loose alliance of activists who would work together to ensure that men of sound Christian morals were elected to office. But his words were widely interpreted to mean much more. Petitioners seized on Ely's language as signaling a deep-seated ambition to revive the discredited establishments of the past, with their religious tests for office and persecution of dissenters. Another feature of Sabbatarian arguments to arouse suspicion was the frequent reference to England. Sabbatarians used the example of London, a great mercantile city where the post office was closed on Sundays, to prove that Sabbath laws were no obstacle to commercial prosperity.[72] But anti-Sabbatarians detected in these allusions to England a secret desire on the part of their opponents to enact an Anglican-style establishment at home. On the question of religious liberty, America had nothing to learn from its former colonial master. "Following too much the example and practice of that church and state government," as a meeting at Tammany Hall resolved, "has been the bane of our free institutions and the misfortune of our country."[73]

If further proof was needed of the devious nature of their opponents, anti-Sabbatarians seized on the means by which they prosecuted their case. Here, they tackled squarely the imbalance in the number of petitions sent to Congress by both sides. John G. West has calculated that 81% of petitions sent to the House from 1827 to 1830 were against Sunday mails. How, then, could anti-Sabbatarians claim that theirs was the majority view and that an unscrupulous elite was subverting the popular will? One response might have referred to timing. The Sabbatarians' overall lead was largely due to their initial flurry of petitioning during the 20th Congress (1827–1829). Once anti-Sabbatarians began to mobilize in earnest in the next session, the balance, while remaining favorable to Sabbatarians, began to shift. In 1830, the proportion of petitions against and for Sunday mails narrowed to 61–39%.[74]

Still, the bare evidence of petitions pointed to a Sabbatarian majority. In response, anti-Sabbatarians cast doubt on the reliability of the petition as a barometer of public opinion. One way to do this was to minimize the significance of the raw number of signatures. In a note attached to a Philadelphia petition, Joseph Carter stated that he had been tasked with obtaining signatures at a public meeting held in the Northern Liberties district on January 25, 1830. This he accomplished without difficulty. Having collected more than a hundred in less than four hours, he stopped, satisfied, as he put it, that "not one in twenty ... had any desire to discontinue the Mail on that day."[75] It would be a mistake, Carter implied, to read the final tally of names as corresponding to the state of community feeling. For a start, he could easily have gathered more. But more importantly, just as telling as the number of names was the ease with which they were gathered. For Carter, this variable, which was impossible to communicate in a signatory list, was a key indicator of where public opinion lay.

Then there was the difficulty in assessing the motivations of those who signed. In Bradford, Massachusetts, anti-Sabbatarians attacked a rival petition as padded with the names of people who had no interest in the issue and who had signed merely to gratify the person who was soliciting their help. The resulting petition, with its long list of names, might give the impression that there was a "great excitement in the place against the present mail arrangement" but such an impression would be false. Most of the signers "do not care anything at all about it."[76] A Virginian described witnessing a Presbyterian minister solicit signatures from four men. Three refused, but the fourth signed without even reading the text.[77] Occasionally, the signers of anti-Sabbatarian petitions confessed to such thoughtlessness on previous occasions. In a note next to his signature, Benjamin McCann of Kentucky wrote that he had once signed a Sabbatarian petition "without thought," but now wished to record his true opinion that the mail should run "at all times necessary."[78] On the same petition, other men also recanted their previously expressed view.

Throughout the century, commentators would continue to wrestle with the problem of evaluating the true worth of mass petitions. Complicating the question further was the suspicion of fraud. Again and again, anti-Sabbatarians accused their opponents of inflating their lists of signatures with fictitious names. In New York, cross-referencing the names on a large Sabbatarian petition against the city directory revealed only 3013 of 6286 to be genuine.[79] Another common charge was that children were forced to sign. A Reverend Mason in New York allegedly brought a petition into the Sunday School attached to his church in Cedar Street for this purpose.[80] In yet another mark of their ruthlessness, Sabbatarians were accused of threatening those who refused to support their cause. This charge was leveled at none other than the Tappan brothers, Arthur and Lewis, who together financed so many evangelical activities. In a claim that was widely circulated, a New York tailor named Thomas Holden claimed that Lewis Tappan had entered his store armed with a Sabbatarian petition, threatening a boycott unless he agreed to sign.[81] Referring to such incidents, the Tammany meeting recorded its "solemn protest" against the "unrighteousness" of its opponents.[82] Others were even blunter. In Nantucket, petitioners attacked such efforts to "make a show of strength by an appearance of numbers" as both "disgraceful to themselves, and an insult to Congress."[83] To draw a contrast with this duplicity, anti-Sabbatarians sometimes made a public show of their integrity. A Pennsylvania petition in 1830 with 891 signatures arrived in Congress with a section missing. An accompanying note explained that, having detected several duplicate names, and not wishing to misrepresent in any way the views of the community, the organizers of the petition had voluntarily excised them.[84]

Even when conceding that the weight of petitions had tipped against them, anti-Sabbatarians found an explanation in the machinations of a group that they identified simply as the "Clergy." The list of sins attributed to the Clergy was almost endless. To cite the petitions, its members were "arrogant and domineering," "corrupt," "intolerant," "enterprising and ambitious." The lesson of the past was that the goals and behavior of the Clergy were at all times and in all places unbending. As petitioners in Alstead, New Hampshire warned, "in all ages, down to the present, the Clergy have been enterprising and ambitious,—seizing eagerly upon power, and exercising it without reason and without mercy."[85] Faced with such an opponent, anti-Sabbatarians were called upon to respond with determination and courage. For the "safety of civil society," as North Carolina petitioners argued, it was imperative to mount a fierce resistance to this clergy which everywhere had "made such a terrible and butchering use of law."[86]

So devious was this clergy that it began to resemble the Catholic priesthood. In a foretaste of a trend which would escalate significantly once mass Catholic immigration ensued in the 1840s and 1850s, anti-Sabbatarians drew on the rhetoric and imagery of anti-Catholicism to conceptualize the nature of their opponents. Petitioners from Poughkeepsie made this association very clear. Unless the Sabbatarians were stopped, they warned, "an ecclesiastical hierarchy will be established in this country, as oppressive and dangerous in its effects as ever was exerted by the pope of Rome."[87] The nature of the threat could be conveyed in one word: priestcraft. Originally a product of anti-Catholic prejudice, priestcraft now denoted any clergy, Protestant or Catholic, which twisted religion for political ends.[88] Just as in the eighteenth century, petitioners deployed the great symbol of fanaticism, the Inquisition, to convey the scale of the threat. The Sabbatarians, one Ohio petition thundered, were "scorpion-tailed inquisitors"; if their campaign were to succeed, petitioners in North Carolina envisaged nothing less than "bigotry, persecution, tyranny, blood and death, in the most horrid and cruel forms which human ingenuity could invent."[89] Sabbatarian priestcraft threatened to stain the New World with the bloody excesses of the Old.

These attacks came together in visual form in one lithograph. The Philadelphia engraver and cartoonist James Akin was notorious for his attacks on President Jackson, whom he routinely depicted in regal gowns and poses.[90] But in *"The Holy Alliance," or, Satan's Legion at Sabbath Pranks* (Fig. 3.1), produced at the height of the controversy, Akin took aim at the Sabbatarians. Dominating the image is the depiction of a group of clergy waylaying a Sunday mail carriage, a reference to the incident in Princeton, New Jersey which had so enraged William Heighton. Akin references many of the sinister aims and strategies condemned in the anti-Sabbatarian petitions. The desire to crush religious liberty is shown in the figure of a clergyman sitting astride a church on what is labeled the "Great State saddle." The link to Old World intolerance is evident as well. Frenzied clerics in different garbs are constructing an inquisitorial pyre, while the accompanying text warns of chains, dungeons, and scaffolds. Even petition fraud is shown in a long Sabbatarian protest snaking along the foreground of the image, its list of names inflated by 2500 Sunday School children. Akin adds a dose of misogyny. Seated on pews, the Sunday School women holding the petition look shrewish and fierce; one complains of the difficulty of finding a husband. The intended meaning is clear. By stepping beyond the sheltered space of the home, where their influence might properly exert itself, and instead engaging in the manly world of public politicking, these women have forfeited their feminine charm and with it their natural destiny of becoming wives and mothers.

THE JOHNSON REPORTS

The anti-Sabbatarian complaints about petition fraud and deception are from this distance impossible to verify. Anti-mail campaigners could respond that they were a smokescreen to divert attention from an inconvenient truth: that the public wished Sunday mails to end. Yet it would also be a mistake to assume that opinion corresponded neatly to petition numbers. Sabbatarians were a motivated group aiming to effect change rather than to maintain the status quo and backed up by an efficient organizational machine. For these reasons, they were always likely to win the petition war.

The level of support for the anti-Sabbatarian position would be shown when the government finally adjudicated on the issue in two reports issued by Colonel Richard Mentor Johnson of Kentucky, chair of the

Fig. 3.1 James Akin, *"The Holy Alliance," or, Satan's Legion at Sabbath Pranks* (1830) (Courtesy of American Antiquarian Society)

Senate and then the House Committee on the Post Office and the Post Roads. The first, on January 19, 1829, forcefully asserted a strict separationist position. Having noted the practical benefits of Sunday mails, and the disruption to commerce that would result from their abolition, the report proclaimed the fundamental principle that religious questions were outside the cognizance of the state. "Our government is a civil," the report declared, "and not a religious institution." The report then raised the specter of religious despotism. Whenever "extensive religious combinations" sought "to effect a political object," it was only a matter of time before government came under their control.[91] The lesson was clear. The Sunday mail controversy was merely the opening shot of a deeper plot against American liberties. "If the principle is once established, that religion, or religious observances, shall be interwoven with our legislative acts," the report warned, "we must pursue it to its ultimatum." The government would begin funding the construction of cathedrals and paying the salaries of priests, and soon the New World would resemble the Old. The only safeguard against such a fate was to adhere to the Constitution, a document which created a government as a "civil institution, wholly destitute of religious authority."[92]

Johnson's authorship of the report has long been called into question. Contemporaries thought it improbable that a man so lacking in education and intellectual accomplishment could mount such a sophisticated constitutional argument. Several accounts later in the century would identify the true author as Obadiah Brown, a Baptist who was a clerk in the post office.[93] Arguably, however, more significant than its authorship is the fact that the report reproduced and affirmed the arguments made by the petitioners. In this sense, they were the true authors, and their appreciation was palpable. A public meeting at Tammany Hall declared its "fullest approbation" of the report which had so forcefully defended the "civil and religious rights of the people."[94] Many now assumed the matter to be closed and were astounded when the Sabbatarian campaign resumed in the next session of Congress. Praising the "unanswerable arguments" contained in the report, Nantucket petitioners saw a sorry lesson in the Sabbatarian refusal to give up. "The intolerant spirit of Religious Bigots," they lamented, "is the same in all ages."[95]

A longer and even more emphatic report the next year stilled the anti-Sunday mail clamor. This report hardened its attacks on religious zealotry, echoing the harsh denunciations of the Clergy contained in the petitions. Nothing was so "incessant in its toils, so persevering in its determinations, so appalling in its course, or so dangerous in its consequence."[96] The danger for the community was particularly acute when zealotry took on a political hue. No faith, even the most peaceable, could resist the temptation to arm itself with political authority. "Every religious sect," the report warned, "however meek in its origin, commenced the work of persecution as soon as it acquired political power."[97] Reflecting the importance of the Revolutionary legacy to the petitioners, the report ended with a vigorous appeal to the hardy spirit of the Founders. Citing the Boston Tea Party, the report reminded Americans that the Founders "did not wait to be oppressed" but instead took a "bold stand." Their successors should be just as intrepid.[98]

The Johnson reports are significant for several reasons. Firstly, they served as a reference for later generations of secularists. At the end of the century, evangelicals were still lamenting their influence, while advocates of a secular state were celebrating their arguments. The response to them provides as well a glimpse of the transatlantic dimension to church-state controversies. As the Sunday mail controversy raged, Great Britain was experiencing its own agitation on the question of religious liberty. There the question was the political rights of Catholics. The passage of the 1829 Roman Catholic Relief Act completed a long process of emancipation by granting Catholics the right to sit in Parliament. In the midst of the debate over this measure, the *Liverpool Mercury* quoted Johnson's ringing affirmation of the civil character of the American state. England, it suggested, should emulate the enlightened doctrine set out in the report and grant full civic equality to religious minorities. American papers then relayed this commentary to their readers. The *Trumpet and Universalist Magazine* cited the *Mercury's* comments as evidence of a growing transatlantic consensus that a modern state should distance itself from sectarian division. The paper also took the opportunity to highlight the retrograde character of the Sabbatarian campaign. How could anyone make the state a machine of religious proscription when the most civilized nations of the world were moving toward greater religious freedom? Not for the last time, secularists used the international dimension to attempt to paint their opponents as swimming against the tide of progress.[99]

The Johnson reports point as well to the linkage between religious liberty and race. The manner in which a defense of the secular state could align with white supremacism would become most clear on the question of slavery. But though left unstated in the reports, for Johnson and his supporters the so-called Christian party in politics was a threat to one of their cherished policies, Indian removal. In late 1829 evangelicals launched another petition campaign, this time to prevent the federal government colluding with the state of Georgia to seize Cherokee lands and expel indigenous peoples west of the Mississippi. For years afterward, furious Democrats denounced the evangelical mobilization on behalf of the Cherokee and other tribes as yet more unwarranted clerical meddling in national politics. In 1838, Georgia Congressman Wilson Lumpkin castigated the pro-Cherokee petitioners as a "religious party in politics" seeking to "blend Church and State." The "opponents of the Government and their pious friends," he lamented, "will not let the Indians go."[100]

The ways in which the Sunday mail and Indian removal issues blended together was clear as well in the tributes to Colonel Johnson. Having praised his record fighting Indians in the 1812 war, one campaign biographer went on to celebrate his stance against religious bigots in Congress. The "same determined spirit," the author declared, led Johnson to oppose both the "open foe on the battlefield" as well as the "secret enemies in the Senate chamber."[101] Indian removal was not the primary reason that Jacksonian Democrats mobilized against evangelicals or proclaimed the need to distance religion from politics. But there is no doubt either that the issue sharpened their hostility to what they characterized as illegitimate and dangerous clerical interference in public affairs.

Historians who argue for the dominance of the informal establishment underplay the evangelical defeat on Sunday mails. David Sehat suggests that the contest did not demonstrate the "speciousness of the ideal of the Christian nation."[102] It is certainly the case that Sabbath laws continued to be enforced in other areas and jurisdictions and that evangelicals rebounded quickly to press for moral legislation elsewhere. But nor should we minimize its significance. The outcome showed that, for all the vitality of evangelical activism, significant divisions existed within the Protestant community on the question of the public role of religion. Many anti-Sabbatarians insisted that their faith was as strong as that of their opponents. But religion, in their view, jeopardized its inherent purity when it strayed too close to state power, becoming in the process a vehicle of fanaticism rather than enlightenment. Civil government, too, was deformed when it sanctioned specific religious doctrines. The chief business of government, as one pro-mail meeting declared, was "maintaining the civil rights and promoting the temporal interests equally of every citizen of the United States, whether he be Christian, Heretic, or Infidel."[103] When it became concerned instead with actively promoting faith, these petitioners argued, the nation was well on the way to a union of church and state.

For many reasons, then, the Sunday mail battle was a key moment. The question that remained, however, was whether this mobilization was the last gasp of a Revolutionary-era impulse or an enduring impulse that might thwart proponents of the Christian nation ideal in the decades ahead.

Notes

1. Re-printed in *Vermont Gazette*, January 27, 1829. Also *Gospel Advocate and Impartial Investigator*, February 21, 1829; *Christian Repository*, April 1829; *National Philanthropist and Investigator*, March 12, 1829. A pamphlet edition appeared in Washington, DC the previous year.
2. Noll, *America's God*, 166, 169.
3. "Letter from the Postmaster-General Transmitting a Statement of the Post Routes Within the United States, on which the Mail is Transported on Sunday." March 4, 1830. House Doc 73, 21st Congress, 1st session.
4. *Laws and Regulation for the Government of the Post-Office Department* (Washington, DC: Alexander & Barnard, 1843), 7–8.
5. *Torch Light & Public Advertiser* (Hagerstown, MD), December 9, 1830; *Newbern Sentinel* (NC), June 24, 1831.
6. Lyman Beecher, *Lectures on Political Atheism and Kindred Subjects* (Boston: J.P. Jewett, 1852), 116.
7. *Minutes of the General Assembly of the Presbyterian Church in the United States of America*, vol. 6 (Philadelphia: Jesper Harding, 1826–1829), 239.
8. John G. West, *The Politics of Revelation and Reason: Religion and Civic Life in the New Nation* (Lawrence: University Press of Kansas, 1996), 261 (no. 10).
9. *An Account of Memorials Presented to Congress During Its Last Session by Numerous Friends of Their Country and Its Institutions: Praying That the Mails May Not Be Transported, nor Post Offices Kept Open, on the Sabbath* (New York: T.R. Marvin, 1829), 17. Italics in original.
10. Timothy Dwight, *Theology Explained & Defended, in a Series of Sermons*, vol. 3 (New York: G&C Carvill, 1828), 231.
11. Ibid., 231.
12. Rec. December 18, 1828. H.R. 20A G14.2. Unless otherwise noted, the petitions that follow are housed at the National Archives, Washington, DC.
13. *Account of Memorials Presented to Congress*, 13.
14. No date. H.R. 20A G14.2.

3 "PROSTRATING OUR RIGHTS ON THE ALTAR OF SUPERSTITION ...   59

15. No date. H.R. 20A G14.2.
16. Alexis de Tocqueville, *Democracy in America*, vol. II (New York: Vintage, 1990), 341.
17. Rec. January 12, 1829. H.R. 20A G14.2.
18. Peter Neilson, *Recollections of a Six Years' Residence in the United States of America, Interspersed with Original Anecdotes* (Glasgow: D. Robertson, 1830), 145.
19. On the Sabbatarian crusade, see Richard R. John, "Taking Sabbatarianism Seriously: The Postal System, the Sabbath, and the Transformation of American Political Culture," *Journal of the Early Republic* 10, no. 4 (1990): 517–67; James R. Rohrer, "Sunday Mails and the Church-State Theme in Jacksonian America," *Journal of the Early Republic* 7, no. 1 (1987): 53–74; Wayne E. Fuller, *Morality and the Mail in Nineteenth-Century America* (Urbana: University of Illinois, 2003); and Bertram Wyatt-Brown, "Prelude to Abolitionism: Sabbatarian Politics and the Rise of the Second Party System," *Journal of American History* 58, no. 2 (1971): 316–41.
20. On anti-Sabbatarians, see John, "Taking Anti-Sabbatarianism Seriously," 548–54; Alexis McCrossen, *Holy Day, Holiday: The American Sunday* (Ithaca: Cornell University Press, 2000), 26–30; and Wyatt-Brown, "Prelude to Abolitionism," 334–36.
21. *United States Gazette* (Philadelphia), January 14, 1829.
22. Rec. January 16, 1829. H.R. 20A G14.2.
23. Signed December 16, 1828. H.R. 20A G14.2.
24. On women petitioning, see Susan Zaeske, *Signatures of Citizenship: Petitioning, Antislavery and Women's Political Identity* (Chapel Hill: University of North Carolina Press, 2003); Rosemarie Zagarri, *Revolutionary Backlash: Women and Politics in the Early American Republic* (Philadelphia: University of Pennsylvania Press, 2007).
25. Westmoreland County. Rec. November 11, 1785. Virginia State Library.
26. Alisse Theodore Portnoy, *Their Right to Speak: Women's Activism in the Indian and Slave Debates* (Cambridge: Harvard University Press, 2005), 53–54; Mary Hershberger, "Mobilizing Women, Anticipating Abolition: The Struggle Against Indian Removal in the 1830s," *Journal of American History* 86, no. 1 (1999): 15–40.
27. Signed January 1830. HR 21A-G15.3.
28. Rec. January 14 1829. H.R. 20A G14.2.
29. Rec. January 14, 1829. H.R. 20A G14.2. On Rochester, see Paul Johnson, *A Shopkeeper's Millennium* (New York: Hill and Wang, 1978), esp. 83–94; 105–24.
30. Signed December 19, 1828. H.R. 20A G14.2.
31. Signed December 10, 1828. H.R. 20A G14.2.

32. Rec. January 14, 1829. H.R. 20A G14.2.
33. Cairo, NY, undated. H.R. 20A G14.2.
34. In John Barkley Jentz's analysis of an 1827 Sabbatarian petition in New York, merchants constituted no less than 39.5% of the signers. See "Artisans, Evangelicals and the City: A Social History of Abolition and Labor Reform in Jacksonian New York" (Ph.D. dissertation, City University of New York, 1977), 81.
35. Signed December 10, 1828. H.R. 20A G14.2.
36. October 10, 1831. HR 22A G16.4.
37. William G. McLoughlin, *New England Dissent, 1630–1833: The Baptists and the Separation of Church and State*, vol. 2 (Cambridge: Harvard University Press, 1971), 1112, 1266.
38. *American Baptist Magazine*, vol. 8 (Boston: Lincoln & Edmands, 1828), 274.
39. *An Account of Memorials Presented to Congress During Its Last Session*, 30.
40. *Course of Popular Lectures as Delivered by Frances Wright with Three Addresses on Various Public Occasions* (New York: Free Enquirer, 1829), 145.
41. Signed February 12, 1830. HR 21A-G15.3.
42. Philip Foner, ed., *William Heighton: Pioneer Labor Leader of Jacksonian Philadelphia* (New York: International Publishers, 1991); A. Kristen Foster, *Moral Visions and Material Ambitions: Philadelphia Struggles to Define the Republic, 1776–1836* (Lanham: Lexington Books, 2004), 98–107; and Bruce Laurie, *Working People of Philadelphia: 1800–1850* (Philadelphia: Temple University Press, 1980), 75–79.
43. *Mechanics' Free Press*, December 27, 1828.
44. Jama Lazerow, *Religion and the Working Class in Antebellum America* (Washington, DC: Smithsonian Press, 1995); William R. Sutton, *Journeymen for Jesus: Evangelical Artisans Confront Capitalism in Jacksonian Baltimore* (University Park: Pennsylvania State University, 1998).
45. Ronald Schultz estimates that three-quarters of the Universalist congregation were workingmen. "God and Workingmen: Popular Religion and the Formation of Philadelphia's Working Class, 1790–1830," in *Religion in a Revolutionary Age*, eds. Ronald Hoffman and Peter J. Albert (Charlottesville: University Press of Virginia, 1994), 132. On the hostility to pious elites within the Democratic Party, Daniel Walker Howe, "The Evangelical Movement and Political Culture in the North during the Second Party System," *Journal of American History* 77, no. 4 (1991): 1216–39.
46. Ronald Schultz, *The Republic of Labor: Philadelphia Artisans and the Politics of Class, 1720–1830* (New York: Oxford University Press, 1993), 218–19; Laurie, *Working People of Philadelphia*, 33–52.

47. *Mechanics' Free Press*, May 2, 1829. Sean Wilentz found a similar hostility to evangelicals among New York's artisans. *Chants Democratic: New York City and the Rise of the American Working Class, 1788–1850* (Oxford: Oxford University Press, 1984), 84.
48. *Mechanics' Free Press*, January 23, 1830.
49. No date. HR 21A-G15.3.
50. Rec. March 15, 1830. HR 21A-G15.3.
51. Rec. February 8, 1830. HR 21A-G15.3.
52. Rec. February 1, 1830. HR 21A-G15.3.
53. Philadelphia. Rec. February 8, 1830. HR 21A-G15.3.
54. *Democratic Press* (Philadelphia), July 29, 1829.
55. Rec. January 18, 1830. H.R. 21A G15.3.
56. Michael Kammen, *A Season of Youth: The American Revolution and the Historical Imagination* (Ithaca: Cornell University Press, 1978), 26.
57. Lehigh County, Pennsylvania. No date. HR 21A-G15.3.
58. Salina, Ohio. Rec. February 1, 1830. HR 21A-G15.3.
59. Various petitions from Bucks County, PA. Rec. February 22, 1830. HR 21A-G15.3.
60. Poughkeepsie, NY. Rec. January 18, 1830. H.R. 21A G15.3.
61. Rec. January 25, 1830. HR 21A-G15.3.
62. Rec. January 18, 1830. HR 21A-G15.3.
63. Rec. February 8, 1830. HR 21A-G15.3.
64. Erie County, PA. Rec. January 25, 1830. HR 21A-G15.3.
65. *An Exposé of the Rise and Proceedings of the American Bible Society, during Thirteen Years of Its Existence* (New York: 1830), 29, 32.
66. *Democratic Press* (Philadelphia), July 29, 1829. On the Jacksonian hostility to powerful elites, see Neem, *Creating a Nation of Joiners*, 140–41.
67. Rec. February 1, 1830. HR 21A-G15.3.
68. Signed December 23, 1828, HR 20A-G14.2.
69. *Connecticut Courant*, November 3, 1829.
70. Rec. January 4, 1830. HR 21A-G15.3.
71. On Ely, see Joseph L. Blau, "The Christian Party in Politics," *Review in Religion* 11 (1946–1947): 18–35. 2.
72. *An Account of Memorials Presented to Congress*, 22.
73. Signed January 8, 1830. HR 21A-G15.3.
74. West, *Politics of Revelation*, 260, note 9. For 1830, West puts the number of anti-mail petitions at 308. My count of pro-mail petitions to the House is 198. The signature count would be even closer.
75. Rec. February 15, 1830. HR 21A-G15.3.
76. Rec. January 12, 1829. HR 20A-G14.2.
77. *Trumpet and Universalist Magazine*, February 13, 1830.
78. Signed January 1830. HR 21A-G15.3.

79. The analysis was carried out by the *New York Telescope*. Reproduced in the *Religious Inquirer*, November 14, 1829.
80. *Workingman's Advocate*, January 30, 1830; *Exposé of the Rise and Proceedings of the American Bible Society*, 29.
81. *Workingman's Advocate*, January 30, 1830; *Free Enquirer*, March 13, 1830.
82. Signed January 8, 1830. HR 21A-G15.3.
83. Rec. February 10, 1830. HR 21A-G15.3.
84. Rec. February 22, 1830. HR 21A-G15.3.
85. Signed December 15, 1829. HR 21A-G15.3.
86. Rec. February 15, 1830. HR 21A-G15.3.
87. Signed January 22, 1829. HR 20A-G14.2.
88. Eric R. Schlereth, *An Age of Infidels: The Politics of Religious Controversy in the Early United States* (Philadelphia: University of Pennsylvania Press, 2013), 22.
89. Brown County, Ohio. Signed December 16, 1829, HR 21A-G15.3; Rec. February 15, 1830. HR 21A-G15.3.
90. Maureen O'Brien Quimby, "The Political Art of James Akin," *Winterthur Portfolio* 7 (1972): 59–112.
91. [Johnson], "Report of a Committee of the Senate", January 19, 1829. 20th Congress, 2nd session, 2.
92. Ibid., 4.
93. *Autobiography of Amos Kendall* (Boston: Lee and Shepard, 1872), 307; John, "Taking Sabbatarianism Seriously," 559.
94. "Preamble and Resolutions Adopted at a Meeting of the Citizens of New York, against the passage of a law prohibiting the transportation and opening of the Mail on the Sabbath." Rec. February 9, 1829. This petition was unusual in being tabled and ordered to be printed.
95. Rec. February 10, 1830. HR 21A-G15.3.
96. [Johnson], "Sunday Mail," March 4, 1830. 21st Congress, 1st session, 3.
97. Ibid., 4.
98. Ibid., 6.
99. *Trumpet and Universalist Magazine*, April 18, 1829. Also reproduced in *Dover Gazette & Strafford Advertiser* (New Hampshire), April 28, 1829; *United States' Telegraph* (Washington, DC), April 14, 1829.
100. 25 *Congressional Globe* 376 (1838).
101. William Emmons, *Authentic Biography of Colonel Richard M. Johnson, of Kentucky* (New York: H. Mason, 1833), 65–66. See also Ryan P. Jordan, *Church, State, and Race: The Discourse of American Religious Liberty, 1750–1900* (Lanham, MD: University Press of America, 2012), 51–52.
102. Sehat, *Myth of American Religious Freedom*, 59.
103. Salina, Ohio. Rec. February 1, 1830. HR 21A-G15.3.

CHAPTER 4

"Exposing Priestcraft and All Its Cognate -isms": Chaplains, Temperance and Sunday Travel

Evangelicals treated their defeat on Sunday mails as a temporary setback on the path to a truly Christian nation. In 1833, the formal separation of church and state was completed when voters in Massachusetts rejected religious taxes. The scope for informal cooperation between church and state, though, seemed as promising as ever. Thwarted at the national level, Protestant reformers threw their energy into local and state causes, aided by an expanding cross-denominational network of missionary societies, Sunday Schools, Bible, tract and reform societies that became known as the Benevolent Empire. In 1829, the American Temperance Society counted 200 auxiliaries across the nation. Six years later it could boast 1.5 million members organized into 8000 affiliates.[1] By 1850, the American Tract Society was blanketing the nation with short, cheap missives of moral uplift, producing some five million works every year from its five-story headquarters in Manhattan.[2] Evangelical reformers pursued an allied set of goals. Individual men and women were exhorted to cleanse themselves of sinful behavior. But attacking national sins by harnessing the power of the state was just as important. Whether lobbying for new laws, as in the case of temperance, or the enforcement of existing statutes to prevent Sabbath-desecration, evangelicals put forth a powerful vision of the inherent harmony between their faith and the state.

This expansion stoked a fierce backlash. Some Protestants denounced reform societies as un-Biblical and driven by worldly ambition more than spiritual zeal. Mass Catholic immigration sharpened the fear that Protestant churches were aping the worst tendencies of papists.

© The Author(s) 2019
T. Verhoeven, *Secularists, Religion and Government in Nineteenth-Century America*, https://doi.org/10.1007/978-3-030-02877-0_4

And whenever clerical zeal seemed to impinge on individual freedoms, the result was an outpouring of hostility. In this era, when the reform ambition of evangelicalism was at its height, religious and secular forces combined to mount a powerful defense of a strict separation of church and state.

ATTACKING LEGISLATIVE CHAPLAINS

A major flashpoint was an institution that many evangelicals assumed to be popular and entrenched, Congressional chaplains. Both the House and the Senate elected a chaplain whose role varied from opening each morning session with prayer to conducting religious services to catering to the spiritual needs of lawmakers. For these services, chaplains received an annual salary, set at $500 by law. For evangelicals, the significance of chaplains extended far beyond their pastoral function. There could be no more public and powerful sign of the nation's dependence on the Almighty than its elected representatives bowing their heads in prayer and calling on His counsel.

The symbolism of the office extended beyond America's shores. Protestants were keenly aware that some European observers read the peculiar features of American religion—the absence of a state church, the hodgepodge of sects, the apparent ease with which men and women swapped one church for another—as signs of a shallow faith. The physical presence of Christ's representatives at the heart of government was a stark rebuttal to anyone who doubted America's religious credentials. In a lecture to the Berlin Evangelical society in 1854, the Swiss-born theologian and church historian Dr. Philip Schaff conceded that some in his audience might equate formal disestablishment with a "renunciation of Christianity by the nation."[3] Nothing, he reassured them, could be further from the truth. The appointment of chaplains at public expense showed clearly that Protestantism was the very heartbeat of the American republic.

Schaff depicted the office of legislative chaplains as uncontroversial. This was not true. At state level, the picture was mixed. In the early Republic, the legislatures of several states, including Pennsylvania, Virginia, and Kentucky, had no paid chaplains. The New York Assembly ended daily prayers in 1833, before reinstating them five years later.[4] In the 1840s, the focus of controversy shifted to Washington. John Pettit was an Indiana Democrat whose obsessive dislike for paid chaplains was legendary. Pettit of Indiana, the *New York Times* noted in 1853, gives one speech a year, and always against chaplains.[5] In 1844, he delivered a long speech to the House arguing that churches were using state-paid chaplains to create an establishment by stealth. The people were unanimous that "the church formed no part of our government," yet through the chaplaincy, it was attempting to "steal its way into the citadel of the state." Furthermore, it was an injustice to force taxpayers to subsidize the salaries of clergymen whose faith was not their own. Pettit ended by challenging his fellow lawmakers to prove their commitment to chaplains by paying from their own pocket; as a start, he pledged five dollars.[6]

Pettit was notorious for his attacks on religion. As a delegate at the 1850 state Constitutional Convention, he opposed the recognition of God in the preamble. His subsequent appointment to the Indiana Supreme Court did not dim his anticlericalism. In 1876, a Republican paper alleged that a drunken Pettit had barged into a religious meeting and assaulted the preacher with his cane.[7] But if Pettit's dislike of organized religion made him an outlier in Congress, there were soon signs that his attack on chaplains had struck a chord with parts of the public. In 1845, twenty petitions demanding that legislative chaplains be abolished arrived in Congress. Some appear to have been directly inspired by Pettit's stance. Four hundred residents of Cincinnati, Ohio, mailed him their petition, though he was not their representative. He was, however, the champion of a cause that was controversial. The first four antichaplain petitions were immediately tabled, which meant that they were neither debated nor referred to committee. Those that followed went to the Judiciary Committee. This was the beginning of a petition campaign that would escalate significantly in the years ahead.

Two features of these 1845 petitions stand out. The first is their insistence that chaplains were by definition sectarian. In establishing by law the salaries of chaplains and drawing the funds from all taxpayers, Congress was violating both the establishment and free exercise clauses of the First Amendment, which the petitioners cited in full. But it was also privileging one sect over another. Comparing the population to the estimated strength of each denomination, the petitioners showed that Congress, by appointing the clergy of a particular church to the office of chaplain, was obliging large numbers of taxpayers to contribute to a faith which they believed to be false. A Baptist chaplain might represent the five million adherents of that faith. But the remaining 12,069,453 citizens found themselves taxed to promulgate a doctrine they regarded as pernicious. The injustice was even greater for Jews and Infidels, who were never represented at all. Defenders of the office of chaplain might argue that all Protestant denominations were equally represented, but this should not disguise its inherent and unmistakable sectarianism.[8]

The second noteworthy feature of this small batch of petitions is the presence of female signers. As we have seen, the anti-Sabbatarian movement was rigid in excluding women. Their opponents might stoop, as they saw it, to enrolling women and children in their campaign, but the defenders of the secular state would never do so. By the 1840s, a relaxation of attitudes had occurred, and the cause was no doubt the explosion of female petitioning through the antislavery movement. The campaign against slavery mobilized women in their thousands as organizers, agents, and signers. By 1845, the practice, if still controversial in many quarters, was at least no longer shocking, and the petitions against legislative chaplains reflect the shift. Women, though still a tiny minority of signers, were now a recognizable presence. One Chester County petition counted two female names among its twelve signers.[9] Then, in December 1845, an all-female petition containing twenty names arrived in Congress.[10] Both petitions escaped the fate of being tabled and were referred to the Judiciary Committee.

Together these petitions failed to spark a public debate over legislative chaplains. Some tried to convey the impression of widespread public opposition. A collector of signatures in Akron, Ohio, boasted that "I could get names without end if I had time to carry it around."[11] But all up the petitions totaled only 1837 names. The next phase, however, would have a greater impact. For the first time, the groundswell of opinion against the office of legislative chaplain reached such proportions that Congress was forced to explicitly consider its constitutionality. Popular mobilization through petitioning produced another national-level debate over the meaning of the First Amendment as well as the shape of true religion in the American republic.

The Primitive Baptists

This phase began in 1848, when a petition from North Carolina arrived in Congress calling for the abolition of legislative chaplains at public expense. In contrast to those of 1845, this petition was more overtly religious in tone. The Church of God, the petitioners argued, required no "aid of human laws" for its "further existence or advancement." When such aid was enacted, the result was hideous, an "ecclesiastical despotism totally at variance with the simple laws, mild reign and spiritual kingdom of the King of kings." The petitioners then took aim at the pastors who sold their services for money. Such men, they thundered, were "hirelings" who had traded away their spiritual authority for profit.[12] This was a provocative attack on public ministers. But the North Carolina Whig, George Badger, presented the petition, albeit reluctantly, to the Senate. Though not agreeing with its views, he found "nothing execrable" in its language and thus saw no reason to table it.[13]

This petition was a striking display of the ways in which a particular vision of true religion could align with the demand for a secular state. It came from Primitive or anti-mission Baptists, a church which set itself against the theological underpinnings of the Second Great Awakening. The rising evangelical churches which formed the core of the Benevolent Empire espoused an optimistic vision of individual and social redemption. Revivalists such as Charles Grandison Finney stressed the moral responsibility of sinners, their capacity to choose freely salvation or damnation, and their agency in accepting or rejecting the Holy Spirit. Primitive Baptists rejected this shift away from Calvinism and its doctrine of predestination. The Bible to their mind was clear: atonement was inherently limited, for Jesus died to save only the elect. Another point of difference with the evangelical mainstream concerned the role of missions. For Primitive Baptists, salvation was the result of God's will alone. Grace was irresistible; no individual could freely choose to receive or to resist the Spirit of the Lord "If salvation is not by grace," as one Primitive paper declared, "there is no such thing as salvation at all."[14] Missions, theological and Sunday Schools, Bible and tract societies were all premised on a false doctrine of conversion. But Primitive Baptists detected as well a more sinister motivation at work. If these institutions had no Scriptural grounding, their existence could only be attributed to worldly ambition. Rather than a concern for sinners, a lust for power and for wealth drove the leaders of the Benevolent Empire.

A dread of worldly temptation led Primitive Baptists to call for the distancing of church and state. True religion should fear any alliance with government, for even the most pious souls might be lured into the corrupting snare of political power. A strict separation of church and state, then, was the best means of maintaining a faith that was pure and free. In this regard, Primitive Baptists encapsulated the pietistic impulse within evangelical Protestantism, with its emphasis on private devotion and its essentially negative view of secular government. This attitude did not lead Primitive Baptists, however, to abandon politics entirely. On certain questions, they were happy to mobilize through public meetings, newspapers editorials and above all petitioning. Without falling into "political strife," as one Baptist newspaper suggested, we can rightly seek to "awaken in our lawmakers a sense of justice and right."[15] Though eschewing the trappings of political power, Primitive Baptists set out to persuade legislators of the correctness of their views.

Their first engagement with political controversy was over Sunday mails. Joshua Lawrence was the most forceful and charismatic leader of the Primitive Baptists in the early Republic. At his urging the Kehukee Association of North Carolina in 1827 became the first Baptist association to formally oppose missions, Bible and tract societies, and he would go on to found and to edit the main organ of the movement, the *Primitive Baptist*. In 1830, in a July 4 oration at his church in Tarboro, North Carolina, Lawrence railed against the movement to ban Sunday mails as an attempt to establish what he called "law religion." The nation should dread the sight of the clergy seeking to wield temporal power. "What a monster," he declared, "is a covetous priest when he has law on his side."[16] Not content with speeches, Lawrence organized a petition in favor of Sunday mails. Re-printed in the *North Carolina Whig*, the petition denounced any law against Sunday mails as "possessing a dangerous and oppressive tendency, on civil and religious liberty."[17]

By the 1840s, other leading Primitive Baptists had taken up the fight. Two members of the Beebe family were particularly prominent. Gilbert Beebe became pastor of the church at New Vernon, New York, in 1826, and founded and edited the *Signs of the Times*. His son, Gilbert Judson Beebe did not follow his father into the ministry, but shared his faith as well as his passion for journalism. In 1848, he established the *Banner of Liberty* to defend civil and religious liberty while "exposing priestcraft and all its cognate -isms." Together the papers targeted legislative chaplains. In March 1846, an article in the *Signs of the Times* applauded John Pettit for his bold stance against chaplains and called for a petition campaign against the "abominable anti-Christian system."[18] In January 1848, the paper again praised Pettit, lamenting his isolation on the issue. "It is humiliating," Beebe Sr. wrote, "that Mr Pettit should stand alone from year to year, contending single-handed for the constitutional rights of the people."[19]

The following year, the Primitive Baptists resolved to act. As Beebe Jr. argued, petitioning was "the most direct and frequently effectual remedy" for such legislative abuses. To have any effect, petitions would have to come from all corners of the nation and in large numbers. For this, the Primitive Baptists were ideally placed. The *American Baptist Almanac* put their number in 1855 at 58,000 spread among 155 associations.[20] Just as importantly, this was a church with pockets of strength in the South, through the Appalachians and on to the western frontier. As Beebe Jr. claimed, with readers in every state in the union the *Banner of Liberty* was the perfect vehicle to muster support. The time had come to "disenthrall" the nation of the "slimy folds of priestcraft."[21] Alongside such calls to action, readers found a blank petition complete with instructions as to how and when it should be transmitted to Congress.

This national reach was reflected in the ensuing campaign. From January to March 1850, 105 petitions with 10,460 names attached were sent to the House. The New England states were almost entirely absent, with only Maine sending three petitions. Instead, it was the mid-West and the South that dominated. Indiana was a center of petitioning, sending thirty-three of the petitions, but fourteen came from Virginia, eight from Georgia, and six from Kentucky. In the 32nd Congress, the effort was resumed, with a further sixty-six petitions containing 7700 names referred to the Committee on the Judiciary. The geographical spread was even wider this time, with Pennsylvania leading the way (fourteen petitions), eight coming from both Alabama and Georgia, and six from Iowa. By the 33rd Congress, the campaign was beginning to peter out, with only fourteen petitions reaching Washington. Together 185 petitions were sent to Congress from January 1850 to April 1854. Of these, no less than 81% came from two regions, the South (41%) and the mid-West (40%).[22]

If this breakdown followed the geographic contours of anti-mission sentiment, there was much evidence that the intended audience was far wider. In a precursor to the Adventist petition drives of the 1890s, the Primitive Baptists set out to enroll support from the broader community. The tone of the petition, as Beebe stressed, was "most respectful and courteous," and the arguments those to which no friend of civil and religious liberty could object.[23] In contrast to the 1848 Kehukee petition, the emphasis was now on constitutional theory rather than theology. State-paid chaplains contravened the ban on religious tests, as neither an "avowed infidel" nor a "non-professor of religion" could take up the role. In the majority of petitions, it is difficult to assess the extent of non-Baptist participation. But a few hint at a broad level of support. One signer list from Van Buren County, Iowa, was headed by Alfred Forbes, a prominent Freemason.[24] According to a canvasser in Coweta County, Georgia, "a more respectable petition list could not be obtained." The signers "consist of all parties as well as all the religious denominations." Many specified their occupations, which included attorneys, doctors, merchants, sheriffs, and preachers. This was merely a sample of opinion, the canvasser argued; with only slightly more effort and better organization, a thousand names across the county could have been obtained.[25] Other agents expressed the same confidence. In Bradford County, Pennsylvania, George Walker believed the majority to be in favor.[26] Another in Virginia recorded that, of his acquaintances, only three were opposed to the petition; far more than thirty-eight names might have been added, he went on, if there had only been more time to collect them.[27]

These sorts of boasts were common in petition campaigns, and perhaps betrayed a sense of disappointment at not gathering more support. But legislators judged the campaign significant enough to warrant a response. On March 13, 1850, James Thompson of the House Judiciary Committee issued a report rejecting the petitioners' demand. Having deflected the charge of sectarian bias by arguing that all denominations were represented, the report fell back on custom. The Congresses of 1775 and 1776, as well as that of 1789, it noted, had all featured chaplains.[28] The continued agitation on the question led to an even longer report in 1853 under the name of Senator Badger. Beebe Jr. and his fellow petitioners had argued that paid chaplains differed in degree rather than in principle from the church and state establishments in Europe.[29] Badger rejected outright this comparison. No particular denomination was preferred over others, and no member of Congress was obliged to attend either prayers or religious services.[30] A further report in 1854 hammered home the point. All agreed that "the ecclesiastical and civil powers have been, and should continue to be, entirely divorced from each other." But this did not mean that religion was not needed to ensure "the safety of civil society."[31] Religion was the foundation of free institutions and laws; the fact that ministers mingled with elected representatives was nothing more than a visible display of this harmony between the nation's Protestant creed and its democratic institutions. To the satisfaction of mainstream evangelicals, the office of chaplain, and with it the Protestant character of the republic, had received a ringing affirmation.

The Anti-Temperance Movement

The Primitive Baptists had done their best to enroll public support for their position that legislative chaplains were both unconstitutional and an affront to true religion. Ultimately they failed in their goal. But on issues which touched more directly the lives and liberties of their fellow citizens, the backlash against the Benevolent Empire proved to be far more powerful. This was particularly so for temperance and Sunday travel.

One of the many "isms" that Gilbert J. Beebe abhorred was what he called "Total Abstinence Fanaticism." Across the nation, opponents of the liquor traffic worked at local and state levels through a proliferating network of associations. In a manner that was characteristic of reform in this era, their efforts had a dual goal; to reshape personal behavior, but also to bring the power of the government to bear on a great social evil. In 1851, these efforts bore fruit in the passage of the Maine Law, which banned the manufacture and sale of alcohol, and was backed up by a series of enforcement provisions including forcible searches, seizures, and even imprisonment. For Primitive Baptists, this show of clerical activism was deeply provocative. The following year, Beebe launched a blistering attack on its clerical backers in a debate with the Presbyterian Reverend McNeir before a large audience at Clinton, New Jersey. Existing public laws were more than sufficient, Beebe argued, to protect families and the community from drunkenness. Given this, the origin of the Maine Law must lie elsewhere. For Beebe, the true motive was an ingrained lust for power. The temperance crusaders, he warned, aimed at nothing less than "to lick up the blood of freemen as greedily as in the darkest days of priestcraft."[32] The Maine Law, along with all other "fiery edicts of fanaticism," was little more than a vehicle for an ambitious clergy to arm itself with the powers of government. This clergy, Beebe concluded, had as much in common with a true Christian minister as a serpent with a dove.[33]

Beebe and the Baptists were not alone in their hostility. From the outset, the temperance movement was confronted with the core objection that while moderation should be encouraged, outright bans were draconian and self-defeating. Not only was prohibition impossible to police, but it was based on the premise that citizens could not be trusted to act responsibly. For large swathes of the Democratic Party, this distrust of the individual was undemocratic. As an anti-Maine law circular in New Hampshire argued, "Democrats assert and believe that man is capable of self-government."[34] When religion and state power combined, the threat to democratic liberty was even more acute. Coursing through the anti-Maine Law movement was a deep hostility to a religious elite which co-opted the powers of the state to impose its moral vision. The pulpit, as the New Hampshire circular argued, should be devoted to "the work of love." Instead, hundreds of fiery preachers were excoriating innocent drinkers as sinners and criminals. Worse, these self-appointed enforcers of public morals were self-righteous hypocrites or, in the term that resonated powerfully, Pharisees. Far from being genuinely concerned with stamping out drunkenness, they wished above all to make a public show of piety. Such moral preening was far worse than the odd tipple. Better, the author concluded, "all the graves of all the drunkards that ever perished in the land, than a generation of Pharisees."[35]

This opposition did not deter Maine law activists, who pushed similar laws through twelve northern states from 1852 to 1855. But in a pattern that would be repeated for the rest of the century, a breakthrough for prohibition was followed by resistance and then retreat. Across the North, agents charged with enforcing the law came under verbal and sometimes physical attack. Anti-Maine law organizations sprang up, often under the auspices of saloon owners and liquor dealers. And wherever temperance advocates flooded state legislatures with petitions, counter-petition campaigns soon sprang to life. In a submission to a special committee of the Massachusetts State Legislature, the Reverend Joseph C. Lovejoy explained why he had signed a petition calling for repeal of the state's prohibition law. He began on Scriptural grounds, arguing that the Old Testament sanctioned the consumption of alcohol, before moving to practical difficulties of enforcement. But most of all, Lovejoy worried about the "approximation of religion and politics" behind the law.[36] Both state and church had made a corrupt bargain in joining forces for temperance and both were likely to suffer a loss of public respect as a result. There certainly seemed much evidence that temperance success was tarnishing the image of the clergy. Lithographers delighted in unmasking the hypocrisy they saw at work. In New York, John L. McGee (Fig. 4.1) showed a portly and red-nosed clergyman clasping a bottle in a saloon. In his pocket is a petition in favor of the Maine law; balanced on the bar is a much longer petition against. Here was the modern Pharisee in action. By 1860, four states had rescinded Maine Laws; elsewhere, they were largely unenforced.

Fig. 4.1 *"Hypocrisy and Rum"*, John L. McGee (1852) (Courtesy of American Antiquarian Society)

Activists Against Sabbath Laws

Even more than temperance, the enforcement of Sabbath laws inflamed popular emotion in the decade before the Civil War. In the wake of their defeat at the national level over Sunday mail delivery, evangelicals shifted their focus to the states, where Sabbath statutes were common. In Pennsylvania, for example, a 1794 law banned all worldly activities, except those of necessity and charity, with offenders liable to a fine of four dollars. Yet by the 1830s, there were signs everywhere that such laws were becoming dead letters. In 1835, a Committee of the General Assembly of the Presbyterian Church lamented that "the profanation of the Sabbath is a sin of giant growth in our land." Aside from mails, the most visible sign of Sabbath violation was travel. Sunday traveling upon railroads, stages, canals, and steamboats was so rampant that even ministers had begun to succumb. As the Committee noted with "great regret," several members of the General Assembly had "traveled in the ordinary public conveyances on the Sabbath" on their way to the meeting.[37] The cancer of Sabbath desecration was spreading even within the Benevolent Empire.

In typical fashion, Sabbatarians responded through organization. The Philadelphia Sabbath Association was formed in 1840; its equivalent in Baltimore in 1843. In the same year, the American and Foreign Sabbath Union was established to coordinate the work of city and state-based associations. Across the nation, county and state conventions brought activists together.[38] At the Lord's Day Conference in Baltimore, former President John Quincy Adams urged Americans to seize an unprecedented opportunity. "The world has never witnessed," he declared, "the spectacle of an universal obedience to the Sabbath." The nation could be invigorated by a surge of moral energy and set a shining example to all other nations as the first to enjoy fully the Sabbath's redeeming power.[39]

The question was whether such activism would trigger the fear of a union of Church and State which was so widespread in the Jacksonian era. Initially, the opposition was limited. In November 1840, a handful of men and women gathered at the Chardon Street Hall in Boston to "examine the validity of the views … as to the divine appointment of the first day of the week as the Christian Sabbath."[40] The figure behind this gathering was the abolitionist William Lloyd Garrison. In some ways, Garrison was an unlikely figure to lead an anti-Sabbatarian crusade. His hatred of slavery put him at odds with the pro-slavery Democratic Party which was the political home of anticlericalism. Far from applauding Richard M. Johnson and his famous report on Sunday mails, Garrison was outraged that a southern slave-owner would dare to speak of republican liberty and virtue. Even worse than a hypocrite, Johnson embodied the sexual vice and moral corruption at the heart of the slave system. He had two daughters with a family slave, Julia Chinn, whom he openly treated as his wife. For Garrison, this was yet a further abomination. When Johnson ran for vice-president in 1836, Garrison attacked him in the pages of his newspaper, the *Liberator*, as a "lewd and filthy amalgamator" whose election would be a travesty of republican principles and a moral stain on the nation.[41]

Nevertheless, Garrison could not hide his delight that even Johnson, a "slaveholder and debauchee," had dispersed the Sabbatarian forces in 1829–1830.[42] His animosity to them stemmed from a range of sources.

In a manner akin to the Primitive Baptists, Garrison was suspicious of the motives of reformers, who seemed more entranced by the prospect of power then by the simple reward of virtuous work. This led him to oppose legislative chaplains; in 1849, the *Liberator* re-printed the Kehukee petition in full, with Garrison calling it "sensible."[43] Even worse, in Garrison's eyes, was the manner in which Sabbatarians enshrined a false conception of religion. Theirs was a faith of outward show and observance. As he explained to fellow abolitionist Samuel May in 1838, not only was there no Scriptural basis for treating the first rather than the seventh day as the true Sabbath, but the very practice of elevating one day over another was the mark of a merely ceremonial religion. "The soul that is sanctified," he wrote, "sanctifies all time."[44]

But the great stain on Sabbatarian churches in Garrison's eyes was their hypocrisy on the question of slavery. He could not stomach what he regarded as cant about public virtue from churches which refused to condemn outright the institution of slavery and which welcomed slave-owners into their fold. In 1836, Garrison launched an attack on Lyman Beecher in the wake of his call for a national crusade for Sabbath observance. By refusing to agitate for the immediate end of slavery, Garrison argued, Beecher was countenancing a national sin far graver, and far more likely to bring down Divine punishment, than Sabbath violation. It was, he argued, a "dreadful mockery" for Beecher and his fellow Sabbatarians to preach observance of the fourth commandment while "conniving at a system which violates every commandment of the Decalogue, habitually, systematically, exultingly."[45]

Though no official account of the Chardon Street Convention was published, several participants recorded their impressions. Ralph Waldo Emerson left a slightly mocking picture of an eclectic group of reformers. "If the assembly was disorderly, it was picturesque," he wrote, bringing together "men of every shade of opinion, from the straightest orthodoxy to the wildest heresy."[46] The poet John Greenleaf Whittier similarly saw a "queer gathering of heterogeneous spirits."[47] Among these was the reformer Bronson Alcott, and radical abolitionists such as Theodore Parker and Edmund Quincy. Most were against Sabbath laws, but at least one attendee spoke in their favor. The Reverend Amos A. Phelps defended Sabbath laws in a speech lasting some four hours.[48] But Garrison was not swayed; Phelps and his fellow Sabbatarians were the embodiment of a shallow faith preoccupied with public display rather than inner piety. Christ, he wrote, "came to deliver us from the burden of rites, and forms, and holy days."[49] Perhaps not surprisingly, the meeting adjourned after three days without agreeing on a resolution.

Through the 1840s, it was left to religious minorities to take up the fight against the enforcement of Sabbath laws. Seventh-Day Baptists were a prominent voice. For these Baptists, whose origins went back to the seventeenth century, the institutionalization of the Sunday Sabbath was an un-Scriptural innovation foisted on the early church by the papacy. Though numbering only several thousand adherents, Seventh-Day Baptists produced hundreds of tracts and pamphlets and founded a weekly newspaper, the *Sabbath Recorder*, to disseminate their views. In its first issue, the paper rejected legislative enforcement of any Sabbath day as self-defeating. Since Sabbath observance was imposed on the people, their commitment to it was grudging and shallow, a fact that explained the growing incidence of Sabbath violation across the nation.[50] In addition to their principled opposition, Seventh-Day Baptists had a direct interest in opposing laws under which they were fined and imprisoned. Occasionally they won exemptions on religious grounds. In November 1847, New York revised its statutes to exempt those religious groups which kept the Saturday Sabbath from military or jury duty on that day, except in times of invasion, insurrection or war.[51] The next year, however, the Pennsylvania Supreme Court upheld the conviction of a Seventh-Day farmer for laboring on the Sunday.[52]

By the 1840s, another religious minority was also venturing into public debate on the issue. Defenders of Sunday mails had often referred to Jews in their petitions. Now, however, Jews themselves began to agitate at the local and state level. In August 1845, the City Council of Richmond, Virginia passed an ordinance which raised the fine for Sabbath violation from $1.67 to between five and ten dollars. Like many Sabbath statutes in the South, the ordinance had a racial more than a religious motivation. Its aim was to stamp out public gatherings of free blacks and slaves on Sundays, a trend which alarmed a white population forever fearful of slave uprisings. When several Jews were caught up in its enforcement, a petition campaign ensued. On October 13, 1845, a petition from Abram Levy and other Jews argued that the ordinance, by "assigning to Sunday-keeping Christians more legal protection than is accorded to Jews," violated the guarantees of religious liberty contained in the state and federal constitutions. Furthermore, it was a first step to a tyranny which would strip non-Jews of their rights as well. The efforts on the part of the clergy to seek the aid of civil power in enforcing their dogmas was, the petitioners argued, a "revolution backwards."[53]

The petition won the backing of a leading force in the prewar Jewish community, Isaac Leeser. A longtime opponent of Sabbath laws, Leeser re-printed the petition in his *Occident and American Jewish Advocate*.[54] In April 1846, the paper applauded an Ohio judge who overturned the conviction of several Jews for transacting business on a Sunday.[55] A similar decision in Charleston, which rescinded a fine imposed on a shopkeeper who had sold a pair of gloves, was also celebrated as a triumph for religious liberty. There was no doubt, Leeser argued, that a day of rest was "promotive of happiness." But in seeking to dictate which day should be kept holy, and enforcing this through fines and other punishments, Sabbatarians were guilty of an "assumption of tyrannical and unconstitutional power against the claim to equality."[56]

The next year two Jews who had fallen foul of the Richmond ordinance, Jacob Ezekiel and his brother-in-law Jacob A. Levy, sent another petition. Ezekiel had a long history of battling against anything that smacked of the Christian nation ideal. In 1841, he wrote to President John Tyler protesting his use of the term "Christian people" in his call for a day of mourning after the sudden death of President William Henry Harrison.[57] Now he railed against Sabbath penalties. Continental Europe showed that such laws were not needed. There the Sabbath was much less stringently observed than at home, but public morals, in Ezekiel's assessment, were just as sound. Furthermore, their enforcement demanded a system of police surveillance which was unworthy of a free republic. To prove that Sabbath work was being carried out in the privacy of the home required the "inquisitorial and prying visits of evil disposed informers," a development which should alarm all citizens.[58] These arguments won over the Council, which in November 1846 repealed the ordinance. While the maintenance of public order was a proper concern of government, the Committee conceded, the enforcement of a religious doctrine, Christian or otherwise, was not. The question of the best way to observe the Sabbath lay solely between believers and their God.[59]

In 1848, anti-Sabbatarians came together for another convention at the Melodeon Hall in Boston. Garrison was again the driving force, and was joined by, among others, Lucretia Mott, Theodore Parker, Elizur Wright and Henry C. Wright. Several speakers argued that there was no Scriptural basis for any Sabbath. The hypocrisy of the Sabbatarian clergy was another prominent theme. The public auction of slaves aroused no protest, Henry C. Wright observed, as long as it came to an end on Saturday evening.[60] But now a different strain in the anti-Sabbatarian argument came to the fore: the emphasis on rational recreation. Several speakers argued that Sunday should be a day apart, but challenged the Sabbatarian grip on its meaning. Theodore Parker insisted that Sunday should be regarded as the day in the week especially consecrated to moral uplift, but that this purpose could be accomplished by wholesome secular activities. Instead of a day which was "stern, dark, and disagreeable," Parker looked forward to a Sunday devoted to "innocent and inoffensive callings."[61] Visits to libraries and museums would provide as much moral elevation as attending a church service.

The Sunday Travel Controversy

Through the 1840s, then, a diverse set of activists together challenged the Sabbatarian grip on the first day. What was missing was an issue which, in the manner of Sunday mails, might stir public anger and spark mass protests. Such an issue emerged with a revolution in urban transit, the horse-drawn streetcar. For decades, the most common form of transportation in the nation's cities had been the omnibus, a wheeled carriage jolting over cobbled streets. Passengers complained of the uncomfortable ride; operators bemoaned the expense of maintaining the large teams of horses required to pull the hefty carriages. The breakthrough came with the streetcar, which solved these problems by running on a fixed rail. Thanks to the rail, the cars could be both larger and at the same time more lightly built, and required at most two horses to operate. Running costs fell, patronage increased dramatically, and for the first time urban dwellers had access to a transportation system that was fast, efficient, and relatively safe.[62]

The result was a national streetcar craze. Philadelphia was one of the last major cities to introduce streetcars, but just twelve months after the first line opened in January 1858, five companies were operating on fifty miles of track. Two years later, the number of companies had jumped to eighteen, and more than 160 miles of track had been laid.[63] In 1863, the chief engineer and surveyor of Philadelphia, Strickland Kneass, reported that nine lines had carried 30,841,000 passengers in 309 cars over the preceding twelve months.[64] For the private companies which were chartered to build and operate the lines, streetcars were a goldmine. In 1861, the Green and Coates Street line carried over two million passengers and recorded a net profit of $32,671.79.[65]

The revolution, however, came to a halt on Sundays. Philadelphians had access to other forms of Sunday travel, from private carriages to steamboat excursions. But unlike Brooklyn where, after a brief petition battle, Mayor Samuel S. Powell approved the service in 1857, Sunday streetcars were banned. Sabbatarians were determined to hold the line.[66] Allowing the cars to run on Sunday would, the Pennsylvania *German Reformed Messenger* argued, "open the door to a progeny of other sins, which would crimson the cheek of any professedly Christian community."[67] No exceptions were possible. The Presbyterian John Holmes rejected Sunday travel even if undertaken for wholesome reasons. Agnew gave the example of a husband returning home to spend the Sabbath with his family; in such a case, Agnew argued, the husband was at fault for not better planning his trip.[68]

With no prospect of a change in regulations, two companies decided to challenge the ban. On Saturday July 9, 1859, the Greene and Coates Street line and the Ridge Avenue and Manayunk Railway Company announced their intention to run cars the next day.[69] Both lines passed by the recently developed park at Fairmount which stood on the fringes of the consolidated city, and which was already a favored picnic spot for Philadelphians. The announcement won immediate praise from leading commentators in the city. One of the most fervent supporters was Thompson Westcott, a journalist, historian, and editor of the *Sunday Dispatch*. He applauded what he saw as a direct challenge to the dominance of the city's Sabbatarians. "The fanatical spirit of persons who proclaim that because *they* desire to go to church, nobody else shall be allowed to go elsewhere," Westcott declared, "has tyranized [sic] over the community too long."[70] The Sunday service immediately won a large patronage. One reporter who rode in the cars noted that they were overcrowded and that a doubling of services would be required for the demand to be met. Some of the cars contained, he estimated, no less than sixty to seventy passengers.[71]

The evidence of popular support, however, did not deter Sabbatarians from mobilizing. Their main target was the Green and Coates Streets line which ran through the built-up areas of the city. Worshippers at the Green Street Methodist church led a delegation to Mayor Alexander Henry complaining that their services had been disrupted by the jangling of the horse-car bells and the noise of passengers. Public meetings composed of the "friends of the Sabbath" were held on July 12 and July 16, with many present calling for boycotts of those lines which had violated

80　T. VERHOEVEN

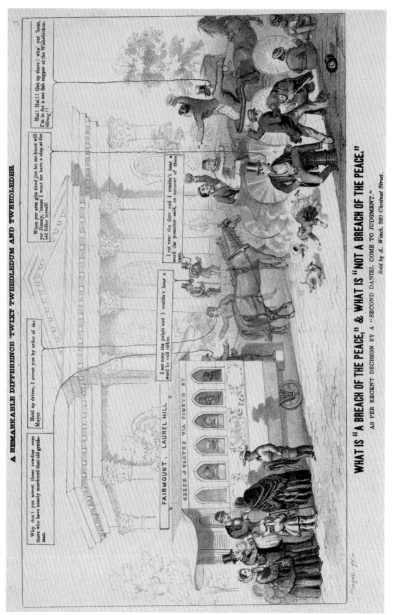

Fig. 4.2 *A Remarkable Difference 'Twixt Tweedledum and Tweedledee* (1859) (Courtesy of New York Public Library)

the Sabbath, and sermons in defense of the Sabbath were preached throughout the city. In response to this evangelical campaign, Mayor Henry instructed his police chief, Samuel G. Ruggles, to prevent the passage of any cars on the following Sunday, July 17, on the grounds that the running of cars "necessarily disturbs the religious observance and the rest of that day," and thus by its nature constituted a breach of peace.[72] That Sunday, the first car had only traveled three blocks before it was stopped.

The shutting down of Sunday cars only intensified the agitation. "Wherever we went," the *North American* reported the following day, "people were engaged in discussing the question ... Go where you might, this was the general topic."[73] Many ridiculed the notion that the running of streetcars filled with respectable men and women could in any way constitute a breach of peace. One printmaker (Fig. 4.2) pointed to the far greater disturbance caused by private carriages. It shows the police stopping a Sunday car bound for Fairmount Park and the Laurel Hill Cemetery, to the dismay of the well-dressed and clearly respectable passengers. Accusing these men and women of a breach of peace is clearly absurd; even worse, the police are ignoring much more flagrant public disorders, including a gang of thugs beating a gentleman and two racing private carriages which have trampled a girl in the street. Meanwhile, two old men leaving a church complain that the preacher's words were lost in the hubbub.

Over the next weeks, two mass protest meetings were held to demand the reinstatement of Sunday cars. The second, held at Independence Square on July 30, 1859, was described by a journalist as one of the "most numerous and orderly assemblages we have ever seen."[74] Thousands cheered as speaker after speaker denounced the Sabbatarians. Their opposition to Sunday travel was based, one speaker declared, on little more than "religious intolerance, Pharasaical pride and sectarian bigotry."[75] The meeting ended with the election of a committee to push for the passage of a law specifically allowing Sunday travel. "We never witnessed," wrote one reporter, "such enthusiasm as characterized the feeling exhibited by the populace assembled last night."[76]

As in the Maine Law agitation, anti-Sabbatarians sought to brand evangelicals as fanatics who were a threat to the interests both of religion and of democracy. The argument that true religion required no external display of piety was heard again and again. As the Unitarian William Furness argued in a pamphlet in favor of Sunday travel, a faithful

Christian saw through such "artificial observances."[77] But the true mark of fanaticism was its disregard for democratic freedoms. As in the Sunday mail clash, supporters of Sunday cars saw an ambitious religious elite conspiring to bring the machinery of government under its control. For Thompson Westcott, the "fanatics" behind the attack on Sunday cars were intent on establishing nothing less than an "ecclesiastical tyranny" which would deprive all Americans of their civil as well as their religious liberty.[78] Their success in shutting down a service which the majority of Philadelphians desired was proof that democratic freedoms were now at risk.

In the case of the Quaker William Logan Fisher, theological and secular arguments converged. The founder of the Wakefield Mills Manufacturing Company, Fisher was a longstanding opponent of Sunday laws who signed a pro-Sunday mail petition and attended the Melodeon Hall gathering in 1848. Although poor health prevented him from taking part in the 1859 controversy, one of his works, *History of the Institution of the Sabbath Day*, was republished in an expanded version that year. For Fisher, the Sabbath was a Jewish custom which, in his reading of Scripture as well as the practices of the early church, was not binding on Christians.[79] But he also rejected Sabbath laws on Constitutional grounds. The Constitution, he wrote, was "a civil contract, having no relation to religious rites."[80] Any attempt to use the machinery of government to enforce a religious doctrine would insert Christianity into a purely secular document. Fisher's stance put him at odds with many of his fellow Quakers. The *Friend*, for example, was uncompromising. Taking a car to go to a religious service might seem reasonable, its editors argued, but in no way made up for the "dissipation and demoralization" wrought by Sunday travel.[81] Fisher, however, was adamant that Sunday laws were a step toward a merging of church and government.

THE ROLE OF ANTI-CATHOLICISM

These were familiar arguments, but by 1859 their force was amplified by a phenomenon which had transformed Philadelphia along with other northern cities, mass Catholic immigration. By 1850, the city's population had reached 409,000, some 30% of whom were foreign-born, with a large proportion Irish Catholic. Hostility to the Catholic Church was deeply ingrained in American political culture, but this massive influx brought it to a new pitch. Nativists in the city published scores of pamphlets and tracts warning of a popish plot to seize control of the bedrock institutions of the republic, from legislatures to schools to the press. Catholics, in turn, defended their church against what they regarded as crude slurs and vilification. In July 1844, tensions between nativists and Catholics exploded into violence. Three days of street battles left fifteen people dead and some fifty wounded. A decade later, nativism flared again. Across the nation the anti-Catholic Know-Nothing Party achieved a series of stunning electoral victories, electing eight governors, more than 100 congressmen, and mayors in Boston, and Chicago, as well as thousands of local officials. In Massachusetts, Connecticut, Rhode Island, and New Hampshire, Know-Nothings controlled the executive and legislative branches. In Pennsylvania, the movement achieved a majority in the House, while in Philadelphia Know-Nothing Robert Conrad was elected mayor.

This surge in both Catholic migration and nativist sentiment fueled the drive to reinstate a Godly Sabbath. Sabbatarians had long been appalled by the advent of what they termed the "Continental Sabbath" in their city, with its dances, beer-gardens, and concerts. In the words of the General Assembly of the Presbyterian Church, "The larger part of our foreign population, having been trained in communities where the sacredness of the Lord's Day is utterly unknown, endeavor to bring in upon us the wretched immoralities of European society."[82] Once elected, Mayor Conrad began a strict enforcement of Sabbath laws. In a reflection of the close links between Sabbatarianism, anti-Catholicism, and temperance, taverns which sold liquor on Sundays were raided. Lithographers mocked this obsession with Sabbath piety. One 1855 print entitled "Beauties of the Sunday Law" (Fig. 4.3) showed the full range of activities to be banned in Conrad's Philadelphia. Among these are putting out a fire, selling medicine to the sick, or allowing a man suffering from bellyache to "do his business" in a water-closet. Included in the list is Sunday travel. One man is trying to ride a carriage so he can attend a funeral some twenty miles into the countryside. The policeman, however, will not permit him to embark, telling him he must walk instead.

At first glance, these crusades showed a curious contradiction. At the same time as they set about enforcing morality through law, nativists proclaimed their belief in the separation of church and state. An 1855 polemic stated that the American Party, as the Know-Nothings were then known, was firmly against "a union of church and state in any and every

Fig. 4.3 *Beauties of the Sunday Law* (1855) (Courtesy of Library Company, Philadelphia)

form."[83] It had been the movement's consistent policy to oppose "all sectarian intermeddling with politics or political institutions."[84] The key to this apparent contradiction was that "sectarian" applied to Catholic but not to Protestant meddling. For the Know-Nothings, Catholicism was alien and autocratic; Protestantism, in contrast, shared with republicanism a core commitment to individual liberty.

Anti-Catholicism was a powerful force. But as Sabbatarians would discover, it was also an unpredictable force that could rebound in unexpected ways. Almost immediately, defenders of Sunday cars argued that the most pressing threat to church-state separation came less from the Catholic Church than from evangelicals who were mimicking the Vatican's political ambition. Several newspapers used the term "Protestant Jesuits" to refer to Sabbatarians. The specter of the Inquisition was often raised. "A new Inquisition is set up," Thompson Westcott warned, "and Presbyterian Jesuits on the bench and in the pulpit are its officers."[85] For the editors of the *Sunday Atlas*, Sabbatarians were "far more dangerous, at least more bigoted, than the American Catholics have ever been."[86] The Baptist William Cathcart accused the opponents of Sunday cars of seeking to build a Vatican-style theocracy. To reinforce his point, he asked his readers to imagine a Philadelphia Puritan who, on a visit to Rome, came under arrest for violating the public rituals of Good Friday. How could he plead the right of free conscience before a papal tribunal, Cathcart asked, when in his native Philadelphia the laws enshrined a Sabbath which not all citizens adhered to?[87] Through the rhetoric of anti-Catholicism, then, defenders of Sunday travel cast their opponents as barely disguised fanatics who threatened the core tenets of American republicanism.

The Sabbath Question and Class

Mass immigration also sharpened the element of class resentment that across the century routinely hampered the Sabbatarian cause. Perhaps mindful of their failure in the Sunday mail controversy, Sabbatarians in 1859 made a great effort to win over Philadelphia's workers. To do so, they appealed less to religious sentiment than to self-interest. Allow the Sabbath to become a day of secular activity, they warned workers, and you will lose your best defense against greedy employers and their lust for profit. In a sermon, which was subsequently reprinted in many of the city's newspapers, the Reverend Joseph Berg claimed that, without the Sabbath, "the poor man is at the mercy of a heartless employer." Rescinding the laws protecting the Sabbath, Berg continued, would "put a rod of iron into the hands of covetous, soulless corporations."[88] Such arguments were also made in the City Council, which debated a draft ordinance prohibiting Sunday cars. In an address in favor of the ban, George F. Gordon pleaded for an alliance between Sabbatarians and the city's workers. The sacrifice of the Sabbath for commercial gain, he declared, would result in the "debasement and enslavement of the working masses." Were Sunday cars to be instituted, the poor would be compelled to labor for the profit-hungry company owners, and at the same time denied the chance "for more leisure, more relief from toil and more enduring happiness."[89]

This was potentially an effective strategy. The physical and psychological benefits of a mandatory day of rest were already apparent to labor reformers and would emerge after the Civil War as a powerful union cause. But the appeal for worker support was undercut by the popular perception of Sabbatarians as servants of the wealthy. After all, there had been little outcry when elegantly dressed men and women paraded through the streets on Sundays in their private carriages. The "aristocratic churches," one letter declared, had long blocked up the city streets with their "silver-mounted carriages."[90] Meanwhile, with the ban on Sunday cars, the "poor needle woman or shop girl" could no longer travel to the countryside so that "the sweet breath of heaven may visit her sallow cheek."[91] Even worse, leading Sabbatarians were among the worst offenders. In Philadelphia, the *Sunday Dispatch* printed lists of "Sunday-riding clergymen" to show the hypocrisy of the Sabbatarian leaders.[92]

The Sunday car clash thus brought to the fore the deep-seated resentment of a clergy which was both politically ambitious and socially privileged. Presbyterians and Methodists bore the brunt. Several speakers at the mass rallies pointed to the irony of the driver of the Sunday car, William Jeandell, standing accused of breaching the peace when churches made so much noise on Sundays. Imagine, one speaker told his audience, a poor workingman who, after six days of hard labor, tries to sleep in on Sunday morning, only to be woken by the "jingling of church bells." The raucousness of the Methodist service was a focus of ridicule. One correspondent to the *Public Ledger* recounted that he had been forced to change residence by the repeated "howling, groaning and screaming" from a nearby Methodist Church. A journalist reported hearing one man in the crowd complain of being kept awake by the "hideous howling and ranting of those going through the second birth."[93] In contrast to this racket, the noise of a passing streetcar was a trivial matter.

For now, this sentiment was not forceful enough to save Sunday cars in Philadelphia. The *Public Ledger* reported that the majority of letter writers were for the service.[94] But Sabbatarians could muster a great deal of support in the city. The strongest evidence for this was the decision of the stockholders of the Green and Coates street line to back down. Defying the Sabbath laws would, as one stockholder argued, "offend the religious sentiments of a large portion of the community" and, by inciting boycotts of the line, result in a "significant pecuniary loss."[95] In his annual address, Mayor Henry congratulated the companies for their "commendable spirit."[96] The Philadelphia Sabbath Association recorded its satisfaction with the outcome. "The question," according to the Reverend J. Miller, "is now *settled*."[97] This proved a hasty judgement. But Philadelphians would have to wait until after the Civil War for the return of Sunday cars.

Historians often paint the two decades before the Civil War as a peak era of the informal establishment. The web of churches and reform societies that made up the imposing Benevolent Empire reached, Mark A. Noll argues, "a higher point of public influence than at any previous time in America history."[98] Yet the scale of the protest in Philadelphia shows that, on the question of religion and government, contest rather than consensus remained the rule. Through the 1840s and 1850s, secularists of various stripes mobilized on a range of issues. One lesson is that Protestant churches were far from a united front. The Primitive Baptists attacked legislative chaplains as a corruption of true faith, while Seventh-Day Baptists denounced Sabbath laws which infringed their civil as much as religious liberty. What also emerges from a study of this period is that broader trends were paving the way for secularism to become a popular cause. Mass Catholic immigration provided secularists with a powerful rhetorical weapon against Sabbatarians and their supporters. The explosion in the number of workers crowding into great cities created another pool of support. The key was to find an issue that touched the daily lives of citizens. The payment of chaplains in the nation's capital was too distant to arouse any but the most committed secularists. Shutting down streetcars was a different matter. As the ensuing backlash showed, there was always scope for popular resentment of clerical activism to burgeon into a large-scale protest movement.

On the day that the stockholders of the Green and Coates Street line voted, the abolitionist John Brown's raid on Harpers Ferry was coming to its bloody end. Across the 1850s, the slavery controversy intersected with the question of church-state relations through what was labeled "political preaching." The outspoken stance against slavery on the part of the New England clergy prompted a series of spirited exchanges which laid bare the peculiar amalgam of sentiments and ideologies driving the case for a strict separation of church and state.

NOTES

1. Michael P. Young, *Bearing Witness Against Sin: The Evangelical Birth of the American Social Movement* (Chicago: University of Chicago Press, 2006), 4.
2. Paul Boyer, *Urban Masses and Moral Order in America, 1820–1920* (Cambridge, MA: Harvard University Press, 1978), 26.
3. Philip Schaff, *America: A Sketch of the Political, Social, and Religious Character of the United States of North America, in Two Lectures, Delivered at Berlin* (New York: C. Scribner, 1855), 91–92. On the legal significance of the modern chaplaincy, particularly its place at the center of a new set of church–state entanglements, Winnifred Fallers Sullivan, *A Ministry of Presence: Chaplaincy, Spiritual Care and the Law* (Chicago: University of Chicago Press, 2014).
4. James S. Kabala, "'Theocrats' vs. 'Infidels': Marginalized Worldviews and Legislative Prayer in 1830s New York," *Journal of Church and State* 51, no. 1 (2009): 78–101.
5. *New York Times*, October 1, 1852.
6. Appendix to the *Congressional Globe*, 28th Congress, 2nd session, January 1845, 128–29.
7. *Cambridge City Tribune* (IN), June 24, 1876. Linda C. Gugin, James E. St. Clair, eds., *Justices of the Indiana Supreme Court* (Indianapolis: Indiana Historical Society, 2010), 85–87.
8. Rec. December 15, 1845. HR29A G8.2. Unless otherwise noted, the petitions that follow are housed at the National Archives, Washington, DC.
9. Signed December 1845. HR29A G8.2.
10. Ibid.
11. Rec. January 27, 1846. HR29A G8.2.
12. "Memorial of the Kehukee Primitive Baptist Association in North Carolina," Rec. December 11, 1848, Senate Miscellaneous Documents No. 2, 30th Congress, 2nd session. On the Primitive Baptists, James R.

Mathis, *The Making of the Primitive Baptists: A Cultural and Intellectual History of the Antimission Movement, 1800–1840* (New York: Routledge, 2004); John G. Crowley, *Primitive Baptists of the Wiregrass South: 1815 to the Present* (Gainesville: University of Florida Press, 1998).
13. *Niles' National Register* 74 (1848–1849): 397.
14. *Signs of the Times*, February 1, 1846.
15. Ibid., April 1, 1849.
16. *A Patriotic Discourse: Delivered by the Rev. Joshua Lawrence, at the Old Church in Tarborough, North Carolina, on Sunday, the 4th of July, 1830* (Tarborough: Free Press, 1830), 10.
17. Rec. February 15, 1830. HR 21A-G15.3.
18. *Signs of the Times*, March 15, 1846.
19. Ibid., January 15, 1848.
20. *The American Baptist Almanac for the Year of Our Lord 1857* (Philadelphia: American Baptist Publication Society, 1857), 47.
21. Editorial re-printed in *Signs of the Times*, March 1, 1852.
22. This count is based on petitions to the House Committee on the Judiciary in the 31st, 32nd, and 33rd Congresses, held at NARA (Washington, DC).
23. Editorial re-printed in *Signs of the Times*, March 1, 1852.
24. No date. HR32A G10.2. *Proceedings of the Grand Lodge of Iowa*, vol. 1 (Muscatine: Raymond, Foster & Eystra, 1858), 141.
25. Rec. December 21, 1853. HR33A-G10.2.
26. Rec. February 15, 1850. HR31A-G9.4.
27. Rec. February 15, 1850. HR31A-G9.4.
28. House of Representatives, 31st Congress, 1st session, "Chaplains", March 13, 1850, 4.
29. Editorial re-printed in *Signs of the Times*, March 1, 1852.
30. Senate, 32nd Congress, 2nd session, January 19, 1853.
31. House of Representatives, 33rd Congress, 1st session, "Chaplains in Congress and in the Army and Navy," March 27, 1854, 8.
32. *Maine Liquor Law Debate, at Clinton, New-Jersey, Wednesday, October 9, 1852* (Middletown: Banner Office, 1853), 12. On Beebe and anti-Maine law agitation, Kyle G. Volk, *Moral Minorities and the Making of American Democracy* (New York: Oxford University Press, 2014), 176–85.
33. Ibid., 20, 31.
34. *Circular, Maine Law* (New Bedford, NH, 1858), no page number.
35. Ibid.
36. *Speech of Rev. J.C. Lovejoy, before the Committee of the Legislature of Mass: On the Petition of Thomas H. Perkins, and Others, for the Repeal of the Liquor Law, March 15, 1853* (Boston: R.C. Nichols and H.W. Muzzey, 1853), 9.

37. Harmon Kingsbury, *The Sabbath; a Brief History of Laws, Petitions, Remonstrances and Reports, with Facts, and Arguments, Relating to the Christian Sabbath* (New York: Robert Carter, 1840), 353.
38. McCrossen, *Holy Day, Holiday*, 30–32.
39. *Abstract of the Proceedings of the National Lord's Day Convention Held in the City of Baltimore on the 27th and 28th November 1844* (Baltimore: Evangelical Lutheran Church, 1854), 35.
40. *Liberator*, October 16, 1840.
41. *Liberator*, August 20, 1836.
42. *Liberator*, July 23, 1836.
43. *Liberator*, December 29, 1849.
44. Garrison to May, September 8, 1838, available at: http://archive.org/stream/lettertomydearbr00garr4#page/n0/mode/2up. On Garrison's hostility to evangelicals, Sehat, *Myth of American Religious Liberty*, 87–89.
45. *Liberator*, July 23, 1836.
46. *The Complete Works of Ralph Waldo Emerson*, vol. 10 (Boston: Houghton Mifflin, 1903), 374.
47. Letter to Ann Elizabeth Wendell in *The Letters of John Greenleaf Whittier*, ed. John B. Pickard, vol. 1 (Cambridge, MA: Belknap, 1975), 469.
48. Amos A. Phelps, *The Sabbath* (New York: M.W. Dodd, 1844).
49. Ibid., 21.
50. *Sabbath Recorder*, June 13, 1844.
51. *Statutes at Large of the State of New York: Comprising the Revised Statutes*, vol. 4 (Albany, 1863), 45.
52. *Specht vs Commonwealth*, 8. Pa 312.
53. Petition reproduced in *Occident and American Jewish Advocate*, February 1846.
54. Ibid.
55. *Occident and American Jewish Advocate*, April 1846.
56. *Occident and American Jewish Advocate*, March 1847.
57. "Jacob Ezekiel," *Publications of the American Jewish Historical Society* 9 (1901): 160–63.
58. Signed February 16, 1846, available at: http://www.virginiamemory.com/collections/petitions.
59. Herbert T. Ezekiel and Gaston Lichtenstein, *The History of the Jews of Richmond from 1769 to 1917* (Richmond: H. T. Ezekiel, 1917), 109–11. On the Seventh-Day Baptists, Jews and Sabbath laws, see Volk, *Moral Minorities*, 46–52. In 1849, the revised state code exempted Jews from any penalty for violating the Christian Sabbath.
60. *Proceedings of the Anti-Sabbath Convention, Held in the Melodeon, March 23rd and 24th* (Boston, 1848), 90–91.
61. Ibid., 47.

62. Clay McShane and Joel A. Tarr, *The Horse in the City: Living Machines in the Nineteenth Century* (Baltimore: John Hopkins University Press, 2007).
63. Frederick W. Spiers, "The Street Railway System of Philadelphia, Its History and Present Condition," *Johns Hopkins University Studies in Historical and Political Science* (1897): 17; Charles W. Cheape, *Moving the Masses: Urban Public Transport in New York, Boston and Philadelphia, 1880–1912* (Cambridge: Harvard University Press, 1980), 157–62.
64. John Noble, *Facts Concerning Street Railway: The Substance of a Series of Official Reports from the Cities of New York, Brooklyn, Boston, Philadelphia* et al. (London: P.S. King, 1866), 56.
65. *Annual Census Reports of Railroads*, November 1861. RG 14, Series 15 (Pennsylvania State Archives, Harrisburg).
66. *Brooklyn Daily Eagle*, January 6, 1857; McShane and Tarr, *Horse in the City*, 99–100.
67. *German Reformed Messenger* (Chambersburg, PA), July 27, 1859.
68. John Holmes Agnew, *A Manual on the Christian Sabbath* (Philadelphia: Presbyterian Board of Publication, 1852), 150.
69. Harold E. Cox, "'Daily Except Sunday': Blue Laws and the Operation of Philadelphia's Horsecars," *Business History Review* 39 (1965): 228–42.
70. *Sunday Dispatch*, July 10, 1859.
71. *Public Ledger*, July 11, 1859.
72. *Evening Bulletin*, July 21, 1859.
73. *North American*, July 18, 1859.
74. *North American*, August 1, 1859.
75. *Public Ledger*, August 1, 1859.
76. *Sunday Atlas*, July 31, 1859.
77. *Sunday Travel: A Discourse Delivered Sunday Morning, April 28, 1850, in the First Congregational Unitarian Church in Philadelphia* (Philadelphia: C. Sherman, 1850), 10.
78. *Sunday Dispatch*, July 24, 1859.
79. William Logan Fisher, *History of the Institution of the Sabbath Day* (Philadelphia: T.B. Pugh, 1859), 9.
80. Ibid., 211. On Fisher, see William Logan Fisher and Nicholas B. Wainwright, "Memoir of William Logan Fisher (1781–1862) for His Grandchildren," *Pennsylvania Magazine of History and Biography* 99, no. 1 (1975): 92–103.
81. *Friend*, July 30, 1859.
82. *Minutes of the General Assembly of the Presbyterian Church*, vol. 15 (Philadelphia: Presbyterian Board of Publication, 1859), 534.
83. John Hancock Lee, *The Origins and Progress of the American Party in Politics* (Philadelphia: Elliot and Gihon, 1855), 21.

84. Ibid., 227.
85. *Sunday Dispatch*, December 4, 1859.
86. *Sunday Atlas*, July 10, 1859.
87. Cathcart, *Lord's Day Not the Sabbath*, 25.
88. *Philadelphia Evening Bulletin*, July 28, 1859.
89. *Journal of the Common Council, of the City of Philadelphia, for 1858–1859* (Philadelphia: Inquirer, 1859), 343.
90. *Public Ledger*, July 13, 1859.
91. Ibid., July 14, 1859.
92. *Sunday Dispatch*, July 24, 1859.
93. *Public Ledger*, August 1, 1859.
94. *Public Ledger*, July 18, 1859.
95. *Public Ledger*, October 19, 1859.
96. *Journal of the Common Council, of the City of Philadelphia, for 1859–60* (Philadelphia: Inquirer, 1859), 295.
97. *Philadelphia Sabbath Association, 19th Annual Report* (Philadelphia: William P. Geddes, 1860), 6.
98. Mark A. Noll, *The Civil War as a Theological Crisis* (Chapel Hill: University of North Carolina Press, 2006), 28.

CHAPTER 5

"God's Vice-Regents": Political Preachers and the Crisis Over Slavery

In February 1856, *Harper's Monthly* made a wry commentary on the modern-day craze for "political preaching." One of the journal's correspondents reported overhearing the following exchange on a streetcar. A passenger asked the conductor what was new in the world of politics. The conductor, however, could give no answer for, as he told the passenger, "*I haven't been to church* for the last two Sundays."[1]

On one level, this was a light-hearted dig at ministers who hectored their congregations on political matters. But the joke carried, as the editors wrote, a "pretty sharp point," namely whether or not ministers should use their pulpits to speak out on the controversy overshadowing all others, slavery extension. Antislavery preachers argued that it was their duty to condemn the spread of a sinful institution. But their newfound boldness raised a series of troubling questions about the relationship between religion and politics. Critics charged that by engaging in partisan politics, ministers were putting at risk the public esteem enjoyed by their profession. Even worse, by adding religious zeal to an already combustible political atmosphere, they were hastening an impending national catastrophe.

The debate over political preaching reveals how the call for a secular state could be deployed as a means of upholding racial privilege. The fiercest opponents of political preachers were southern defenders of slavery and their allies in the North. For white supremacists, the best means of silencing antislavery ministers was to invoke a strict separation of church and state. Furthermore, the contest over political preaching

© The Author(s) 2019
T. Verhoeven, *Secularists, Religion and Government in Nineteenth-Century America*, https://doi.org/10.1007/978-3-030-02877-0_5

enshrined a distinctively southern conception of the relationship between religion and politics. From the perspective of white southerners, the activism of the northern clergy highlighted the virtues of their own section, where widespread piety was accompanied by a studious effort to steer clear of political controversy. This may have been, as critics pointed out, a highly selective reading of sectional difference. But whether accurate or not, white southerners articulated their conviction that clerical politicking was a northern disease. This would prove an enduring sentiment. Well into the Progressive era, moral legislation would run into the opposition of southern legislators, who associated such measures with the hated political preachers responsible for poisoning sectional relations before the Civil War.

Finally, the political preaching controversy was yet another vehicle through which religious-political activism came to be branded as fanaticism and as such a threat to true faith. In this case, it was history that became the site of contest. For their opponents, abolitionist preachers were the modern-day inheritors of a long theocratic tradition that had its origin in the European settlement of New England. In the debate on political preaching, then, we see coming into focus the vexed figure of the Puritan.

The Limits of Pulpit Politicking

One of the reasons for the backlash against political preachers was the sense that they were deploying the pulpit in a new and radical fashion. Before the issue of slavery extension emerged with such force in the 1850s, the majority of northern Protestant ministers approached explicitly political questions with a great deal of wariness. Sabbatarians might urge their flock to sign petitions or attend public meetings. But political partisanship on the part of men of faith seemed to arouse deep misgivings both within and outside the ministry. Alexis de Tocqueville noticed this as he toured the nation after the Sunday mail controversy. Clerics, he observed with some surprise, largely stayed out of the political fray. Religion was a powerful force, providing a moral counterbalance to the individual freedom at the heart of democracy. Law, he wrote, "permits the Americans to do what they please," but Christian morality "forbids them to commit, what is rash or unjust." In this sense, as Tocqueville famously concluded, religion was "the first of their political institutions."[2] But clerical influence had clear limits. Tocqueville saw that public opinion prevented ministers taking sides in political disputes, a constraint that most willingly accepted. The vast majority, he wrote, "keep aloof from parties and from public affairs" and make it "the pride of their profession to abstain from politics."[3]

Even as the Benevolent Empire extended its reach, outright politicking on the part of the clergy was frowned upon. Homiletic manuals advised avoiding, both in content and in style, anything that smacked of partisanship. James W. Alexander suggested that while discussion of broad moral principles was appropriate, ministers should tread carefully when discussing their practical application, and be absolutely steadfast in avoiding the heated language of the political arena. The pulpit, he wrote, "soils itself" when it mimics the "unworthy passions" of political debate.[4] Alexander then directed his readers to a Swiss theologian, Alexandre Vinet, whose *Homiletics: or, the theory of preaching* was published in several American editions before the Civil War. The preacher must be willing to tackle contentious issues, Vinet argued, because the Christian religion touched all phases of life. But he should be careful to avoid the perception of taking political sides and always employ the sober, moderate language appropriate to his position.[5] Although Vinet and others did not put it in these terms, this prudence was also a function of the voluntary system. While he might supplement his income by publishing tracts or joining the lecture circuit, a preacher's livelihood was almost entirely determined by the size and goodwill of his congregation. In this situation, many preachers were understandably wary of running too far ahead of public opinion or expressing views which might not be shared by all.

The rise of abolitionist agitation did not make ministers more outspoken on slavery. Through the 1830s and 1840s, the vast majority echoed public opinion in denouncing radical abolitionists and their call for immediate emancipation. As a number of scholars have demonstrated, support for outright abolition, though probably increasing through the 1850s, remained a minority position in the northern churches as late as the outbreak of the Civil War.[6] But slavery extension was a different matter. The first sign of opposition came in the Mexican-American war, a war which many northern clerics interpreted as part of a southern strategy to open up new fields for slavery. However, it was the Fugitive Slave Law, passed on September 18, 1850, which emboldened much of the northern clergy to speak out. As soon as its details became known in the northern states, public outrage flared. The law circumvented state autonomy by giving federal commissioners the right to issue warrants for the arrest and return of runaway slaves. But more provocatively, it drew citizens into the odious task of sending men and women back into bondage by allowing federal marshals to press bystanders into their service. For the first time, northerners were brought into direct contact with an institution that many had regarded as objectionable but distant. "We are all," as the headline of one newspaper proclaimed, "slave-catchers."[7]

Henry Ward Beecher Enters the Debate

This was the moment when the debate over political preaching sprang to life, and the spark was provided by the then little-known Reverend Henry Ward Beecher. The son of Lyman Beecher, Henry graduated from the institution headed by his father, Lane Theological Seminary, in 1837, and a decade later took up the position from which he would eventually win a national audience, Plymouth Congregational Church in Brooklyn. Beecher's stance on the slavery question was typical of the northern ministry. Though always convinced that slavery was immoral, he was an advocate of gradual emancipation and was content to leave slavery where it existed, trusting that it would wither away. "We only ask," he wrote, "that a line be drawn about it." Slavery "must find no new sources, new fields, new prerogatives."[8] But with the passage of the 1850 law, Beecher suddenly saw slavery as a national problem which could no longer be ignored. From that moment, Beecher would recall decades later, "I was thoroughly roused."[9]

Beecher's response was to pen an anonymous article for the Congregationalist weekly, the New York *Independent*, which appeared on March 21, 1850, and in which he denounced the Fugitive Slave Law as a "monstrous inhumanity." This was not overly controversial. But Beecher went further by attacking the politicians behind the measure. These men were moral cowards driven only by ambition, "statesmen of their own advancement" as he put it, and the worst of them was the leader of the Whig Party, Daniel Webster. Beecher was outraged that a scion of New England could cede, as he saw it, to southern intimidation. In so doing, Webster had "betrayed the faith and honor of the Commonwealth of the Pilgrims." That a man of God would level a charge of treachery against a figure as distinguished as Webster was in itself provocative. But Beecher did not stop there. With the political class corrupted by ambition and beholden to slave-owners, the advocates of justice and morality could only look to one place for leadership, the pulpit. Across the North,

Beecher boasted, ministers were exhorting the faithful to oppose the new law. "TEN THOUSAND PULPITS," he declared, "are every week pouring light upon the public mind." Beecher ended with a dire warning of Divine retribution for those who continued to defend this immoral measure. "They who cast off Right," he concluded, "cast it against God, and He will give it an Omnipotent rebound."[10]

Beecher's outspoken stance immediately came under attack from the New York *Journal of Commerce*, a paper which ironically had been founded and financed by the great supporter of evangelical causes, Arthur Tappan, as a moral counterweight to what he saw as the salaciousness of New York's leading dailies. For decades, its editors David Hale and Gerard Hallock upheld Tappan's principles by refusing to carry advertisements for theaters or lotteries and by banning all editorial work and printing from midnight on Saturday to midnight on Sunday. On slavery, the *Journal* combined a hostility toward abolitionist agitation with a consistent advocacy of colonization as the best solution both for slaves and for the nation.[11] By 1850, Hallock, who was now sole editor after Hale's death the previous year, was growing alarmed at what he saw as the spreading influence of abolitionists within northern churches. Beecher's call to arms was a provocation that he could not ignore. On April 12, the *Journal* denounced Beecher for bringing politics into the pulpit. The minister's primary duty was to tend to the souls of his flock, and by making this the focus of his efforts, he would maintain their respect and esteem. Those that followed Beecher's example, Hallock charged, would find that "their black coats will most likely be rolled in the dirt."[12] On April 18, the *Independent* responded that preachers could properly use the pulpit as a platform for antislavery principles without descending into political partisanship.[13] The *Journal* was not convinced. A sermon might begin with a general discussion of slavery, it asserted, but before long the unwitting congregation would find itself the objects of a free-soil harangue.[14] Over the next months, the *Independent* and the *Journal* continued to spar over political preaching before calling a truce.

POLITICAL PREACHING AND MANLINESS

Far from going away, the controversy over political preaching was set to escalate. If Beecher had been roused by the Fugitive Slave Law, the passage of the Kansas-Nebraska Act in 1854 prompted many more northern ministers to follow his example. That bill repealed the 1820 Missouri Compromise which had barred slavery north of the 36°30′ parallel and allowed the residents of Kansas and Nebraska to decide whether slavery would be allowed there. The prospect of slavery seeping into the vast free-soil territories triggered public outrage in the North, and ministers shared the indignation. In the most dramatic act of clerical protest to date, more than three thousand clergymen from New England signed a petition to Congress protesting the Kansas-Nebraska Act.

Across the North, preachers railed against slavery extension from their pulpits. Apart from Beecher, perhaps the most prominent was George Barrell Cheever, pastor of the Church of the Puritans in New York. The man of God was obligated, Cheever declared, to preach not just on the sinfulness of extending slavery but also on the immorality of any vote in favor of it.[15] He saw signs that most now understood this. As hateful as the Kansas-Nebraska Act was, it had at least shaken the ministry from its passivity. As he wrote to his sister, the controversy had "done much to open the mouths of ministers, and give freedom to their pulpits."[16] Cheever was now confident that ministers across the free states would rally their congregations against slavery extension.

Though aware of the risk of a backlash, preachers like Cheever seemed in fact to relish the opportunity to prove their independence. As George M. Fredrickson has suggested, many ministers chafed under the restraints of the voluntary system, particularly their dependence on the goodwill of parishioners for their living.[17] Speaking out against slavery was a chance to throw off the shackles. One of the editors of the *Independent*, Leonard Bacon, prickled at the notion that a man of God might stifle his conscience for fear of jeopardizing his income. Such a man, he wrote, may as well "go out with Judas and hang himself."[18] Nor should he allow the secular press to dictate the content of his sermons. With a typical rhetorical flourish, Henry Ward Beecher argued that he would be as likely to look to "Greenland for tropical plants" or to "Australia for literature," as to rely on the *Journal of Commerce* for guidance as to what was a fitting topic for the pulpit.[19]

In their diaries and letters, individual preachers expressed the same thrill at throwing down the gauntlet to their flocks in the name of a holy cause. One example is a man who would become a secularist leader after the Civil War, William J. Potter. In 1859, Potter began preaching at the New Bedford Unitarian congregation. Initially, he was deeply insecure about his performance as a preacher. In July 1859, he expressed his anxiety in a letter to his friend George W. Bartlett: "Sermons, sermons, nothing but sermons! They are eating me up, soul and body," he complained. "Preaching will do me, but I cannot do it."[20] On the cusp of the Civil War, the great cause of antislavery steadied his nerves. Writing to Bartlett, he described giving a sermon to a packed congregation. It was "rather cruel," he admitted, but he had seized the opportunity to "throw an antislavery bomb."[21] He did not, unfortunately, record their reaction.

It is not hard to detect in this newfound audacity an assertion of manliness. In her study of preaching manuals, Roxanne Mountford argues that evangelicals sought to cement their position in national life by projecting a virile image. Preachers, she argues, were urged to "develop themselves as *men* so that their congregations would recognize them as civil leaders."[22] Central to this ideal of manliness was autonomy. The true man, according to the conventions of the time, relied above all on his own initiative and was beholden to no other.[23] This was a challenge for preachers whose livelihood was largely dependent on satisfying their flock. But the antislavery cause offered a way to project a bold independence. By striding into a political storm and braving the outcry from the press, the political preacher could carve out a position of social leadership while boosting his sense of manliness. All the "inducements," as Cheever wrote, were "on the side of ease, quiet, and silence." But the greater rewards were on the side of speaking out. Were he to remain silent, Cheever declared, he would "never lift my head as a man, a free man."[24] Cheever was far from alone in seizing the opportunity provided by the Kansas-Nebraska controversy to affirm his manly credentials.

In fact, the craze for political preaching brought together old foes. As we have seen, William Lloyd Garrison was a fierce opponent of the Benevolent Empire and its reform drive, in part because he detested the hypocrisy of preachers who condemned Sabbath-breaking while staying mute on the far greater sin of slavery. Throughout the 1840s, Garrison and other abolitionists such as Gerrit Smith challenged ministers to put aside their scruples about mixing religion and politics and preach against slavery from the pulpit. The clergy, Smith lamented, had been trained to "draw a line between religion and politics, and to regard religion as one thing, and politics as another." The only result of this squeamishness, Smith argued, was to "consign Civil Government to the Devil."[25] When the northern ministry at last raised its voice, abolitionists applauded their newfound courage. The *Liberator* published articles from the secular and religious press advocating clerical activism on the subject of slavery.[26] Black abolitionists joined the appreciation. In June 1850, Frederick Douglass' *North Star* re-printed a long article defending Beecher in his contest with the *Journal of Commerce* and urging other preachers to follow his example.[27] The political preaching controversy would not convert Garrison or Douglass into wholehearted supporters of the Benevolent Empire. After the Civil War, and with slavery at last abolished, Garrison would return to opposing the strict enforcement of Sabbath laws, for example, or the attempt to Christianize the Constitution. William J. Potter went on to become a vocal proponent of the secular character of the American government. But while the threat of slavery extension hovered over the union, areas of common ground came clearly into view.

The Backlash Against Political Preachers

Preachers like Potter and Cheever were right to fear a backlash. The *New York Herald*, edited by the notoriously racist James Gordon Bennett, lambasted what it termed "pestiferous political parsons."[28] But opponents went beyond personal abuse to make a series of arguments about religion and government. As ever, a vision of pure religion was a powerful rallying point. Faith would only be sullied by contact with the vile world of politics; anyone who truly believed in the timeless truth of Christianity would stay aloof from grubby political battles. Religion, as a writer in the *Democratic Review* argued, "is a pure white dove descending like flakes of snow from the skies, and cannot touch anything earthly without being defiled."[29] For these critics, the minister's primary duty was not to mold public opinion or to rally resistance to laws but simply to tend to his flock's spiritual needs. In this way, he would follow the example of Jesus Christ who, as several writers asserted, never broached political topics.

This was a familiar argument for a strict separation of church and state. More novel was the way in which its advocates descended from the higher plane of religion as a whole to the level of the individual congregation. In churches across the North, the injection of politics into the Sunday sermon was wreaking discord among once harmonious flocks. Tired of being bludgeoned with antislavery harangues, some in the pews might stop listening. Daniel Webster, the Massachusetts Whig whose support for the 1850 compromise bill had drawn the ire of Henry

Ward Beecher, confessed to adopting this strategy of passive resistance. "Many of the Ministers of the present day," he was reported as saying, "preach from the newspapers. When they do so, I prefer to enjoy my own thoughts rather than to listen."[30] But others were thought likely to react with much more vehemence, transforming the church from a haven of communion to a pit of dissension. As one commentator in the *Boston Evening Transcript* remarked, very few communions were marked by political unanimity, and while churchgoers would accept being lectured on their sins, they were unlikely to sit calmly through an attack on their political opinions. The writer then painted such a warring congregation. The faces of some in the pews were marked by "hatred and revenge," others by "malice and uncharitableness." At the end of the sermon, a portion was "ready for three cheers," while the rest were "ready to fight."[31] Political preaching appeared to be turning the house of God into something which resembled the fractious atmosphere of Congress.

But there was a difference between a church and a legislative assembly which made political sermons even more galling. Members of Congress could endure the blows of their opponents because they knew that they would soon have their turn to respond. But in church, there was no mechanism for a rejoinder. Denied the right to interject, churchgoers were condemned to suffer in silence. Preachers were bringing politics into the pulpit without adopting the democratic mechanisms which governed other political forums. The only recourse for the disgruntled parishioner was to call for the minister to be replaced or to shift to a different congregation. As the press reported, precisely this sort of small-scale rebellion was happening across the northern states. A congregation in Jerseyville Illinois was reported as having resolved to no longer support any minister who preached politics.[32] Citizens in Camden, Maine, called a meeting to consider raising funds for a minister who would act exclusively as a teacher of religion.[33] In Pennsylvania, a farmer was said to have stood up in the midst of a free-soil sermon and demanded that in future half of the time be devoted to the Democratic Party.[34] Across the north, congregations seemed to be fracturing.

In response, antislavery preachers argued that parishioners would have little interest in attending a church which ignored the most pressing questions of the day. A minister who tried to stay above the slavery controversy would find his pews emptying. As Beecher argued in the *Independent*, "when men have learned that their weightiest interests are more Christianly met out of the Church than in it—in lectures, societies, and divisions—then where will be the Church?"[35] But his opponents insisted that the real threat to a flourishing church lay in the intrusion of political squabbling. The New Hampshire *Patriot and State Gazette* was a fierce critic of what it termed "political priests" who had transformed their pulpits into "political rostrums." One of the effects of such behavior was to drive away the faithful. The paper cited a report by the local association of Congregational ministers lamenting the "spiritual drought" which had settled over the state. Revivals were scarce, and congregations were shrinking. The cause, for the *Patriot and State Gazette*, was clear. Ministers had "abandoned their posts" as well as the "cause of religion," and instead "given their chief attention to politics."[36] They would do well to lower their gaze toward the men and women thirsting for spiritual guidance in such troubled times.

Underlying these arguments was a fundamental division over the public role of clerics in a republic which had discarded formal religious establishments. For evangelicals, the absence of formal ties between church and state made the guiding hand of religion even more indispensable to the politics of the nation. The reason was, as the *New Englander and Yale Review* argued, that the Founders had separated church and state but not religion and politics. Echoing Tocqueville's argument decades earlier, the *Review* saw Christian morality as providing the essential ballast to any republican democracy. There could be no "healthy and safe politics," the journal argued, "not controlled by the principles of religion." The result of stripping religion from the public sphere would be first lawlessness and then tyranny. Within this conception of the relationship between religion and the state, ministers had a privileged role. They must constantly remind voters as well as their representatives of their ultimate accountability to God and "preach the gospel in its application to politics" at every opportunity. "For politicians to repel their influence," the journal concluded, "is as ungrateful for the past as suicidal for the future."[37]

But for many Americans, this notion of a distinct if unofficial public role for pastors raised the specter of a union of church and state. The Founders had intended the separation of the two to be, as the *Democratic Review* argued, an "impassable barrier." Any intersection between them would be "equally fatal to the purity of one and the freedom of the other."[38] This conception of separation demanded that churches and their representatives be kept at arms-length from the organs of government. No church or religious organization, the New

Orleans *Picayune* argued, "stands on any connection, or relation with the political authorities."[39] This did not mean that ministers should be excluded entirely from the political sphere. They could, for example, stand for election. By the Civil War, all states bar three had abandoned any formal disqualification on ministers of religion sitting in state legislatures. In their capacity as citizens, they might petition legislatures or address political meetings. But once they claimed to be acting as representatives of God or sought special authority on the basis of their profession, they were guilty, as one southern paper put it, of a "pure and unmitigated assumption."[40]

STEPHEN A. DOUGLAS ATTACKS THE NEW ENGLAND CLERGY

These divisions over the political role of the clergy were expressed with great clarity when the remonstrance of the three thousand New England clergymen against the Kansas-Nebraska Act was presented to the Senate. The response of Stephen A. Douglas, the most famous Democrat in the nation and a key architect of the law, was furious. In signing the petition, the clergymen had, he thundered, "prostituted the sacred desk, to the miserable and corrupting influence of party politics." Their stance was hypocritical. They castigated members of Congress for abrogating the Missouri Compromise, a move which they described as a breach of trust, but felt no compunction in urging the faithful to defy laws which did not please them, notably the Fugitive Slave Act. But Douglas was most incensed by their presumption in claiming a privileged public role as a bridge between government and its citizens. "I do not," Douglas continued, "acknowledge them as an intermediate tribunal."[41]

The ministers had their defenders. The Texan Sam Houston defended their right to petition like any other citizen. "Because they are ministers of the Gospel," he argued to the Senate, "they are not disfranchised of political rights and privileges." It was their civic duty, he continued, to protest against a measure which they regarded as immoral. The Constitution did not give ministers a formal role. But it was widely agreed, Houston continued, that the political ideals of the nation rested on a moral foundation.[42] New Englanders sprang to the ministers' defense. The signers of the petition, Edward Everett of Massachusetts reminded the Senate, were some of the most intelligent, well-educated, and respectable members of the community, men who could rightly expect to have their opinions treated with greater courtesy.[43] But

Douglas was not mollified and took aim at two key phrases in the petition. The first, underlined in black, framed the protest in the "name of Almighty God." The second was a warning that in passing the Kansas-Nebraska Act, Congress had opened the nation up to "the righteous judgements of the Almighty." By making their demand in the name of Almighty God, and even more shockingly underlining this section in black pen, the ministers appeared to be elevating their interpretation of God's wishes over the will of the people as expressed through their representatives. "It is an attempt," he declared, "to establish in this country the doctrine that a body of men organized and known among the people as clergymen have a peculiar right to determine the will of God in relation to legislative action."[44] If it were allowed to pass, he concluded, a clerical minority would in effect have a veto power.

Douglas went on to argue that the Senate should not even receive the petition. In making this case, he was attempting to revive the gag rule. In the 1830s, antislavery organizations began sending thousands of petitions to Congress calling for the abolition of slavery in the District of Columbia. In response, southerners and their allies succeeded in passing a rule requiring the House to table them immediately. No antislavery petition could henceforth be printed, referred to a committee, or debated. Supporters of the gag rule sometimes presented public petitions in support. In 1839, New York representative Ely Moore presented a petition from Washington, DC residents urging the House not to consider any remonstrance against slavery in their district. In his remarks in support of the petition, Moore argued that non-residents of a state or territory had no right to call for Congressional action in other jurisdictions. The right of petition was limited to those citizens who were directly affected by the issue at hand.[45] The gag rule remained in place until 1844.

Douglas' attack on the New England ministers no doubt served his political purposes. An attack on antislavery ministers was a sure means of rallying his supporters and distracting attention from the tensions between the sections on the question of slavery extension. But his intervention showed that the fear of the Clergy, which had been expressed so cogently by the pro-Sunday mail petitioners, was alive and well. As an old Jacksonian, Senator James Mason of Virginia argued, the clergy "are the most encroaching and, as a body, arrogant class of men." It was for this reason that the Founders had erected a constitutional barrier between religion and politics. "The great effort of the American people has been", Mason concluded, "to keep that class away from the Government."[46] An entrenched suspicion of religious power combined with a growing sense of national crisis to spark a backlash against political preaching.

POLITICAL PREACHERS AND FALSE RELIGIONS

To conceptualize the threat, opponents of political preachers evoked other faiths which had been degraded and corrupted by their embrace of temporal power. Islam was one favored point of reference. Following the death of his wife in 1853, Douglas embarked on an overseas tour that included a visit to Turkey. What he saw there provided him with a stock of ammunition to deploy against the New England clergy. He had, he told the Senate, witnessed the manner in which the "successors of Mahomet proclaimed and enforced God's will on earth." He had not expected, he continued, to find Christians in his native land aspiring to a similar position.[47] Asian religions provided another key to making sense of the dangers brewing at home. One newspaper printed an article purportedly written by a missionary in China which likened the New England ministers to the despotic priesthood reigning over Eastern nations.[48] In both cases, a politically ambitious clergy wielded enormous power to the detriment both of spiritual vitality and social and economic progress.

But two faiths much closer to home provided an even more powerful point of comparison. The first was the standard-bearer for politicized religion, Roman-Catholicism. Again and again, opponents of political preaching drew a link to what they saw as the Catholic priest's despotic control over his flock. Political preachers were guilty, in the phrase that captured their affinity with the Catholic clergy, of acting as "God's vice-regents," each of them, in the words of the *Journal of Commerce*, a "Pope in a small way."[49] Just as alarmingly, they were giving Catholics an opening to turn the situation to their advantage. As Protestant clerics assumed a more overtly political role, some Catholics began to argue that it was their faith which was now more in tune with the American understanding of the separation of church and state. Unlike the northern Protestant churches, as Democratic Congressman John Kelly of New York argued, the Catholic Church was "the only one that has taken no part in political strife." At the last Presidential election, he continued, its ministers alone "abstained entirely from political appeals."[50] Nativists were busily denouncing the Vatican for lusting after political power. Perhaps, these statements implied, they should be more concerned with the rise of evangelical ambition.

Yet another aspect of political preaching that raised parallels with the fearsome power of Catholicism was its theatrics. No faith was thought to be more adept at theatricality than Roman-Catholicism. For its opponents, the sensory show of the Mass—its repertoire of candles, incense, music and skillful staging—was a formidable weapon in winning over converts and keeping them under the Church's spell. There was a gendered dimension to this critique. Women, always thought susceptible to appeals to the senses and the heart, were forever vulnerable. Men, deemed to be naturally endowed with reason and willpower, were better placed to resist the Church's blandishments. This was the message of the popular genre of escaped nun tales. In these tales, a young Protestant woman falls under the spell of Catholicism and enters a convent. She soon discovers, however, that she is trapped. Cut off from family and friends, and subjected to harsh discipline, emotional bullying and, in some of the more lurid narratives, sexual abuse and torture at the hands of her fellow nuns as well as priests, she experiences the terrible cruelty of the Catholic Church.

The final act in the captive nun's narrative is her escape, which makes possible the publication of her narrative for a fascinated public. But before taking her place as a credible witness to Catholic wickedness, the escaped nun faced one great challenge. How could she justify her initial decision to abandon the Protestant faith and to join the convent? The answer lay in the visual and emotional appeal of the Mass. One famous escaped nun, Josephine Bunkley, blamed her choice on a vulnerability to spectacle and ritual, or as she put it, on her exposure to the "seductive allurements of a sensual system."[51] This was her weak point, and the Church, so practiced in the art of visual entrapment, exploited it to the full.

Political preachers did not have recourse to such a rich visual and sensory backdrop. But for their critics, their fierce language worked in a similar way to overwhelm the intellect and stimulate strong emotions. The words of the political preacher, as the *New York Herald* put it, "sink deep into the hearts of his hearers."[52] But in the case of political sermons, men just as much as women were at risk. Men faced the loss of that core marker of manliness, the independent intellect. The aim of what the *Herald* called "theatrical performers" like Beecher and Cheever was to make men's minds malleable and therefore subject to control.[53] If he were not careful, a man might be reduced to the same state of fanaticism. "By becoming less manly and intellectual," the *Democratic Review* warned, "he will also be more easily governed, without the aid of that dangerous instrument called human reason, which is a sad stumbling-block in the way of fanaticism."[54] Notions of manliness, then, shaped the political preaching controversy in different ways. Antislavery preachers celebrated their defiance of convention and their willingness to brave the opprobrium of their flocks as in part an assertion of their manly independence. But for their opponents, their fiery and extravagant words were working to emasculate their audience. Once under the spell of such a preacher, a man would have surrendered his cherished independence and become a mere tool of fanaticism.

He would be reduced, in fact, to a state akin to slavery. As Eric Foner has convincingly argued, a range of nineteenth-century activists, from temperance and women's rights advocates to labor leaders, employed the language of slavery as a "master metaphor" for any subordinate, unequal position in society.[55] Anti-Catholics were no different. Anti-Catholic literature often described the hierarchical relationships within the church—the priest over his flock, the Mother Superior over the nun, the Jesuit General over his novices—as directly akin to the dictatorial, ruthless authority enjoyed by the slave-owner over the slave. Again, however, political preachers were accused of acting in the same sinister manner. On the eve of the Civil War, the New York *Illustrated News* compared the intimidating power of the minister to that of a slave-owner. "No one," the paper commented, "can arrest your thought or sway your sentiments more immediately." Through a combination of "stealthy moves" and "subtle reasonings," the preacher had the power to "wear you down to a tame submission." The listener had to be wary, for the outcome would be a form of slavery. "He becomes master of the position," the paper concluded, "and you are his abject serf."[56]

THE SHADOW OF THE PURITANS

Another useful foil for the adversaries of political preaching was a group with even deeper roots in American history, the Puritans. The period of the early Republic saw a newfound interest in the legacy of the Puritan/Pilgrim colonies for the nation.[57] On one side, as Steven K. Green describes, New Englanders celebrated their forebears as the true inspirers of the republican experiment in liberty.[58] The Puritan that emerged from works such as David Ramsay's *History of the United States* (1816) was a brave, industrious, and self-reliant pioneer whose primitive sense of equality had set the nation from its inception on a path to democracy. In seeking the Puritan origins of republican freedom, writers turned to several sources. One was the Mayflower Compact, the 1620 agreement between the Plymouth settlers on the nature of their government. Having remained largely unknown until the late-eighteenth century, the Compact was now praised as a foundational text, an early statement of the social contract theory of governance that would find such glorious expression in the Declaration of Independence. More surprisingly, given their reputation for intolerance, the Puritans also won praise for inspiring the principle of religious liberty enshrined in the Constitution. In a July 4 address to the citizens of Springfield, Massachusetts, the historian George C. Bancroft reminded his audience that these men and women had come to America not in pursuit of wealth but as "exiles for conscience sake." Furthermore, they had shown that democracy and faith were a powerful combination. Their religion sprang from the people and not from princes; they were, he argued, "PLEBEIANS ALL."[59] From that moment onwards, Bancroft asserted, "popular liberty in its infancy in America, had religion to rock its cradle."[60] The fusion of popular piety and democracy that so astonished foreign observers was very much a Puritan legacy.

But for many other writers, the Puritans cast a much darker shadow. In making its Revolution, the nation had not brought Puritan principles to perfection, but rather thankfully discarded them. This was particularly the case for freedom of conscience, an area where the Puritan record seemed abysmal. Far from pioneers of religious liberty, the Puritans in this reading were bigots and theocrats, mercilessly rooting out and punishing dissenters while limiting political rights to those who conformed to their creed. "With all due respect to their many noble characteristics," the *Democratic Review* argued, "we are free to say, that of all enlightened people we ever heard or read of, they appear to have least understood, or, at any rate, practiced, the true principles of civil and religious liberty." So intense was their desire to crush rival faiths that they were akin, the journal argued, to the followers of "Mahomet."[61]

A full-scale debate on the Puritan legacy would not occur until after the Civil War. But already in the antebellum era, the figure of the Puritan captured and conveyed the dark ambition of political preachers. The New England clergy who signed the petition against the Kansas-Nebraska bill appeared to be the direct descendants of the Puritan settlers of the region, animated by the same intolerant spirit and just as oblivious to the distinction between religion and politics. "This strain of blood," the *New York Herald* suggested, "has not died out in New England," where the clergy remained "addicted to superstition and fanaticism."[62] The modern-day descendants of the Puritans were still determined to meld faith and politics in their ruthless campaign for power.

POLITICAL PREACHING AND THE SOUTH

Such invocations of the Puritans resonated particularly strongly in the South, where the rejection of political preaching became a key component in the construction of a distinct sectional identity. Across the slaveholding states, commentators were unanimous in drawing a contrast between the hateful political activism on display in northern pulpits and what they saw as the resolutely non-political position of southern preachers. "Fortunately in this section of the Union," as one paper in Mississippi commented, "we are but little cursed with pulpit politics and ecclesiastical interference with secular matters."[63] "During the whole exciting period of the last Presidential contest," the editor of the *Richmond Enquirer* asserted, "when New England pulpits were thundering anathemas against Buchanan, Fillmore and the South, not a single pulpit in all the southern States was desecrated by political preaching."[64] The *New Orleans Daily Crescent* agreed that southern preachers would not budge from their purely spiritual role, adding that "If northern ministers would but conform to their example, an immense amount of good would follow."[65] When they reflected on the benefits of such a stance, southern commentators came to another distinction between the two sections. In the North, the transformation of the pulpit into a political rostrum had produced the blight of atheism. A leading southern journal, *DeBow's Review*, blamed the "mingling religion and politics" for leading to the "gradual relaxation in the popular mind of any very strong religious faith."[66] In the South, however, where the pulpit had not been tainted by political rancor, popular faith was strong, and atheism virtually unheard of.

Northern ministers did not remain silent in the face of such arguments. Many pointed to the obvious hypocrisy in the southern claim to be free of political preaching. The southern pulpit had never refrained from offering theological justifications of slavery and from assuring southerners that their institutions were divinely blessed. What was this, after all, if not political preaching? "To preach against slavery is of course political preaching," as the *New Englander and Yale Review* observed, "but to preach for it ... with the host of southern preachers, is what such Christians as the *New York Journal of Commerce* and its allies call preaching the Gospel."[67] This was a telling point. Southern evangelicals, as Edward R. Crowther argues, "tried to disguise their political ranting as instruction in the Christian duties of citizenship or to bury it deeply in theological defense of slavery."[68] But it was political preaching nonetheless.

Still, southern propagandists did not concede the point. Their hostility to political preaching, they argued, predated the slavery controversy and had its roots in the Revolutionary era. In 1857, the *Weekly Standard* (North Carolina) recounted the story of a Revolutionary-era preacher who had dared to deliver a sermon in favor of the British. Some days later the preacher discovered a bucket of tar and a bag of feathers in his pulpit and, wisely heeding the message, fled the country.[69] Another key moment in this southern genealogy occurred in the early Republic. On the eve of the Civil War, some southerners were still recalling with bitterness the New England clergy's opposition to the 1812 war. Southern states were among the strongest advocates of the war, which propelled Andrew Jackson to national fame. Yet in the same manner as antislavery preachers, the New England clergy of the day, the *Times-Picayune* (New Orleans) reminded its readers, "set aside the exercise of their holy function" in order to "indulge in the heated partisanship of their time." By denouncing the war as unjust and immoral, the New England clergy succeeded only in stirring up discord at a moment of national peril. The political preachers of today, the paper concluded, should "read this lesson to their profit."[70]

To reinforce the point that their hostility to political preaching was not merely self-serving but a matter of principle and tradition, southerners drew on the writings of political theorists. A favorite authority, and one cited by the *Times-Picayune*, was the eighteenth-century British conservative Edmund Burke. Educated southerners had long been fond of Burke, in large part because he judged their devotion to the cause of liberty to be stronger than that of northerners.[71] In the 1850s, it was his warnings against political preaching that resonated most in the South. "Politics and the pulpit," Burke wrote in his *Reflections on the Revolution in France* (1790), "are terms that have little agreement." Clerics were poor guides to politics for they were "wholly unacquainted with the world in which they are so fond of meddling." Even worse, political sermons corrupted the spirit of the Sunday service. Churchgoers had the right to expect a "one-day truce" from the "dissensions and animosities of mankind." For the good of all, then, political conflict should be left at the church door.[72]

THE IMPACT OF THE CIVIL WAR

With the outbreak of the Civil War, there was good reason to believe that the political preaching controversy would die away. As Sean A. Scott argues, northerners understood the conflict in providential terms. The Union was to them a sacred instrument of God's purpose and therefore had to be preserved at all costs.[73] In this atmosphere, political preaching became an act of Christian patriotism, and northern preachers put their pulpits at the service of the cause. During the 1864 election campaign, the majority of sermons were virtually stump speeches for the Republican Party.[74] Dissenting voices remained. Reverend Ferdinand C. Ewer, pastor of Christ Church in New York, set forth to his congregation his reasons for refusing to endorse any of the candidates. Preachers should not ignore great events of the day. But only an arrogant man, he told his congregation, would claim to know which candidate was divinely favored. Furthermore, such pretension was a step toward an Old World model of church-state union. Mixing politics with the pulpit, Ewer concluded, would work to "endow this continent with a European confusion of fifteen centuries, and to stab at the heart of true freedom."[75] But Ewer was in the minority. Very few northern clerics refrained from endorsing Abraham Lincoln and the Republican Party.[76]

On the Confederate side, preachers were just as wholehearted in rallying support and in reassuring their congregations of the righteousness of their cause. But even in the midst of war, some southerners continued to resent overtly political appeals from the pulpit. The diaries of southern women make this clear. In May 1863, Amanda McDowell Burns of Tennessee recorded her frustration with the political sermons she now heard every week. Instead of the Gospel, the preacher filled his sermons with calls to resist the northerners invading their homes. "It seems to me," she wrote, "rather strange that a man who says he is called to preach the religion of Christ should think of any political topic whatever worthy to be even introduced."[77] In Georgia, Mary C. Nisbet was similarly frustrated "Our pastor," she complained, "gives us political sermons every Sabbath Day." All she could do was go to another church until he changed his approach.[78]

Was the Civil War, then, a turning point? Having put their pulpits at the service of their respective sections, would ministers in both north and south feel free to agitate on political questions without fear of a backlash? The antislavery preachers certainly hoped so. In April 1865, and with an eye on the political controversies to come, Henry Ward Beecher denounced ministers who spoke of nothing but Moses and the prophets and steered clear of the great public issues of the day as "little men" unfit for their office.[79] Foreign observers saw a pulpit which resembled a political tribune. In the immediate aftermath of the Civil War, the Englishman Louis John Jennings, a correspondent of the London *Times*, declared that Tocqueville would be amazed to witness the change in the political activism of the clergy. In no other country in the world, he wrote, "is the pulpit used for hustings purposes so systematically."[80] The clergy had shed its aversion to party politics and looked set to enter post-Civil War America as a partisan force.

To the disappointment of Beecher, however, hostility to political preaching proved to be resilient and came from both expected and unexpected quarters. The *Old Guard* (New York) was a mouthpiece for anti-war Democrats, or Copperheads; in its first issue in 1863, editor Charles Chauncey Burr viciously attacked Beecher and his fellow antislavery preachers as having blood on their hands.[81] After the South's defeat, he condemned these same preachers for continuing to whip up sectional hatred. Their reckless and bloodthirsty calls for vengeance on the South were akin to those of the "followers of Mahomet." Like the priests of that faith, they had told their flocks that death in combat was to be welcomed as "a sure passport to heaven."[82]

But more moderate organs were also beginning to shift their position on religion and politics in the pulpit. In 1860, the *New York Times* had declared that a rigorous application of Christianity was needed in public affairs and that any divorce of religion and politics would weaken American democracy. In the aftermath of the North's victory, the paper struck a very different note. "The introduction of religion into secular affairs," the editors now announced, "is certainly in bad taste." Rather than inculcating moral and religious truths, too many preachers were drumming up support for parties and candidates, and undermining the dignity of their profession.

"To really devout minds," the editor continued, "this impingement upon the priestly function has a strong odor of *cant*."[83]

Other northern papers agreed that the War, far from establishing the legitimacy of political preaching, had been an aberration. During the conflict, the *North American Review* argued in July 1865, political preaching had served a patriotic purpose. But the crisis had passed, and the fundamental problems which had always accompanied political preaching were once again in plain sight. Religious ministers were ignorant on questions of science and of economy; indeed, overall their knowledge was "limited." Together with their isolation from secular affairs and their absorption in the spiritual realm, this made them "unsafe guides in the decision of great questions of government." Furthermore, the public mood was against them. The tendency of the times, both at home and abroad, was to diminish their public influence. Only the "exceptional nature" of the slavery issue, and the "unusual weight of moral affairs" it entailed, had endowed the pulpit with an aura of public authority.[84]

In the defeated Confederacy, the antebellum hostility to political preaching returned with even greater vigor. The fiery abolitionist preacher became a stock figure in southern accounts of the onset of the Civil War. It was his fanatical sermons, in this narrative, which more than anything else had stirred up popular hatred against the southern people and sabotaged any chance of compromise between the sections. But in the immediate aftermath of the war, it was the role of northern preachers in imposing a harsh and vindictive Reconstruction that vexed white southerners the most. In 1866, the *New Orleans Daily Crescent* attacked the northern clergy who seemed determined to punish and humiliate an already defeated people. It was not Union soldiers, the paper argued, who were "clamoring for negro suffrage and confiscation," as well as the "perpetual exclusion of southern representatives from Congress." Instead, it was the "meek ministers" spreading their "gospel of the halter and the guillotine." The result in terms of a loss of popular piety was the same. From a decline in churchgoing to an increase in crime and violence, the paper reported, the northern states were a case study in how politicizing the pulpit led to the spread of irreligion.[85] The South, needless to say, had been spared that affliction.

In a sign of the political and social changes taking place across the South, the *Crescent* immediately came under attack from the *New Orleans Advocate*. Founded in 1866 by a white Methodist from the

North, John P. Newman, the *Advocate* was one of a handful of Louisiana papers to support the local Republican Party. It ridiculed the *Crescent's* position as a tired and predictable effort by apologists for slavery and secession.[86] Nor did Newman miss the opportunity to unmask the hypocrisy behind such views. Weeks later, the *Advocate* reported a long public speech by a prominent white minister denying that slavery was the cause of the Civil War and calling on the South to resist Reconstruction. Here, Newman charged, was the very embodiment of a political preacher seeking to "meddle with the affairs of State," a task for which he has "neither the intellect nor education."[87] Yet since his views were at one with the white majority, he escaped public censure.

For the African-American community in the defeated South, meanwhile, even the appearance of engaging in political preaching was extremely dangerous. In 1871, an ex-slave named Elias Hill recounted his story to the congressional committee investigating the wave of terror unleashed across the South by the Ku Klux Klan. Despite being crippled by a childhood disease, Hill forged a career as a teacher and Baptist preacher, and was active in local politics in York County, South Carolina as a republican and unionist. One night six members of the Klan raided the farm where he lived with his brother and sister-in-law, and began interrogating him about his political activities. What seemed to particularly infuriate them was their belief that he had been preaching "political sermons." Having whipped Hill, the men spared his life on condition that he stop working for the Republican Party and that he, as he told the committee, "quit preaching."[88]

The Civil War, then, had done little to transform attitudes. Across the South, whites continued to characterize political preaching as a deformation of true religion that marred the North and jeopardized their rule. And despite the efforts of Henry Ward Beecher, northern ministers by and large returned to a traditional reticence to engage in partisan politics. Admittedly, a handful of postwar preaching manuals dared young ministers to be brave. Austin Phelps was a professor of oratory at Andover Theological Seminary; in more than thirty years in the post, he taught homiletics to over 1000 students. In one of his popular works on the theory of preaching, he dismissed the notion that preachers who tackled political questions were desecrating their pulpit. Adopting martial imagery, Phelps advised young ministers to make their pulpit a "battery," sending moral shots where they were needed most. As in the antebellum era, this was in part a question of manliness.

The true preacher, Phelps wrote, "must be neither an angel nor a brute." He must instead, Phelps wrote, "be a *man*."[89] In his lectures to theology students at Yale, Howard Crosby adopted a similarly vigorous stance. "Let no coward," he declared, "enter the ministerial ranks." The failure of ministers to tackle great public issues like political corruption or municipal reform was fostering an impression on the part of the public of effeminacy. The preacher was now seen, he lamented, as "a sort of male woman." The only remedy was to "go to the front" and to join in "the thickest of the fight."[90]

Such martial imagery could not, however, disguise the fact that the golden age of northern ministerial activism associated with the Civil War was long gone. "It was good," as the Episcopal clergyman and writer Phillips Brooks recalled to the Divinity school at Yale, "to be a minister during the war of the Rebellion." There was a great moral issue at stake, and preachers had their role "as sharply marked as the soldiers."[91] But as Brooks regretfully conceded, this was no longer the case. Now it was common to hear that ministers had no influence over politics.

The attack on political preaching was an important chapter in the ongoing debate about the meaning of church-state separation. It showed, firstly, the extent to which questions of religion and politics were wrapped up in some of the greatest issues of the day, in this case slavery. Secondly, it brought to light a powerful argument for distancing religion and politics, the defense of white racial privilege. Convinced that the northern ministry was a hotbed of abolitionism, white southerners and their allies in the North articulated some of the fiercest denunciations of clerical politicking heard across the century. Secularism drew on a diverse set of cultural sources and could be deployed for a range of purposes. In this case, the argument for separating religion and politics served to silence opponents of slavery and drew its energy from racial prejudice.

The Civil War had wrought immense changes in American society. But it had not made political preaching acceptable. For one group of northern evangelicals, though, there was now a chance to draw on the great sacrifices of the War and put the nation on a firm Christian footing. The focus of their effort was not the pulpit but the Constitution.

Notes

1. *Harper's New Monthly Magazine* 12, no. 69 (1856): 426. Emphasis in original.
2. Tocqueville, *Democracy in America*, vol. 1, 305.
3. Ibid., 304, 309.
4. James W. Alexander, *Thoughts on Preaching: Being Contributions to Homiletics* (New York: Scribner, 1860), 270.
5. Alexandre Rodolphe Vinet and Thomas H. Skinner, *Homiletics: Or, the Theory of Preaching* (New York: Ivison & Phinney, 1854), 86–87.
6. John R. McKivigan, *The War Against Proslavery Religion: Abolitionism and the Northern Churches, 1830–65* (New York: Cornell University Press, 1984).
7. Columbus *Standard*, re-printed in *Anti-slavery Bugle*, October 5, 1850.
8. *Independent* (NY), November 14, 1850.
9. Joseph Howard, *Life of Henry Ward Beecher: The Eminent Pulpit and Platform Orator* (Toronto: Joseph Robertson, 1887), 492.
10. *Independent*, March 21, 1850. Emphasis in original.
11. Joseph P. Thompson, *Memoir of David Hale* (Hartford: E. Hunt, 1850). On Hallock, *Life of Gerard Hallock* (New York: Oakley, Mason, 1869).
12. *Journal of Commerce* (NY), April 12, 1850.
13. *Independent*, April 18, 1850.
14. *Journal of Commerce*, May 4, 1850.
15. George B. Cheever, *God Against Slavery: And the Freedom and Duty of the Pulpit to Rebuke It* (Cincinnati: American Reform Tract & Book Society, 1857), 59.
16. Cheever to Elizabeth Cheever, July 2, 1854, Cheever Family papers, Box 11, Folder 2, American Antiquarian Society.
17. George M. Fredrickson, "The Coming of the Lord: The Northern Protestant Clergy and the Civil War Crisis," in *Religion and the American Civil War*, eds. Randall M. Miller, Harry S. Stout, and Charles Regan Wilson (New York: Oxford University Press, 1998), 112.
18. *Independent*, April 18, 1850.
19. *Independent*, April 25, 1850.
20. Potter to Bartlett, July 2, 1859. William J. Potter papers, HM 37380, Huntington Library. Emphasis in original.
21. Potter to Bartlett, January 1861? William J. Potter papers, HM 37386, Huntington Library.
22. Roxanne Mountford, *The Gendered Pulpit: Preaching in American Protestant Spaces* (Carbondale: Southern Illinois University Press, 2003), 41.
23. As E. Anthony Rotundo writes, "a man was expected to be jealous of his autonomy and free from reliance on external authority." *American Manhood: Transformations in Masculinity from the Revolution to the Modern Era* (New York: Basic Books, 1993), 3–4.

24. Cheever, *God Against Slavery*, 61.
25. Gerrit Smith, "Speech of Gerrit Smith, made in the National Liberty Party Convention at Buffalo, September 17th, 1851" (Peterboro, NY, 1851), no page, in *Collected Printed Papers by Gerrit Smith in the American Antiquarian Society*.
26. For example, March 24, 1854; April 21, 1854; October 26, 1855.
27. *North Star*, June 13, 1850.
28. *New York Herald*, November 25, 1860.
29. *United States Democratic Review* 34, no. 2 (1854): 114.
30. Samuel P. Lyman, *Life and Memorials of Daniel Webster* (New York: D. Appleton, 1858), 247.
31. *Boston Evening Transcript*, June 14, 1851.
32. *Daily National Intelligencer* (Washington, DC), March 11, 1857.
33. *Boston Recorder*, November 22, 1855.
34. *Columbia Democrat and Bloomsburg General Advertiser* (PA), February 27, 1858.
35. *Independent*, April 25, 1850.
36. *New Hampshire Patriot and State Gazette*, August 13, 1854.
37. "Politics and the Pulpit," *New Englander and Yale Review* 12, no. 46 (May 1854), 265, 274.
38. *United States Democratic Review* 34, no. 2 (1854): 115.
39. *Times-Picayune* (New Orleans), June 11, 1854.
40. *Daily Picayune* (New Orleans), November 11, 1854. See William M. Hogue, "The Civil Disability of Ministers of Religion in State Constitutions," *Journal of Church and State* 36, no. 2 (1994): 329–55.
41. *Congressional Globe*, 33rd Congress, 1st session (1854), 621.
42. Ibid., 619.
43. Ibid., 620.
44. Ibid., 621.
45. *Remarks of Mr. Ely Moore, of New York, in the House of Representatives, February 4, 1839* (Washington, DC, 1839).
46. *Congressional Globe*, 33rd Congress, 1st session (1854), 618.
47. Ibid., 659.
48. *New Hampshire Patriot and State Gazette*, March 11, 1857.
49. *Journal of Commerce*, May 4, 1850.
50. *Appendix to the Congressional Globe*, 34th Congress, 3rd session (1857), 364.
51. Josephine M. Bunkley, *The Testimony of an Escaped Novice from the Sisterhood of St. Joseph, Emmetsburg* (New York: Harper, 1855), 14.
52. *New York Herald*, November 25, 1860.
53. *New York Herald*, March 27, 1857.
54. *United States Democratic Review* 26, no. 143 (1850): 391.

55. Eric Foner, "The Meaning of Freedom in the Age of Emancipation," *Journal of American History* 81, no. 2 (1994): 438.
56. *New York Illustrated News*, December 29, 1860.
57. The Pilgrims of Plymouth and the Puritans of Massachusetts Bay were technically distinct in that the former wished to separate entirely from the Anglican church, whereas the latter sought to reform it. Yet in other aspects such as theology they were almost indistinguishable, and the difference became almost meaningless once the Massachusetts Bay colony was established in 1629. Throughout the nineteenth century, the two groups were routinely conflated.
58. Steven K. Green, *Inventing a Christian America: The Myth of the Religious Founding* (New York: Oxford University Press, 2015), 227–39.
59. George Bancroft, *An Oration Delivered before the Democracy of Springfield and Neighboring Towns, July 4, 1836* (Springfield: George and Charles Merriam, 1836), 21–22. Emphasis in original.
60. Ibid., 23. On Bancroft and the Puritan legacy, see Jan C. Dawson, *The Unusable Past: America's Puritan Tradition, 1830 to 1930* (Chico, CA: Scholars Press, 1984), 26–32.
61. *United States Democratic Review* 26, no. 143 (1850): 390.
62. *New York Herald*, December 22, 1860.
63. *Semi-weekly Mississippian*, March 9, 1855.
64. *Daily Dispatch* (Richmond), April 2, 1857.
65. *Daily Crescent* (New Orleans), April 13, 1857.
66. "Southern Education for Southern Youth," *DeBow's Review* 19 (1855): 464.
67. "National Sins and Their Retribution," *New Englander and Yale Review* 14, no. 56 (1856): 528.
68. Edward R. Crowther, "'Religion … Has Something to Do with Politics': Southern Evangelicals and the North, 1845–60," in *Religion and the Antebellum Debate Over Slavery*, eds. John R. McKivigan and Mitchell Snay (Athens: University of Georgia Press, 1998), 331.
69. *Weekly Standard* (Raleigh), April 1, 1857.
70. *Daily Picayune*, April 23, 1854.
71. On Burke's influence, Elizabeth Fox-Genovese and Eugene D. Genovese, *The Mind of the Master Class: History and Faith in the Southern Slaveholders' Worldview* (Cambridge: Cambridge University Press, 2005), 76, 728.
72. Edmund Burke, *Reflections on the Revolution in France, and on the Proceedings in Certain Societies in London Relative to That Event* (London: J. Dodsley, 1791), 14. For just one example of southerners citing Burke's words approvingly, see *De Bow's Review* 21 (1856): 508.
73. Sean A. Scott, *A Visitation of God: Northern Civilians Interpret the Civil War* (New York: Oxford University Press, 2011).

74. George C. Rable, *God's Almost Chosen Peoples: A Religious History of the American Civil War* (Chapel Hill: University of North Carolina Press, 2010), 356. For a fuller analysis of political preaching, Timothy L. Wesley, *The Politics of Faith During the Civil War* (Baton Rouge: Louisiana State University Press, 2013).
75. *A Rector's Reply to Sundry Requests and Demands for a Political Sermon: Preached in Christ Church, Fifth Avenue, N.Y. by Rev. F.C. Ewer, on the Morning of the Sixteenth Sunday after Trinity, 1864* (New York: Francis Hart & Company, 1864), 7. For more evidence of opposition to political preaching, Scott, *Visitation of God*, 166–67.
76. Harry S. Stout, *Upon the Altar of the Nation: A Moral History of the American Civil War* (New York: Viking, 2006), 283.
77. Amanda McDowell Burns, May 18, 1863 in *Fiddles in the Cumberland*, eds. Amanda McDowell and Lela McDowell Blankenship (New York: Richard R. Smith, 1943).
78. Mary C. Nisbet to Mary Jones, January 17, 1861 in *The Children of Pride: A True Story of Georgia and the Civil War*, ed. Robert M. Myers (New Haven: Yale University Press, 1972).
79. *Liberator*, April 7, 1865.
80. Louis John Jennings, *Eighty Years of Republican Government in the United States* (New York: C. Scribner, 1868), 200.
81. *Old Guard* (New York), January 1863.
82. *Old Guard* (New York), December 1865.
83. *New York Times*, August 28, 1865. Emphasis in original.
84. *North American Review* 101, no. 208 (1865): 128.
85. *New Orleans Daily Crescent*, February 28, 1866.
86. *New Orleans Advocate*, March 3, 1866. On Newman, see Reginald Francis Hildebrand, *The Times Were Strange and Stirring: Methodist Preachers and the Crisis of Emancipation* (Durham, NC: Duke University Press, 1995), 92–93.
87. *New Orleans Advocate*, March 10, 1866.
88. *Report of the Joint Select Committee Appointed to Inquire into the Condition of Affairs in the Late Insurrectionary States*, vol. 1 (Washington, DC: Government Printing Office, 1872), 45–46. Hill emigrated to Liberia and died shortly afterward.
89. Austin Phelps, *Men and Books; Or Studies in Homiletics* (New York: C. Scribner's Sons, 1882), 29. Italics in original.
90. Howard Crosby, *The Christian Preacher: Yale Lectures for 1879–80* (New York: A. D. F. Randolph, 1879), 161, 162.
91. Phillips Brooks, *Lectures on Preaching, Delivered Before the Divinity School of Yale college in January and February, 1877* (New York: E.P. Dutton), 141–42.

CHAPTER 6

How Christian Were the Founders? God and the Constitution After the Civil War

At the end of the Civil War, one of the many questions yet to be resolved concerned the future relationship between Protestantism and the national government. For northern evangelicals, there were both promising and disquieting portents. Many hoped that victory over the South would be a springboard to a new era of Christian republicanism. With the national sin of slavery wiped away, the covenant between God and the American nation could be restored with all its power. Now was the moment to refashion the social system along godly lines by launching a campaign against the scourges of Sabbath-breaking, drinking, prostitution, and gambling. In this task, reformers aimed to call on a vastly expanded federal government whose leaders had signaled more than once during the conflict their trust in Divine providence, putting "In God We Trust" on coins, setting aside the last Thursday in November as a day of thanksgiving for God's grace, and issuing an executive order calling on the northern armies to respect the Sabbath. As George M. Fredrickson notes, the lesson of the war seemed to be that the surest path to national redemption lay in the mobilization of government power.[1]

Yet as the turn away from political preaching after 1865 demonstrated, it was not clear if the War would prove a turning point. There was no disguising the fact that religious authority had received a blow. The Bible, the nation's most revered text, had become entangled in the conflict over slavery, with both sides using it to justify their cause. Protestants had long been accustomed to seeing the Bible as a repository of simple and literal truths. Now, with Scripture being deployed in support of two radically different positions, the problem of interpreting and applying the Bible seemed far more complex.[2] Then there was the challenge of holding fast to faith in the midst of so much misery and bloodshed. The families of all those killed or maimed may have accepted their sacrifice as a necessary act of penance for the sin of slavery. Yet at least for some northern intellectuals, the sheer scale of suffering prompted an intense crisis of faith, setting the stage for the rise of liberal theology that would become so dominant in the postbellum era.[3] With the conflict barely over, some Protestant clerics were warning of other trends which threatened their authority. In 1865, Philip Schaff told a German audience that mass immigration was once again imperiling the sacred character of the American Sabbath.[4] Furthermore, it was clear to all that the center of national energy would continue to shift west as new territories opened to white settlement. In these communities, far from the established strongholds of religious orthodoxy in the northeast, a heterodox set of reformers would find the space to prosper.

In the midst of this confusion, a group of Protestant clerics seized the chance to affirm the Christian character of national government in clear and ringing terms. Their focus was a document which, after decades of calm, was now undergoing a flurry of revision. From 1865 to 1870, the ratification of the 13th, 14th, and 15th amendments to the national Constitution abolished slavery, defined citizenship rights, set the terms for the readmission of the Confederate states, and extended voting rights to freedmen. Now, these Protestant activists argued, it was time to correct another flaw in the Constitution, that fact that, aside from a perfunctory reference to the "Year of our Lord, one thousand seven hundred and Eighty seven," it contained no explicit acknowledgment of God or Jesus Christ. A nation saved from ruin should demonstrate its gratitude by writing the Almighty into its guiding text.[5]

The campaign for a Christian amendment to the Constitution produced reactions which ranged from indifference to mockery to alarm. Some of the secular and religious press saw an eccentric distraction from the pressing problems of a nation still recovering from a catastrophic war, a proposal with as much chance of succeeding, as one speaker put it, as a railway to the moon.[6] Others struck a gentle note, dismissing the campaigners as sincere but misguided, a "forlorn band of well-meaning persons" running a campaign which would surely peter out in the face of public apathy.[7] But many saw a well-organized and powerful movement which stood a real chance of succeeding. With the slave power at last vanquished, they warned, religious power now threatened to twist the Constitution for its own ends.

These fears were vivid enough to prompt a range of organizations to campaign actively against the Christian amendment. Some of their arguments were familiar from previous battles. But the clash over the amendment inspired a public discussion of two questions which, though present in earlier controversies, now attained an unprecedented level of attention. The first concerned the intentions and beliefs of the men who framed the Constitution. Protagonists on both sides were forced to grapple with the fundamental question of why the Revolutionary heroes had left God out in the first place. What ensued was a thoroughgoing and heated debate which revolved around one key question: how Christian were the Founders?

The second key point concerned the relationship between the New World and the Old. For decades, defenders of the secular state had made national exceptionalism their rallying cry. Church-state combinations were a medieval relic which disfigured the Old World but which the United States had thankfully left behind. In the post-Civil War era, the example of Europe attained a proportion and an immediacy which had no parallel in earlier battles. Aided by improvements in transport and communications, particularly the completion of a functioning transatlantic telegraph cable in 1866, Americans became more conscious of political and social developments in Europe. The effect of this thickening of trans-Atlantic ties was complex. On the one hand, a greater awareness of Europe reinforced a pride in national difference. This was a continent still marked by state churches: the Anglican establishment, for example, or the *concordat* in France. On the other hand, there seemed promising signs that the Old World was finally casting off its attachment to religious establishments and joining America in embracing a stricter separation of church and state. The trans-Atlantic divide, then, appeared on the point of being bridged, a realization that profoundly shaped the domestic debate on the Christian amendment. These two perspectives, one looking inward to the past and the other outward across the Atlantic, form the focus of this chapter.

The Push for a Christian Amendment

Devout men and women had lamented the absence of any reference to God or Jesus Christ in their nation's Constitution almost from its ratification. But a concerted push for change only emerged in the first years of the Civil War, as the northern cause appeared to be faltering. Amidst the shock and blame-sharing that followed the Union defeat at Manassas in 1861, Congregational minister Horace Bushnell suggested that the government formally acknowledge its dependence on God. This was the best way, he argued, for northerners to repudiate the "false theories under which we have been so fatally demoralized," chief among which was the notion that government authority rested on a secular rather than Divine foundation.[8] Two years later, an even deeper sense of despair led to action. In February 1863, a group of Protestant clergymen meeting in Xenia, Ohio, devised a way to revive the flagging Union cause. The recently passed Emancipation Proclamation promised at last to cleanse the nation of the sin of slavery. But this still left the "crowning, original sin of the nation," the absence of any direct acknowledgment of God in the guiding law of the land. Now was the ideal moment to remove the first of its great "plague spots."[9] On January 27, 1864, a meeting of an organization which would later take the name of the National Reform Association (NRA) called for the preamble of the Constitution to be altered to acknowledge "Almighty God as the source of all authority and power in civil government."

From the outset, the pro-amendment party placed great hopes in Abraham Lincoln. To their mind, no other President had so eloquently and forcefully expressed the nation's dependence upon God. In his proclamation of national days of thanksgiving and prayer, and particularly in his vivid evocations of the designs of Providence in his Second Inaugural speech, the President seemed to have signaled that he too felt in his heart "the want of a distinct and plain recognition of the divine authority in the Constitution of the United States."[10] Yet Lincoln's response was lukewarm. Though meeting with a group of supporters, he promised only to examine their arguments. As the North's fortunes improved, too, the pressing need for a change diminished. By 1865, Horace Bushnell was arguing that the government had been Christianized already by the terrible sacrifice of lives. The "rivers of blood," he declared in 1865, which had "bathed our institutions," made the government once and for all Providential—"no more a mere creature of our human will but a grandly moral affair."[11] As an act of atonement, amending the Constitution paled in comparison.

These setbacks stalled the drive for an amendment, and for several years the NRA held only local rather than national conventions. But the movement gradually regained momentum. The launch of a semi-monthly journal, the *Christian Statesman*, in September 1867, gave it an ongoing platform, and in February 1870 the first in a series of national conventions was held at Pittsburgh. Among the delegates to this and subsequent conventions was a group of extremely influential men. The 1872 Cincinnati Conference welcomed Supreme Court justice William Strong as President, while the list of vice-Presidents and supporters included the Governors of Pennsylvania, Vermont, Kansas, and Rhode Island, presidents and professors of several colleges, as well as justices of state courts. Added to this was a national membership base of around ten thousand.

What drove the resurgence in the campaign was the realization that, even after all the great sacrifices of the War, the much-hoped for moral regeneration of the nation had not transpired. At convention after convention, delegates lamented that the antebellum trend toward secularization had resumed with even greater speed. The sanctity of the Sabbath was violated with impunity by citizens and officials alike. In 1872, one of the editors of the *Christian Statesman*, the Reverend Thomas P. Stevenson, listed just some of the many desecrations of the Holy Day that had recently occurred. On Sunday December 4, scores of Congressmen travelled to the nation's capital to be ready for the next day's session. Many could be seen moving around the capitol in carriages and streetcars; among the Sabbath travelers was none other than President Ulysses S. Grant. On Sunday March 3, 1867, Congress sat all day, concealing the fact by having the *Congressional Globe* refer to a continuation of the Saturday session.[12] Prewar victories were being overturned. In 1867, the Pennsylvania Supreme Court ruled that running streetcars on Sundays did not constitute a breach of peace. In the aftermath of the decision, many of the lines in Philadelphia, including the Green and Coates street line, resumed a Sunday service.

The NRA, then, saw itself not as fomenting controversy, but fighting a rearguard action against the aggressive forces of secularism. "No one can say," as Tayler Lewis, professor of Greek at New York University declared, "that we are fighting shadows."[13] This sentiment is clear in the pro-amendment petitions which soon began flooding into Congress.

According to one from Philadelphia with 9445 signatures, the "theory of secularism" was growing stronger by the day, and its results were clear to see. Sabbath laws went unenforced, the name of God had been stripped from official oaths, and the Bible driven out of schools in St. Louis, Chicago, Rochester, and San Francisco. These agitators were intent, the petitioners lamented, on severing "at every point" the bond "which has always existed ... between the American Government and the Christian religion." And their "most formidable weapon" was the absence of any formal acknowledgment of God in the Constitution.[14] Until this was rectified, laws in favor of Christian morality would have no firm basis, and the nation would continue to drift away from its religious moorings.

THE ANTI-AMENDMENT CAMPAIGN

The NRA's push for a Christian amendment sparked a vast counter-petition campaign. In 1871–1872, thousands of Americans signed a petition protesting an "attempt to revolutionize the government of the United States" by overthrowing two of the nation's great principles: religious liberty and the complete separation of church and state. The petitions themselves reveal who was behind the campaign. Once completed, the blank form read, each petition should be returned to the offices of one of three newspapers: the *Boston Investigator*, the *Index*, or the *Banner of Light*. The first, edited by Horace Seaver, had been a mainstay of freethought since its founding in 1831. The *Index* was a much more recent creation. Its editor was Francis Ellingwood Abbot, a man who, over a long career as a journalist, public speaker, organizer, and agitator carved out a leading if controversial role in the secularist movement.

Abbot came to secularist causes via a religious path. A Unitarian minister, he grew frustrated with the strictures of dogma. In 1869, he resigned his post at Dover, New Hampshire, telling his congregation that men and women should no longer be divided into rival theological camps. Those of "unlike faiths," he declared, may join in good works without "prying into each other's orthodoxy." His God was the Infinite Spirit, his Bible the Universe. "Let those who will, cramp themselves into sectarian straight-jackets," Abbot proclaimed, "I have learned the love of freedom."[15] This love of freedom had led him to co-found the Free Religious Association (FRA) two years earlier. The FRA was one product of the spiritual restlessness that marked post-Civil War society. Appealing to Christians and non-Christians alike, it aimed to free faith from the constraints of dogma and sectarian jealousy. For many of its members, a hostility to religious orthodoxy was an extension of their earlier commitment to abolitionism. The FRA, as one speaker declared, was a "spiritual anti-slavery society."[16] Among its leaders was William J. Potter, the political preacher lobbing abolitionist bombs to his congregation before the War, who now joined what he saw as a crusade for spiritual emancipation.

In a letter to Potter, Abbot called for the establishment of a newspaper which "strives to work out the application of the American Idea to Church as well as State... a bold, free American journal."[17] The result was the *Index*, which appeared in January 1870, and which Abbot would edit for the next decade. In April 1872, the *Index* responded to the NRA's call for a Christian amendment with a nine-point program to make government "more consistently secular" by, among others, abolishing chaplains and tax exemptions for churches and ending the enforcement of Sabbath laws.[18] Abbot also agitated for local liberal leagues join in a national organization that could match the NRA. In 1876, the National Liberal League (NLL) held its first convention at Philadelphia, electing Abbot as President. The delegates agreed that theirs was not an anti-Christian organization, but was "directed simply against certain glaring political usurpations of the Church."[19] It also called for a different Constitutional amendment, the Religious Liberty amendment, to guarantee a strict separation of church and state at federal and state levels. For Abbot and his fellow liberals, the brazen ambition of the NRA represented a priceless opportunity to build support for their nine principles. As Potter wrote after both he and his wife signed an anti-amendment petition, the determination of the NRA to put Christ into the Constitution was sure to "open people's eyes" to the scale of the threat now facing their freedoms.[20] By the end of the decade, the NLL counted more than two hundred local auxiliaries.

Another sign of the post-war impatience with orthodoxy was the burgeoning career of Robert Green Ingersoll. Son of a Presbyterian clergyman, Ingersoll witnessed firsthand the backlash against political preaching as his father was forced out of a series of posts thanks to his antislavery views. Like many post-war freethinkers, Ingersoll remembered a childhood dominated by a strict and gloomy Calvinism. Sabbaths were particularly oppressive. "Nobody said a pleasant word," he remembered. "Nobody laughed; nobody smiled." To be caught even chewing gum was "evidence of the total depravity of the human heart."[21]

From the early 1870s, Ingersoll began to attract a reputation as a brilliant and entertaining lecturer. A champion of Darwinian science, he mocked literal interpretations of the Bible with a roguish good humor that appealed even to some of the devout. Most of all, Ingersoll articulated an optimistic creed that seemed to suit the tenor of the age. Whether eternal reward proved to be true or not, he told his audiences, men and women should strive for happiness on earth.

In its anti-amendment petition campaign, the *Index* was joined by the *Banner of Light*, the organ of yet another product of the ferment of religious inquiry and reform which marked the post-war years, spiritualism. Though its origins in America dated to 1848, spiritualism exploded in popularity after the Civil War, attracting millions of members, sustaining a lively network of speakers and boasting, in the *Banner of Light*, a paper which had a national reach.[22] In May 1872, one of its members in Washington, DC, John Mayhew, used the columns of the paper to call on all spiritualists to petition against the Christian amendment. All Americans, he argued, had an interest in preventing the government coming under the control of a fanatical clique of religious dogmatists. But spiritualists had a particular cause to be concerned. We do not, he reminded his fellow spiritualists, believe in God, Jesus Christ or the Bible in the same way as orthodox Christians; as a result, spiritualists were as vulnerable as Jews or atheists to the loss of civil and political rights which would follow the triumph of the Christian party. The threat, he went on, was real, and required the "*most prompt and decisive action.*"[23] Send your petitions to me, he finished, and I will see that they are presented to Congress without delay.

Cajoling and coordinating produced a deluge of petitions. The highpoint came in January 1874 when Senator Charles Sumner presented the Senate with a monster petition filled with more than 35,000 names. For the purposes of analysis, however, individual petitions are much more revealing. The records of the Senate Judiciary committee in the 42nd Congress (1871–1873) contain 458 anti-amendment petitions with 24,655 signatures.[24] From their regional origin, it is clear that the center of gravity of secularist mobilization had shifted from the Atlantic states and New England to the mid-West (see Appendix B). Fifty-five percent of the petitions came from the mid-Western states, with Illinois, Iowa, and Ohio dominant. In the next largest section, New England (19.5% of petitions), Massachusetts outstripped all others, a reflection no doubt of the role of the Boston *Investigator* in coordinating the campaign.

The Atlantic states, so dominant in the pro-Sunday mail campaign, now contributed just 13.5% of petitions.

Where the petitions carried on a prewar trend was in attracting a cross section of community support. Canvassers on the ground made no secret of their affiliation to either freethought or spiritualism. In Downieville, California, John Richardson boasted that there were more freethinkers in his state than anywhere else in the world, relative to population.[25] One organizer asked for copies of Thomas Paine's *Age of Reason* and *Common Sense*; in Columbus, Ohio, Isaac Corbin identified himself as a subscriber to the Boston *Investigator*.[26] But in seeking out support, these agents went well beyond their immediate circle of sympathizers. Several attested that community opposition to the Christian amendment was overwhelming. In Nevada City, Montana, the petition agent stated that he had managed to fill the form without even leaving his place of business.[27] It was the same in Tabor, Iowa, where the organizer declared confidently that almost everyone he met was opposed to the amendment.[28] The great obstacle to collecting even more names was public apathy. There was a general feeling that putting God into the Constitution was a foolhardy idea with little chance of success. Why, then, even bother to sign a protest? In Middlefork, Indiana, the canvasser swore that he could have obtained thousands of signatures, but most of the community did not believe the "rascals" would dare to carry out their plans.[29] In Washington, DC, nine clerks in the census office put their names on a petition; in New Orleans, it was eleven employees of the Charles Theatre. In Fremont, Nebraska, the forty-six signers gave their occupations, which ranged from barbers, shoemakers, and gunsmiths to clerks, councilmen, attorneys, and a probate judge.[30] In Randolph New York, farmers were more prominent, making up eleven of thirty-nine signers. But the list included as well mechanics, lawyers, a dentist, sheriff, and civil engineer.[31]

What is clear as well is the manner in which the amendment issue was dividing men and women of faith. Some of the signers, perhaps wary of being mistaken for freethinkers or radicals, took care to add after their names a note professing their piety. One, from Cincinnati Ohio, wrote that he believed in God and in Jesus Christ, but not "in forcing the names of either into a Constitution."[32] Another stated his belief that Jesus reigned over spiritual and not temporal affairs.[33] Some petitioners identified themselves as members of specific denominations. Foremost among these were the Baptists. The list of signers from Houston, Texas included the editor of the *Baptist Herald* as well as the pastor of the First Baptist church. But Baptists were not the only church members to take a public stand against the amendment. The same petition from Houston listed a member of another church with perhaps even more reason to dread the ascendancy of the NRA, the Roman Catholic Church.[34]

Examining the names on the anti-amendment petitions reveals not just religious but gender diversity. The anti-amendment drive gathered women signers in much larger numbers than the antebellum campaign against legislative chaplains. An exact figure is impossible to ascertain, as many signers gave only their first initial. However, the evidence of strong female involvement is unmistakable. Four of the petitions are formally divided into male and female signers. This is the case for a petition from Highland, Oregon, where seven women added their names to those of eight men. At the other extreme, a petition from Augusta Kansas, all eighteen signers were women.[35] Overall, female names, if still a minority, are sprinkled across the petitions, even if in some cases, to judge by the handwriting, husbands signed on behalf of their wives. This level of female involvement was no doubt a testament to the role of spiritualism in organizing the petitions. Women were central to spiritualism as mediums, as speakers and as agents. Furthermore, as Ann Braude has argued, spiritualism was a powerful vehicle for women's rights, taking an early and strong stance in favor of female suffrage.[36]

The presence of women in the anti-amendment campaign was significant because the secularist movement was at that moment divided over the merits of female suffrage. Many freethinkers believed women to be the natural allies of the NRA and worried that giving them the vote would be the surest path to the passage of the dreaded Christian amendment, along with a host of other proscriptive laws. In accounting for what they saw as women's subservience to clerical authority, freethinkers offered a range of explanations. Some pointed to nature. Recycling the biological arguments that had long been deployed against female suffrage and public petitioning, they argued that women's vulnerability to emotional manipulation made them susceptible to clerical control. Others preferred social explanations. Taught from an early age that their peculiar gifts were spiritual rather than rational, and denied the kind of thorough intellectual training given to boys, it was not surprising that women struggled to free themselves from the shackles of theology. But whatever the cause of their devotion to religious causes, the prospect of arming women with the vote struck many freethinkers as near-suicidal.[37]

In an article opposing female suffrage in the *Boston Investigator*, one writer connected this fear to the amendment campaign. Once female suffrage passed, he warned, the religious amendment was certain to follow in its wake.[38]

For his part, Francis Abbot came out in favor of female suffrage. He did so despite his concern, as he wrote in the *Index*, that the Christian party would be boosted as a result. A majority of women, he conceded, would vote in favor of the amendment, while only a "respectable minority" could be counted on to vote against. The result of female suffrage would surely be a "formidable increase of the ecclesiastical party." Yet Abbot could not bring himself to oppose a measure which spoke to his "profoundest convictions of right." If Christianizing men had the vote, Christianizing women surely deserved it just as much. Secularists could only hope that the common sense of the people would in the end prevail.[39] Furthermore, as the petition campaign showed, there were hopeful signs that, given the opportunity, large numbers of women might rally to the anti-amendment cause.

THE PIETY OF THE FOUNDERS

One canvasser added a revealing note to his petition. Nine of ten people he encountered were against the amendment, he stressed, because "they think that the wisdom of our forefathers in regard to this part of our Constitution is all we need at the present time."[40] More than any other church-state battle, the beliefs and intentions of the men who framed the Constitution became a key site of contest. Were they Deists who envisaged their republic as operating independently of Divine support? Or even, as some suggested, infidels? Evangelicals claimed that the Founders were sincere believers in Christian revelation. But if this were true, why had they neglected to make any reference to God, Jesus or the Bible in the nation's founding text? Some NRA members explained this as merely an oversight on their part. Grappling with a host of weighty political issues, the question of God slipped from their minds. But this was hardly a satisfactory explanation. For a start, it suggested a carelessness which jarred with the Founders' reputation for wisdom and foresight. But more fundamentally, it made little sense in the context of a decades-long campaign to claim the Founders as pious and devout men intent on creating a Godly republic.

In the case of George Washington, the shaping of public memory began almost immediately after his death. In life, Washington showed himself to be a dutiful but hardly zealous Christian. The Washington painted by clerical eulogists after his death was very different. Mason Weems' 1800 biography launched the popular image of the Washington who exceeded all others in private and public virtue. Weems' Washington regularly attended church, read Scripture on the Sabbath, and never doubted that his country's fate hung on Divine beneficence.[41] For decades afterward, a host of biographers sought to demonstrate both from episodes in Washington's life as well as his correspondence and speeches that the father of the nation was a devout Christian who wished the laws of the nation to uphold his faith. In E.C. M'Guire's 1836 study, Washington emerges as a frequent churchgoer who scrupulously respected the Sabbath, not perhaps a man of "unusual piety," but blessed with a strong faith nonetheless.[42] Benjamin Morris went further. In his account, Washington's life was ruled by Christian principle; his piety, based on the "truths of revelation," might have been "unostentatious," but was nevertheless "great and decisive in its influences." He would have scoffed at any notion of a divorce between religion and state.[43]

Perhaps the most powerful image of Washington the Christian was the prayer at Valley Forge. The source of this story was once again Mason Weems. In his recounting, a farmer named Isaac Potts was walking through the woods near Washington's headquarters when he came across the Commander-in-Chief on his knees and praying, before then rising and walking away with a look of "angel serenity."[44] Though entirely fictitious, this moment of private and intense piety against a backdrop of the snowy woods distilled for many Americans the sincerity of Washington's faith and his unquestioning attachment to a benevolent and protective Deity. By the time that the Christian amendment campaign emerged, engravings of the scene, many of which were based on Henry Brueckner's 1866 painting, hung in homes across the nation (Fig. 6.1). In addition to Washington's piety, the story of the prayer at Valley Forge captured another important truth for evangelicals, the reality of Divine intercession. This was a moment of crisis in the military campaign. Cold, hungry and weary, the Continental army seemed on the point of disintegrating, taking with it the hopes of the Revolution itself. Then came news of the French alliance, a development which turned the campaign decisively in the Revolutionaries' favor. Washington's prayer had been answered, and a new nation saved.

6 HOW CHRISTIAN WERE THE FOUNDERS? GOD AND THE CONSTITUTION ...

Fig. 6.1 *The Prayer at Valley Forge*. From the original painting by Henry Brueckner (1889) (Courtesy of Library Company, Philadelphia)

The puzzle remained, though, why such a man would subsequently preside over a Convention which left God out of its Constitution. This was particularly baffling because, in the minds of many evangelicals, Washington was far from alone in his godliness. If he needed support, he could call on Benjamin Franklin. For his nineteenth-century biographers, there was little question that the young Franklin was drawn to skepticism. But in their account, this youthful flirtation with irreligion soon gave way to a wise embrace of Christian revelation. In 1826, the *National Intelligencer* published a letter from William Steele describing a conversation with Jonathan Dayton, a delegate to the 1787 Convention which wrote the federal Constitution. Dayton was reminiscing about a dramatic moment when the Convention seemed on the point of failure. The delegates were divided over the voting system for the Senate, with small and large-state advocates refusing to compromise. At that crucial moment, Benjamin Franklin suggested Divine guidance as the only remedy. "As a sparrow does not fall without Divine permission," Franklin advised his fellow delegates, "can we suppose that governments can be erected without His will?" He then moved the appointment of a chaplain to open each session with prayer and to guide the Convention toward a resolution of the impasse.

As recounted in Steele's letter, the proposal was met with general acclaim. George Washington appeared the most pleased. "Never...did I behold," Dayton recalled to Steele, "a countenance at once so *dignified* and *delighted* as was that of Washington!" Only one delegate had the temerity to argue against Franklin's proposal. The impertinent Alexander Hamilton argued that there was more than enough talent and wisdom assembled in the Convention to achieve its goal without the help of the Almighty. There was no necessity, as he cuttingly remarked, of "calling in *foreign aid*." These words were met with shock and hostility among the other delegates, who immediately approved Franklin's proposal. Following an opening prayer, the Convention resumed its deliberations, and in the ensuing spirit of goodwill and calm a successful compromise was agreed.[45]

Steele's account was for the most part fiction. The records of the convention confirm that Franklin proposed the appointment of a chaplain, and that the motion was seconded by Roger Sherman of Connecticut, a born-again Christian. Alexander Hamilton certainly opposed the motion, though there is no evidence that he delivered an irreverent speech. The Convention then adjourned without the matter being voted on, and no chaplain was appointed. As Franklin's notes indicate, "The Convention, except three or four persons, thought Prayers unnecessary."[46] But the NRA made the episode a centerpiece of its claim that Washington and Franklin would surely have wished to see the Almighty acknowledged in the new Constitution. The fact that this did not occur was due to one factor: an outbreak of that regrettable affliction, French infidelity. At the 1873 Convention in Pittsburgh, the President, Felix Brunot, conceded that "skepticism pervaded the minds of the leading statesmen of the day." The "contagion," as the *Christian Union* called it, led most of the delegates to snub their God.[47] By the time they recovered their senses, the moment had passed.

In the evangelical construction of the Revolutionary past, the Founder most stricken with the disease was Thomas Jefferson. The suspicion of irreligion had hung over Jefferson since his Presidency. When he helped his friend Thomas Paine return to America, the New England clergy denounced the President's sympathy for an avowed enemy of organized religion. By the middle of the nineteenth century, this clerical hostility had cooled. Yet despite the best efforts of his biographers, the black mark of skepticism continued to stain his memory. Henry Randall, author of a three-volume life of Jefferson, was aware of the need to tread carefully on the subject of religion. As he wrote to his friend Hugh Blair Grigsby, "I have got a tough chapter before me on the subject of Mr. J's *religious* beliefs." It could only be approached, he continued, "discreetly but manfully."[48] His solution was to portray a man who had a quiet but firm faith. In his account, the third President regularly attended church, contributed to the building of church edifices, invoked God and Providence in his public writings, including of course in the Declaration of Independence, and refrained from publicly attacking any church or creed. He was also a man of strict moral probity, who was never heard to utter a profanity.[49]

The difficulty for Randall was that Jefferson's private letters and papers, many now published for the first time, showed a man who railed against organized religion. In 1829, Jefferson's grandson, Thomas Jefferson Randolph, published four volumes of memoirs and correspondence and granted George Tucker access to the entire collection for the preparation of his *Life of Thomas Jefferson* (1837). But the bulk of Jefferson's correspondence remained private until, in 1848, the government purchased Randolph's collection and subsequently appointed Henry A. Washington to produce a comprehensive edition. Washington's nine-volume Congress Edition (1853–1854) included a letter which had not resurfaced since its first appearance in 1802. This was Jefferson's now-famous reply to the Danbury Baptist Association, in which he described the first amendment as "building a wall of separation between church and State."[50] Historians often suggest that the "wall" metaphor then largely vanished until 1879, when Supreme Court Chief Justice Morrison Waite revived it in a landmark ruling against Mormon polygamy.[51] This is not wholly accurate. In the 1850s, several newspapers republished the key section of the Danbury letter. As the controversy over political preaching raged in 1855, newspapers in New York, Pennsylvania, Wisconsin and several southern states published an excerpt from the 1802 letter referring to the "wall," and gave its author as Jefferson.[52] The same year, the freethought Boston *Investigator* cited Jefferson's reference to the "wall of separation" as proof that the Fathers opposed any mingling of religion and government.[53] Randall did not directly quote the letter. But he noted that Jefferson's reply to the

Baptist Association carried an emphatic rejection of any alliance between church and state.[54] After the Civil War, the letter appeared once again in the press, when the *Daily Richmond Whig*, followed by the *Israelite* and once more the Boston *Investigator*, printed it in full.[55] The "wall of separation" metaphor was not as famous as the Johnson reports on Sunday mails. But it was circulating in the public sphere well before beginning its long and influential legal career in 1879.

Given the mass of documentary evidence, even sympathetic biographers struggled to depict Jefferson as a friend of religion. Randall, for example, was forced to explain Jefferson's Syllabus on Christianity, appended to an 1803 letter to Benjamin Rush, in which he appeared to reject the Divinity of Jesus Christ. Such opinions, Randall argued, were intended to be kept private and were in any case less a reflection of the President's true beliefs than a product of his anger at the incessant attacks on his Administration by the New England clergy.[56] Other biographers were less circumspect. In his 1874 life of Jefferson, the freethinker James Parton gleefully cited the President's barbs against religion. He rejected Calvinist doctrine as a "blasphemous absurdity," held Presbyterianism—the "haughtiest of all religious sects"—in contempt, and praised Unitarianism as the only faith to abandon the "incomprehensible jargon of the Trinitarian arithmetic." Above all, and in a way that no doubt seemed highly relevant to contemporary battles, Parton portrayed a President at war with religious fanaticism.[57]

All of this suggested another reason why the Founders had left God out of the Constitution: they were not Christians in anything but a nominal sense, and certainly saw no need to introduce a supernatural presence into a secular document. For Francis Abbot, the Founders were not Christian "in the proper sense of the word."[58] But the *Index* also opened up a new front in the battle over the piety of the Presidents. This time the subject was not the founder but the savior of the nation, the martyred President Abraham Lincoln. In 1866, Josiah G. Holland published the first substantial biography of Lincoln, a work which attempted to go beyond the public career and delve into the inner life of the President. In Holland's best-seller, Lincoln emerged as a true if discreet Christian. The President carried a copy of the Bible in his pocket and held religious conviction to be an essential element in statesmanship. This depiction outraged William Herndon, Lincoln's former law partner in Springfield, Illinois. Herndon was no friend of orthodox faith. "Christianity," as he wrote to Abbot, "as applied to mankind is a failure." A "higher religion," as he put it, was now called for.[59] He could not abide his old friend being portrayed as a closet zealot, and set out to put the record straight in the pages of the *Index*. He would show the world, he told Abbot, a man whose "human struggle for life" was far more sublime than any profession of orthodoxy.[60]

Appearing on April 2, 1870, Herndon's account revealed a very different Lincoln to that of Holland. Lincoln's temperament, Herndon began, was far too logical and practical to put much faith in things that could not be demonstrated. As a young man, he had read and absorbed the writings of Thomas Paine and the Comte de Volney, and for the rest of his life would toy with atheism, particularly while in the grip of his regular bouts of melancholy. As he matured, the President came eventually to his own peculiar brand of belief. Lincoln accepted the existence of God and the immortality of the soul. But he explicitly rejected other key tenets of Christianity: the Bible as Divine revelation, the power of miracles, and the divinity of Jesus Christ. Nor did his views on these matters shift under the strain of leading the nation through the Civil War, as Holland claimed. As Herndon wrote to Abbot, the testimony of dozens of men and women who were close to Lincoln from 1860 until his death proved that he had never undergone any such religious conversion late in life.[61] He was in no sense, therefore, a "technical Christian" as depicted by Holland. It was time, Herndon concluded, that Christians stopped trying to enroll the dead in their cause. "Every great man that dies," he lamented, "is instantly dragged into the folds of the Church, and transformed through falsehood into the great defender of the faith."[62]

As this battle over the piety of the Founders raged, many commentators sought a middle-ground. Some of the secular press responded angrily to the NRA's depiction of a group stricken with French infidelity. The *Commercial Advertiser* castigated the NRA for characterizing the Founders as "irreligious old fellows" and came to the defense of Washington, a man who, though not as pious as modern evangelicals, was nevertheless "profoundly sensible of his religious obligations."[63] But the most common response was to argue that, whatever their religious convictions, the Revolutionaries were adamant that their nation was not in any formal sense Christian. Two points of evidence supported this view. On January 24, 1871, the *New York Tribune* published part of the then little-known Treaty of Tripoli, signed in 1796. Declaring that it would be a "hard nut to crack" for the amendment party, the paper drew attention in particular to the phrase which affirmed that the United States *"is not in any sense founded on the Christian religion."* Here, the paper argued, was a clear and credible guide to the views of the Founders. When it was signed, their beliefs and designs were still fresh in the minds of the people, who approved the treaty as encapsulating the nature and purpose of their government. The current amendment agitation was only serving to make clear that conferring special rights or privileges on Christians would be a repudiation of the Founders and their intentions.[64]

Further support for this contention came from the pen of Washington himself. In a letter to Washington in 1789, a group of Presbyterian clergy expressed their regret at the absence of God and Jesus in the "Magna Charta" of their country. This showed, as the *Washington Chronicle* wrote, the parallels between the clergy of that era and their modern-day counterparts. Washington's reply was, in the words of the paper, a "crusher." Faith, he told them, did not require the sustenance of government. The "path of true piety," Washington wrote to the clergymen, "is so plain as to require but little political direction." For the paper, this exchange showed why Washington did not wish to see any reference to God in the Constitution. In common with the other delegates at the Convention, he was content to leave religion to ministers of the Gospel, while government worked in its sphere for the progress of the nation.[65]

The Example of the Old World

In this understanding of the Founders' intentions, the Old World was a constant presence. The revolutionaries, as the *New York Times* argued in a hostile editorial on the Christian amendment, "knew what State religion meant in the Old World, and carefully guarded against its introduction in the new." Through their familiarity with European history, these men had come to a very clear understanding of the fate which awaited their new nation if anything resembling a state religion was allowed to develop: a hollow and lifeless faith based on mindless adherence to external forms, a government forever embroiled in theological quarrels, and a citizenry broken into warring sectarian camps.[66] Thankfully, the *Times* concluded, the wise Founders had set the nation on a very different trajectory.

Unfortunately, the Christian amendment party now seemed intent on forcing the nation down a path of state-sponsored theology which the Founders had so sagely avoided. In a hostile editorial, the *Chicago Tribune* warned that were the amendment to succeed, the majority Protestant faith would become a state creed, and the republic would join the ranks of corrupt theocracies such as Russia.[67] Small incidents suggested that the feared European contagion was creeping into the body politic. In March 1875, a Philadelphia judge refused to naturalize Julius Nieland, despite the fact that he had met the required residency period. His reason was that Nieland was an "infidel." When news of the decision broke, the reaction of much of the press was extremely negative. The *Chicago Tribune* saw the indirect influence of the God-in-the-Constitution party. The judge seemed to have acted as though the religious amendment had been adopted; in refusing naturalization, he was imposing a religious test which was unconstitutional. Following from an earlier incident in which a New York judge excluded the evidence of a witness who refused a religious oath, the paper saw a Europeanizing tendency at work. After all, in England just a few weeks before, a police-magistrate had similarly refused to admit the testimony of a witness on the grounds of his atheism.[68]

The controversy over the Christian amendment thus afforded defenders of a secular state the opportunity to reaffirm the exceptional nature of the United States in having enshrined a true separation of church and state. In 1869, the editors of the *Nation* reflected on its advantage in this regard. In many respects, the journal argued, the New World had imitated rather than innovated. Though Americans liked to believe that their institutions were "essentially distinct" from those of European nations, the truth was that they were "in most things a development of European ideas." But there was one area in which the United States had contributed a new idea to the science of politics: "the complete and organic separation of the state and the church." European nations might tolerate different faiths and forms of worship. But America had gone beyond toleration by erecting a regime in which churches had no distinguishing legal status. American law recognized the existence of church corporations, but in precisely the same manner as it recognized banking or railroad corporations. Taking no interest in the motives, spirit, or beliefs within a church corporation, the state treated it as a "legal, secular organization possessing land, edifices, funds." What made the nation unique was not the nature of the relations between church and state, but more fundamentally, their utter "absence of relations."[69]

The First Vatican Council

There were signs, however, that America's lead was diminishing. On the one hand, the NRA seemed to be importing a European-style meshing of church and state. On the other hand, Europe itself seemed to be copying the American model. One promising sign was the 1869 disestablishment of the Anglican church of Ireland, a reform widely applauded by American commentators as a step in the right direction. But even more significant was an event taking place in Rome whose aftershocks seemed sure to overturn once and for all the European model of state churches. This was the first Vatican Council, a gathering of some 1050 prelates from across the globe, which opened in Rome on December 8, 1869. In a religious age, the Council, the first of its kind since those of Trent in the sixteenth century, appeared momentous even to non-Catholics. The author and social reformer Charles Eliot Norton wrote to his mother that it was certainly "a great historic event" that would "have a large place in the history of the next generation."[70] The poet William Cullen Bryant thought that the Council would "occupy the attention not only of the religious but the secular public."[71] Particularly intriguing was the purpose of the Council. Most commentators assumed that Pope Pius IX would use the Council to define formally the doctrine of papal infallibility. This was a controversial aim even within the episcopacy. But for outside observers, the very concept of infallibility seemed to distill the ridiculous pretensions of Rome. The notion that any man could be considered immune from error was bizarre. Furthermore, if history were a guide, the occupants of the papal chair were poor candidates for infallibility. To reinforce the point, some American papers re-printed a French article listing the number of popes deposed, murdered or declared heretical. As the *Cleveland Herald* suggested, even the American Presidents had a better track record than the allegedly infallible popes.[72]

The Vatican Council engaged the attention of American commentators for many reasons. But in the context of the Christian amendment debate, the key point of significance was the prospect of secular governments taking advantage of the Council to assert their independence from Rome. The reasoning went as follows. European leaders understood papal infallibility as a tool with which the Vatican hoped to assert its control over their citizens. Its core message was that the primary loyalty of Catholics lay not with fallible governments but their infallible Pope.

For this reason, governments across the continent were determined to block what they saw as a brazen grab for authority over their Catholic populations. The *North American and United States Gazette* informed its readers that "the monarchs and liberal statesmen of Europe will do their utmost to thwart the schemes of the Pope."[73] The British premier, William Gladstone, was known to be hostile. The position of the French government, whose troops maintained the Pope's temporal power in the face of Italian nationalists, was particularly important. In a move that was widely reported in America, the French ambassador to the Papal States, the Marquis de Banneville, was instructed to warn the Vatican that any proclamation of infallibility might lead the French government to withdraw its garrison from Rome.[74]

This evidence of opposition to papal authority on the part of European governments signaled that the Old World was finally joining the New in embracing a true separation of church and state. "There is scarcely," one journal claimed in the midst of the controversy, "a country in Europe ... that does not hold the State to be independent in its functions of all interference from the Church."[75] Such hopes were tempered when the Council voted to approve the Constitution defining infallibility in July 1870. But the subsequent withdrawal of the French garrison, an event triggered not by the vote but by the outbreak of the Franco-Prussian war, began a sequence of events that led to the fall of the Papal States just months later. With the annexation of Rome to the Kingdom of Italy, the days of theocracy in Europe seemed well and truly numbered.

In this context, the effrontery of the NRA appeared even more outrageous to its opponents. At the very moment of trans-Atlantic *rapprochement*, here was the NRA mimicking the Vatican by seeking to impose clerical control over the state. The *New York Tribune* saw the irony. Having celebrated the downfall of the Papal States, the paper was now confronted with the sight of Protestant clergy in America resurrecting the doctrine of state-sponsored orthodoxy.[76] In response, the NRA denied again and again that amending the Constitution would produce a form of government that in any way resembled the Papal States. But a slew of commentators were nevertheless of the view that a strange trans-Atlantic reversal of roles seemed to be occurring. European states were busy pushing the church out of the state, the *Banner of Light* reminded its readers, while orthodoxy at home was bringing it back in.[77] "Would it not be a strange example," the editors of the *Daily Inter*

Ocean asked, "if at the very moment when the older and long-despotic and priest-ridden nations are making vigorous efforts to separate the church from the state ... republican American should attempt to coerce men's consciences and to erect a political establishment?" [78] If nothing else, it would strip the nation of one of its proudest points of superiority.

This was an argument made by Jewish leaders, who had much to fear from a Christian amendment. It would be a national humiliation to Christianize the Constitution, one rabbi told his congregation, at precisely the moment when America's principles were sweeping the civilized world.[79] The German-born educator and rabbi Max Lilienthal emphasized that France, Italy, Spain or the German states would never think of writing God into their Constitution. The idea would strike all as hopelessly out of touch with the tenor of the age. If the Christian party were to succeed, America would be transformed in the eyes of the world from a shining example to a laughing stock. To remain in the vanguard of civilization and progress, Lilienthal concluded, America had only to hold firm to the "entire separation" of church and state by rejecting the Christian amendment.[80]

LIBERAL PROTESTANTS AND THE CHRISTIAN AMENDMENT

The Christian amendment also aroused the opposition of a grouping which was beginning a long phase of growth and influence, liberal Protestants. For liberal Protestants, the Christian amendment encapsulated a mistaken notion of true faith. Conservatives might insist on conformity to external rules and rituals; a true believer, in contrast, cultivated the inner resources of spirituality. The nation would only be godly when its citizens made Christ's teachings their daily rule of behavior. Until this occurred, any claim to have built a Christian nation by changing the text of the Constitution was simply affirming hypocrisy as the national creed. Henry Ward Beecher's *Christian Union* argued that there should be a Christian nation, but accused the amendment party of beginning at the wrong end. They were akin to the builder who starts by placing the capstone rather than "building up from a foundation in solid earth."[81] The *Independent* agreed. "If every section of every article of our Constitution had the name of Christ inserted, it would amount to nothing," the editors announced, "but blasphemous vanity." The nation could not be truly Christian until a true love of Christ was "recognized and felt in the people's homes, in their stores, in their beds, from their inmost to their outmost life."[82] Here the *Independent* reluctantly made a common cause with the *Index*, a paper it regarded as irreligious. But "an infidel who tells the truth," the editors argued, was "better than a Christian who does not."[83]

But the NRA was widely deemed to have mistaken more than the nature of a truly Christian nation. For many other commentators, it had also misunderstood the purpose of the Constitution. As the *New York Times* argued, the Constitution was a "political charter" which regulated civil order and set out public rights. It was not an affirmation of a national creed.[84] The Constitution, another paper wrote, was a "civil instrument designed to effect certain civil ends," and for this reason rightly free of all "theological allusions."[85] This argument was put forth in most detail by a Presbyterian minister and contributor to the *Independent*, Samuel Thayer Spear. Spear would gain most prominence as an advocate of secular schools. But he was just as convinced that the Constitution was also secular, a term which he defined not as hostility to religion but as an exclusive focus on temporal ends. "The purposes," he argued, "of a bank corporation or a railway company are not more strictly temporal and secular than those set forth in the preamble of the Constitution."[86] Religion was simply outside the scope of a document of this nature.

This was an argument over the nature of the government itself. For Spear, the Godless Constitution forged a government that was a "political organization for secular and temporal ends, based upon the principle of popular representation, and upon nothing else."[87] The NRA, in contrast, rejected what it saw as a purely utilitarian understanding of government and of the state. The state was far more than an impersonal entity deriving its powers and legitimacy from a social compact and tasked with maintaining order and prosperity. The secular ideal, as the Unitarian Reverend Amory D. Mayo charged, saw the state as little more than a "policeman to keep people from breaking each other's heads."[88] The vision of the amendment party was much more expansive. In their view, the state was a living entity endowed with a moral character and ultimately answerable to the ruler of nations, Jesus Christ. The state, in other words, could sin, and in the same manner as any sinner would have to reckon with Divine punishment. To convey the threat, the pro-amendment party looked, in a similar manner to their opponents, to the Old World. What drew their attention was the bloodshed and destruction of the Paris Commune. The vision of Paris in flames distilled the fate of governments which turned their backs on God. "Could any madness be greater," as one pro-amendment delegate argued, "than that of the men who shriek like howling Dervishes against any national acknowledgment of God, ere yet the glow of burning Paris has passed from yonder heavens?" In France, he continued, Americans had a vivid demonstration of "the results of theories that exclude God from the government of nations and refuse obedience to His law."[89]

The debate over the Christian amendment thus exposed a fundamental difference over the nature of the state and the origin of political authority. For the NRA, the optimism that followed the northern victory in the Civil War had quickly given way to a despairing realization that the nation was still bathed in sin. Abolishing slavery was no guarantee of immunity from Divine punishment. Christians like Spear, on the other hand, saw a state which was largely detached from Divine will. States existed within a divinely constructed framework, but their course was set by independent historical forces, "natural causes," as he put it, "operating under the providential superintendence of God." There was no need, then, to fear Divine vengeance. "The hand of God," he argued, "is no more really involved in the formation, constitution, growth, and government of empires than in the formation and growth of coral reefs."[90] States rose and fell for a range of reasons, but Divine providence was not one.

An example from the recent past proved the point. On March 11, 1861, seven southern states adopted the Confederate Constitution, which in its preamble appealed to the "favor and guidance of Almighty God." No doubt fearful of being tarred with the stigma of rebellion and slavery, the NRA made little mention of this precedent. Their opponents, however, were not as reticent. The *Independent* cited the Confederate example to rebut the contention, made often by the NRA, that the moral tenor of the nation would be improved if the Constitution were to be Christianized. "We have seen," the editorialists argued, "one republic that solemnly acknowledged God in its Constitution, and the example is not an attractive one." Under its religious Constitution, the Confederacy waged an unjust war and committed the worst sins, from stealing the labor of men and women to starving prisoners. Having God in its Constitution had neither redeemed the Confederacy's character nor saved it from destruction.[91]

As in the Sunday mail controversy, the hopes of the amendment party were dashed by a Congressional report. In February 1874, Benjamin F. Butler for the House Judiciary Committee rejected the call for a Christian amendment. Mirroring the national debate on the issue, the report highlighted two key themes: the intentions of the Founders, and the exceptional nature of their republic. In the 1787 convention, they had considered this issue, but decided to make their new nation a refuge for the oppressed of all nations, whether "Christian or Pagan." Foremost in their minds was the example of the Old World, which had suffered so greatly from the union of church and state. It was for this reason that the Founders had rightly left out any reference to faith or creed in their Constitution.[92]

The report won applause from much of the nation's press. The *Chicago Tribune* congratulated the committee for affirming the highest principles of American republicanism: "Politics are not religion. Religion is not politics. We have kept our religion and our politics separate hitherto, and the separation has worked well."[93] The amendment movement would flare again in the 1890s. But for now, defenders of a secular Constitution could congratulate themselves that the threat had been averted. In 1877, the *Nation* reflected with satisfaction that, having withstood more than a decade of agitation, the Constitution remained "absolutely and completely secular." The legacy of the Founders was still intact. These men were "thoroughly imbued" with the principle which for the journal had come to define the nineteenth century, the "entire separation of Church and State."[94]

Notes

1. Fredrickson, "The Coming of the Lord," 124.
2. Noll, *Civil War as a Theological Crisis*.
3. George M. Fredrickson, *The Inner Civil War: Northern Intellectuals and the Crisis of the Union* (New York: Harper and Row, 1965).
4. Philip Schaff, *Der Bürgerkrieg und das christliche Leben in Nord-Amerika* (Berlin: Wiegandt und Grieben, 1866), 57–58.
5. On the Amendment issue, see Steven K. Green, *The Bible, the School and the Constitution: The Clash That Shaped Modern Church-State Doctrine* (New York: Oxford University Press, 2012), 137–78; Tisa Wenger, "The God-in-the-Constitution Controversy: American Secularisms in Historical Perspective," in *Comparative Secularisms in a Global Age*, eds. Linell E. Cady and Elizabeth Shakman Hurd (New York: Palgrave Macmillan 2010), 87–106.

6. *New York Herald*, June 15, 1869.
7. *Critic-Record* (Washington, DC), February 28, 1873.
8. Horace Bushnell, *Reverses Needed* (Hartford: L.E. Hunt, 1861), 26.
9. *Proceedings of the National Convention to Secure the Religious Amendment of the Constitution of the United States, held in Cincinnati, Jan 31 and Feb 1 1872* (Philadelphia: James B. Rodgers Co., printers, 1872), iv. On the NRA, Joseph S. Moore, *Founding Sins: How a Group of Antislavery Radicals Fought to Put Christ Into the Constitution* (New York: Oxford University Press, 2016), 126–145.
10. Ibid., ix.
11. Horace Bushnell, *Building Eras in Religion* (New York: C. Scribner's Sons, 1881), 341.
12. *Proceedings of the National Convention, held at Cincinnati*, 61.
13. Ibid., 45.
14. HR 44A-H8.2. National Archives, Washington, DC.
15. Clipping in Francis E. Abbot papers, bMs 550/8, Harvard Divinity School, Cambridge.
16. *Proceedings at the First Annual Meeting of the Free Religious Association, held in Boston, May 28–29, 1868* (Boston: Adams & Co., 1868), 9, 22.
17. Abbot to Potter, June 18, 1867, Francis Ellingwood Abbot papers, bMs 550/8, Harvard Divinity School, Cambridge.
18. *Index*, April 6, 1872.
19. "Resolutions Adopted by the National Liberal League, July 3, 1876." Box 65, Francis Ellingwood Abbot papers, Harvard University Archives, Cambridge.
20. Potter to Abbot, January 10, 1872. Box 46, Abbot papers, Harvard University Archives, Cambridge.
21. *The Works of Robert G. Ingersoll*, vol. 1 (New York: Dresden, 1900), 377; Susan Jacoby, *The Great Agnostic: Robert Ingersoll and American Freethought* (New Haven: Yale University Press, 2013).
22. Molly McGarry, *Ghosts of Futures Past: Spiritualism and the Cultural Politics of Nineteenth-Century America* (Berkeley: University of California Press, 2008).
23. *Banner of Light*, May 4, 1872. Emphasis in original.
24. The analysis that follows is based on the anti-amendment petitions to the 42nd Congress, housed at the National Archives (Washington, DC).
25. Signed March 31, 1872. SEN 42A-H11.
26. Clifton (IN). Signed March 15, 1872. Columbus (OH). No date. SEN 42A-H11.
27. No date. SEN 42A-H11.
28. Ibid.
29. Ibid.

30. Ibid.
31. Signed February 13, 1872. SEN 42A-H11.
32. No date. SEN 42A-H11.
33. Franklin (NH). No date. SEN 42A-H11.
34. Signed March 1872. For another Baptist signer, see petition from Storm Lake, Iowa, signed February 15, 1872. SEN 42A-H11.
35. SEN 42A-H11.
36. Ann Braude, *Radical Spirits: Spiritualism and Women's Rights in Nineteenth-Century America*, 2nd edition (Bloomington: Indiana University Press, 2001).
37. Evelyn A. Kirkley, *Rational Mothers and Infidel Gentleman: Gender and American Atheism, 1865–1915* (Syracuse: Syracuse University Press, 2000), esp. Chapter 2.
38. *Boston Investigator*, April 12, 1871.
39. *Index*, September 10, 1874.
40. No date or place, SEN 42A-H11.
41. M.L. Weems, *The Life of George Washington; With Curious Anecdotes, Equally Honourable to Himself and Exemplary to His Young Countrymen* (Philadelphia: Mathew Carey, 1809), 182–84; Edward G. Lengel, *Inventing George Washington: America's Founder, in Myth and Memory* (New York: Harper, 2011), 72–105.
42. E.C. M'Guire, *The Religious Opinions and Character of Washington* (New York: Harper and Brothers, 1836), 409. On this and similar efforts to deify Washington, Green, *Inventing a Christian America*, 205–10.
43. Benjamin Franklin Morris, *A Discourse on the Christian Character and Influence of Washington* (Office of the Indiana Blade, 1846), 11.
44. Weems, *Life of George Washington*, 184.
45. *National Intelligencer*, August 26, 1826. Reprinted in Max Farrand, ed., *The Records of the Federal Convention of 1787*, vol. III (New Haven: Yale University Press, 1966), 467–73. All italics in original.
46. Farrand, *Records of the Federal Convention*, I, 452. On this controversy, John M. Murrin, "Fundamental Values, the Founding Fathers and the Constitution," in *To Form a More Perfect Union: The Critical Ideas of the Constitution*, eds. Herman Belz, Ronald Hoffman, and Peter J. Albert (Charlottesville: University Press of Virginia, 1992), 3, 33–34.
47. Cited in *Flake's Bulletin*, May 10, 1868.
48. Randall to Grigsby, May 25, 1856, in *The Correspondence Between Henry Stephens Randall and Hugh Blair Grigsby, 1856–61* (Berkeley: University of California Press, 1952), 50.
49. Henry Stephens Randall, *The Life of Thomas Jefferson*, vol. 3 (New York: Derby & Jackson, 1858), 554–55.

50. The letter appears in volume 8 of H.A. Washington, ed., *The Writings of Thomas Jefferson* (Washington, DC: Taylor & Maury, 1854), 113. On Jefferson's reputation for infidelity, Merill D. Peterson, *The Jefferson Image in the American Mind* (Charlottesville: University of Virginia Press, 1960), 127–30. On Washington, Francis D. Cogliano, *Thomas Jefferson: Reputation and Legacy* (Edinburgh: Edinburgh University Press, 2006), 82–83.
51. Dreisbach, *Jefferson and the Wall of Separation*, 96–97.
52. *Buffalo Courier* (NY), April 9, 1855; *Public Ledger* (Philadelphia), May 2, 1855; *Perry County Democrat* (PA), May 17, 1855; *Daily South Carolinian*, May 4, 1855; *Fayetteville Observer*, May 31, 1855; *North Carolinian*, May 5, 1855; *Daily Gazette and Comet* (LA), May 11, 1855. In Wisconsin, *Kenosha Democrat*, May 18, 1855; *Oshkosh Courier*, April 25, 1855; *Sheboygan Lake Journal*, May 1, 1855.
53. *Boston Investigator*, May 30, 1855.
54. Randall, *Life of Jefferson*, 2.
55. February 6, 1869. Re-printed in *Israelite*, February 26, 1869; *Boston Investigator*, June 9, 1869.
56. Randall, *Life of Jefferson*, 559–60.
57. James Parton, *Life of Thomas Jefferson, Third President of the United States* (Boston: J.R. Osgood, 1874), 711–12.
58. *Index*, March 12, 1870.
59. Herndon to Abbot, no date. Box 45, Francis Ellingwood Abbot papers, Harvard University Archives, Cambridge.
60. Herndon to Abbot, March 19, 1870 in ibid.
61. Herndon to Abbot, May 7, 1870 in ibid.
62. *Index*, April 2, 1870. On Holland, Allen C. Guelzo, "Holland's Informants: The Construction of Josiah Holland's 'Life of Abraham Lincoln'," *Journal of the Abraham Lincoln Association* 23, no. 1 (2002): 1–53.
63. *Commercial Advertiser*, January 16, 1871.
64. *New York Tribune*, January 24, 1871.
65. Re-printed from *Washington Chronicle* in *New Hampshire Sentinel*, January 25, 1872; *Milwaukee Sentinel*, January 12, 1872; *Cleveland Herald*, January 12, 1872.
66. *New York Times*, January 10, 1871.
67. *Chicago Tribune*, March 1, 1873.
68. *Chicago Tribune*, March 20, 1875. Nieland successfully appealed this decision.
69. *Nation*, August 19, 1869.
70. Charles Eliot Norton, *Letters of Charles Eliot Norton*, vol. 1 (New York: Houghton Mifflin, 1913), 381.

71. Bryant to Leonice M. S. Moulton, December 10, 1869, in *The Letters of William Cullen Bryant*, eds. William Cullen Bryant II and Thomas G. Voss, vol. 5 (New York: Fordham University Press, 1992), 347.
72. *Daily Cleveland Herald*, November 19, 1869.
73. *North American and United States Gazette*, December 10, 1869.
74. *New York Times*, December 12, 1869.
75. *Appletons' Journal of Literature, Science and Art*, March 12, 1870.
76. *New York Tribune*, January 24, 1871.
77. *Banner of Light*, May 20, 1871.
78. *Inter Ocean* (Chicago), March 2, 1875.
79. *Israelite*, February 24, 1871.
80. *Israelite*, December 16, 1870.
81. *Columbus Daily Enquirer*, March 10, 1870.
82. *Independent*, February 19, 1874.
83. *Independent*, April 10, 1873.
84. *New York Times*, February 13, 1869.
85. *Milwaukee Sentinel*, March 3, 1873.
86. Spear, *Religion and the State*, 204.
87. Ibid., 212.
88. *Proceedings of the National Convention... Held at Cincinnati*, 37.
89. Ibid., 26.
90. Spear, *Religion and the State*, 177.
91. Cited in *New York Tribune*, January 28, 1871.
92. "Acknowledgment of God and the Christian Religion in the Constitution," House Judiciary Committee, 43rd Congress, 1st session, February 18, 1874.
93. *Chicago Tribune*, February 22, 1874.
94. *Nation*, February 1, 1877.

CHAPTER 7

The Bible Wars: Religion, Morality, and Schools in an International Age

On September 6, 1869, a member of the Board of Education of Cincinnati, Ohio, Samuel A. Miller, set off what would become known as the "Bible Wars." That evening Miller moved a resolution to ban from the city's classrooms all forms of religious instruction, including the customary reading of the Bible.[1] When news of the resolution broke in the city's press, a furious public reaction ensued. Supporters and opponents of Miller's resolution held rival mass meetings, launched petition drives, and filled the columns of the press with letters and commentary. Miller and the Board, as one newspaper put it, had "exploded a bomb which seems to have awakened all Christendom."[2] In the face of this public pressure, the Board sought to defuse the issue by sending it to a select committee for further study. But the question could not be put off indefinitely. On November 1, by a margin of 22 votes to 15, the Board passed Miller's resolution.[3] Pro-Bible forces immediately launched court proceedings in an effort to have the vote overturned, and the issue would not finally be resolved until 1873, when the Supreme Court of Ohio upheld the Board's decision.

Across the nation, commentators depicted events in Cincinnati as both a critical moment in their nation's history and a rehearsal for a series of similar conflicts that were sure to break out elsewhere. The school question, as the *Hartford Daily Courant* argued, was "one of the most important with which we have ever had to deal," and whatever the outcome in Cincinnati, was "sure to rise again in other places."[4] These debates were filled with rancor and with passion, for they brought

© The Author(s) 2019
T. Verhoeven, *Secularists, Religion and Government in Nineteenth-Century America*, https://doi.org/10.1007/978-3-030-02877-0_7

together two cherished institutions, the Bible and the common school. For many Protestants, any talk of banishing the Bible was highly provocative. "The mere mention of it," as the Reverend Henry Martyn Scudder charged, "moves men deeply; it stirs their very blood."[5] At the same time, the common school was celebrated as the bedrock of the republic, the place where boys and girls of all backgrounds and faiths received the training in citizenship that was essential for the stability of the republic. In a nation still binding its divisions after a catastrophic Civil War, the unifying power of the common school appeared more critical than ever.[6]

The Bible and the school had a longstanding connection. The practice of Bible-reading in schools dated back to the period before the Civil War, and the influential reforms put in place in Massachusetts by the founder of the common school, Horace Mann. As secretary of the Massachusetts Board of Education, Mann created the template for the common school system—free tuition, taxpayer funding, and a series of mechanisms to raise and to maintain pedagogic standards. Mann also established the principle of what he regarded as nonsectarian religious instruction. Active proselytism, such as the reading of catechisms or the teaching of specific and potentially controversial doctrines, was forbidden; the teacher must never become, Mann wrote, "an umpire between religious hostile opinions." But the universal truths of what he called the "religion of the Bible" were welcome. Rather than injecting his or her interpretations, the teacher should simply allow the Bible to "*speak for itself*."[7]

As Catholics were quick to discern, Mann's language of a generic Bible-religion masked a preference for Protestantism. The Bible to which common school students were exposed was the King James version preferred by Protestants, and not the Catholic Douai translation. But the sectarian bias went further. The very practice of Bible-reading without clerical guidance or interpretation was foreign to Catholics and steeped in the traditions of the Reformation faiths. To overcome this bias, Archbishop John Hughes of New York called for a division of the school fund so that Catholics could develop properly their own school network. But Mann was unapologetic. A short reading of the King James Bible during opening exercises without note or comment was a reasonable compromise between the demands on the part of certain Protestant leaders for a more thorough course of religious instruction and the complaints by Catholics that the use of the King James Bible was an affront to their faith. In Mann's vision, the King James Bible was not a sectarian text, and the development of common schools went hand in hand with his model of Bible-reading.

Prizing the Bible out of schools, then, was a formidable task that required appeals to principle as well as to fear. One argument was that the repetition of texts without explanation alienated rather than inspired children. For its great truths to be absorbed, the Bible required active and thorough interpretation; even passages that appeared straightforward contained a complexity of language and thought that defied mere recital. Without this, students were likely to be baffled or worse, repelled. The *Milwaukee Sentinel* doubted if any students benefitted from hearing Scripture read during the daily opening exercises; for most, far from a moment of quiet reverence, this was instead a "gala time."[8] The editor of the *Boston Investigator*, Horace Seaver, was similarly dubious. The Bible-reading to which he had been exposed as a child had done nothing to prevent his later embrace of freethought. Nor, in his recollection, had it made much of an impression on his classmates. Most took the opportunity to play up, pinching, teasing, and mocking each other as the teacher droned on.[9]

The evidence that mass immigration was bringing about an ever more diverse nation provided another impulse. This was a factor that clearly weighed heavily on the School Board of New Haven, Connecticut, which in 1878 followed Cincinnati's lead in banning the Bible. In defense of its position, the Board produced strong evidence that the formerly Protestant makeup of the city's school population was a thing of the past. Figures for the week ending January 18, 1878, showed that of a total enrolment of 7900 students, no less than 63.34% were of foreign-born parentage. The Board did not undertake a thorough survey of their religious affiliation. But even on the assumption that every child whose parents were born in the United States or majority-Protestant nations abroad belonged to that faith, a large proportion of the student population—44.94% in the Board's calculation—was likely to object to the imposition of the King James Bible.[10] More and more ministers agreed. The Reverend William Weston Patton was a Congregational pastor and a lecturer in theological seminaries in Ohio and in Illinois. For Patton, Bible-reading was an essential part of any child's education, and he had made sure that his own children were steeped in its great and universal truths. But Patton was just as adamant that the public school was not the appropriate venue for such instruction, and foremost in his reasoning was the shifting composition of the population. This was a population that "once nearly homogeneous in race and in religious faith, has become, by immigration and by changes of opinion, widely heterogeneous."[11]

A visible sign of this diversity was the Jewish population. A decade after the Civil War, their numbers remained small. The New Haven Board counted 282 Jewish pupils across eleven common schools, a figure which represented less than 4% of the total enrolment. Furthermore, as Naomi W. Cohen notes, this was a community which contained a range of opinions on the question of Bible-reading, as well as other church-state controversies. Some Jews, fearful of stirring anti-Semitism, opted for a muted public stance. Conservative organs such as the *American Hebrew* (New York) argued that sectarianism in the classroom was still preferable to no religion at all. Nevertheless, the dominant Jewish position in the decades after the Civil War was strongly in favor of a robust separation of church and state, and several Jewish leaders emerged as prominent actors in the Bible Wars.[12] This was the case in Cincinnati, where two of the leaders of Reform Judaism, Isaac Mayer Wise and Max Lilienthal, threw their support behind the Board's decision. Wise was the editor of the *Israelite*, the leading organ of Reform Judaism, where he strongly argued against mixing religion and public schooling. In a population which was a "conglomeration of nationalities and sects," the only safe and just ground was to make the classroom secular.[13] Lilienthal was a longstanding member of the Cincinnati Board of Education. In a series of letters to the *Jewish Times* in New York, he described a controversy which was generating "an intense excitement in all class of the community." His own position was clear. With a secularist victory, he wrote, "the separation of state and church will be gloriously vindicated," and along with it the great principle of religious liberty, "the brightest gem in the American diadem."[14] Anecdotal evidence suggested that some Jewish parents were prepared to confront what they regarded as sectarian intolerance. In November 1869, the Washington correspondent of the *Jewish Times* reported his anger upon hearing that his daughter's teacher had opened and closed the school day with prayer, and then asked the students to invoke the aid of Jesus Christ. By his account, the issue was quickly resolved. After complaining to the trustees, the objectionable prayer was quickly removed.[15]

In response, defenders of Bible-reading fell back on a majority-rights argument. Rufus W. Clark, a well-known preacher and the author of a hugely popular series of Sunday School primers, summarized the situation. The number of Protestants in the nation was twenty million. Even allowing for mass immigration, the number of Catholics could not be more than seven million, while Jews were still only a tiny minority. To eject the King James Bible from schools was therefore to ignore the wishes of the majority of citizens and to privilege a noisy minority.[16] Relying on blunt numbers was problematic, for it assumed that all Protestants were of one mind on the question, an assumption that was clearly false. But Clark and others could point as well to the evidence of petitions. In New Haven, for example, the school board received twenty-seven petitions demanding the restitution of the Bible with a total of 3972 names attached, a number which far outweighed the opposing camp.[17]

There was still a great deal of doubt, however, about the reliability of the petition as a gauge of public opinion. The majority of the New Haven Board offered a lengthy dissection of the flaws of the pro-Bible petitions in its report on the issue. Even without a thorough examination, it was evident that the duplication of names was rife. Then, there was the question of who could legitimately sign a petition. After decades of female petitioning, it might be supposed that there would no longer be any objection to women signers. But the Board nevertheless dismissed the pro-Bible petitions on the grounds that a large proportion of their signers were women. No less than 1052 were preceded by "Miss" or "Mrs" or a female first name; even without these clear indications, the writers of the majority report claimed to be able to detect a female hand behind many of the signatures. A cursory examination showed as well that many of the signers were boys from the city's schools. Eliminating what it regarded as illegitimate signers, the total number of petitioners in favor of retaining the Bible was closer to 2000, a figure which represented only 18–20% of the voters of the district.[18] The claim to a majority, then, rested on spurious evidence.

CATHOLICS AND THE COMMON SCHOOLS

Overshadowing the entire discussion was the specter of Catholic aggression. In 1870, the *Catholic World* set out the case against the common school system. It was clearly an injustice, the *World* argued, that Catholic taxpayers were forced to support a common school system which was imbued with Protestantism and which was hostile to their faith. But removing the King James Bible was not the solution, for this would produce something even more objectionable, a wholly godless school.

Furthermore, Protestant bias was only part of the problem. The state had no right to tax Catholics for the support of schools which did not actively train their children in the principles of their faith. The common school system was flawed not simply because it taught a Protestant creed, but because it denied Catholics the chance to "freely and fully teach our religion and train up our children ... to be true and unwavering Catholics."[19] The only fair approach was to divide the fund between Protestant, Catholic, and Jewish schools, a system, in other words, of sectarian-based funding.

This claim provoked a storm of hostility. For its opponents, the church's talk of fairness and equality masked its true aim of rearing the rising generation in its autocratic and backward principles. What it desired, they argued, was to create an army of loyal followers that it could then turn against the republic and its freedoms. This, as Henry Martyn Scudder argued, was the real basis of its hostility to children coming into contact with the King James Bible. The papacy could not tolerate the presence of the Bible because it "creates the condition in which men learn to think and act for themselves." The common school, with the Bible at its core, loosened the bonds which tied Catholics to the episcopal hierarchy, an intolerable result for a church which "wishes to subjugate the minds, hearts, wills, consciences, imaginations, bodies and lives of all men and women to itself, so that they shall think, feel and act as it dictates."[20] Though cloaked in the language of justice, the Catholic demand for state funding of its schools was driven by theocratic ambition.

The reaction was fiercest in cities where the church had succeeded in procuring state funds for its schools. In New York in 1872, an outcry ensued when the City Council of Political Reform reported that, thanks to an obscure amendment to the city tax levy passed three years earlier, religious schools had been granted hundreds of thousands of dollars. Particularly infuriating was the revelation that Catholic schools received the lion's share. In a series of editorials, and through the pen of its leading illustrator Thomas Nast, *Harper's Weekly* denounced a well-planned assault on the city's common schools. Just five years earlier, the journal reminded its readers, the public school system of the city was flourishing, to the point that even the "more thoughtful of the Irish Catholics" were beginning to entrust their children to its care. Alarmed as its grip over the Catholic population loosened, the hierarchy then set out with typical zeal and cunning to destroy what it regarded as a growing obstacle to its rule. Aware that a direct assault was likely to spark resistance, the church had instead devised a plan "to create a large number of Romish schools at the expense of the city, and then drive their children into them." Aided by all the forces at its disposal—the clergy, corrupt politicians, pliant newspaper editors—the church had succeeded; all over the city, great educational establishments devoted to the propagation of the Roman Catholic faith were now springing up. And taxpayers were shouldering the cost.[21]

Opponents of Bible-reading were just as hostile to the Catholic demand for state funding, which they also interpreted as a thinly disguised attempt to wreck the common school system. In a petition to the Philadelphia Board of Education calling on it to remove the Bible, the secularist Liberal League warned of the church's "openly avowed warfare" against the common school.[22] But they drew very different conclusions about the appropriate response. For Henry Martyn Scudder, the antidote to Catholic ambition was the King James Bible. Only the "Bible-sunlight," as Scudder termed it, would free the benighted minds of Catholic youth.[23] Secularists, in contrast, argued that the presence of the King James Bible, the reading of the Protestant version of the Ten Commandments, and the singing of Protestant hymns provided the Catholic hierarchy with a powerful line of attack against the common school. The continuing presence of the Bible in schools, as the Liberal League of Philadelphia argued, was "placing a most destructive weapon in the hands of the greatest enemies of our public school system."[24] This belief that Bible advocates were playing into Catholic hands was widespread. As the *Atlantic Monthly* argued, while the obligatory reading of the Bible was maintained, the Catholic call for a division of the school fund was always likely to win public sympathy.[25] The editors of the *Nation* agreed, suggesting that whatever benefits accrued to children from the presence of the Bible, the costs were far higher. In particular, Bible-reading gave Catholics "a constant incentive to intrigue and agitate for the overthrow of our whole educational system."[26]

PRESIDENT GRANT AND THE SCHOOL QUESTION

In the last months of 1875, the issue entered national politics. On September 29, President Ulysses S. Grant addressed a gathering of Union Army veterans at Des Moines, Iowa. In a largely impromptu speech, Grant issued a spirited defense of mass education. The future dividing line in the nation would no longer be the Mason Dixon, he predicted, but "patriotism and intelligence" versus "superstition, ambition and ignorance." Education was the key to national progress, but for this education to be truly national in character it had to be "unmixed with sectarian, pagan or atheistical tenets."[27] The school question then assumed an even greater magnitude when another leading Republican, Maine Senator James G. Blaine, called for the establishment clause of the First Amendment to be applied to the states in the form of a Sixteenth Amendment to the Constitution. The proposed amendment would also prohibit any division of the school fund along sectarian lines, as well as any funding of schools which were, as Blaine wrote to a colleague in Ohio, "under the control of any religious sect."[28] On December 7, President Grant returned to the importance of mass education in his annual address to Congress. In addition to supporting a ban on sectarian funding, Grant once again expressed his opposition to the introduction of "sectarian tenets" into taxpayer-supported schools. But at a key point in the address, his language shifted. It was imperative, he argued, to keep the nation's classrooms free of "religious" tenets.[29]

Grant's intervention in the school question is often interpreted as a politically motivated attack on the Catholic Church. The Republican Party which Grant led had absorbed the Know-Nothing voters of the prewar era; there was no surer way to fire up the base than to launch a crusade against papal ambition. Yet, in broadening his language from sectarian to religious tenets, Grant seemed to draw in the King James Bible as much as the Catholic catechism, and there is some anecdotal evidence that this was his intention. One of Grant's closest friends, William Tecumseh Sherman, later recalled that the President's words at Des Moines were directed not at the Catholic Church but at the Protestant denominations and their "ceaseless clamor for set religious exercises in the public schools."[30] Whatever Grant's motivation, much of the press understood his December address as targeting Protestant and Catholic alike. The *National Republican*, one of the leading organs of the party, concluded that the President was advocating an outright ban on Bible-reading.[31] For the *Daily Graphic* in New York, the President clearly intended to preserve the schools from zealots and extremists of all faiths, whether Protestants pushing their Bible or Catholics seeking state funding.[32] A Pennsylvania paper understood Grant to be calling for all religious texts, whether the Bible, the Koran, or the writings of Confucius to be kept away from the classroom. In this, the paper argued, the President was siding with a large segment of the public.[33] Even *Harper's Weekly*, which had made anti-Catholicism its rallying cry, read the December address in this way. While public opinion was not yet in favor of banning the Bible, there was "no question," the editors declared, "that the President expresses a sentiment which is rapidly increasing." That sentiment was that Bible-reading in the common school "serves no good purpose."[34]

Many Protestants no doubt maintained that the term "sectarian" applied only to alien faiths like Roman Catholicism. But the difficulty in limiting the scope of sectarianism to one faith alone became clear once Congress began debating Blaine's proposed Sixteenth Amendment. On August 11, 1876, the Senate Judiciary Committee issued a revised version. It began with a prohibition on state funding for any institution under religious control. The amendment then outlawed the reading and teaching of any "particular creed or tenets" in public schools. Such broad language might have stoked fears of an end to the King James Bible in the classroom. But any anxieties on this score were calmed by a further clause specifying that this could not be "construed to prohibit the reading of the Bible," a clear reference to the King James. Protestant defenders of Bible-reading seemed on the verge of a dual victory—a constitutional ban on parochial funding allied to a guarantee of Protestant influence over the common schools.

The ensuing controversy showed, however, that "sectarian" was not simply a synonym for "Catholic." Critics lined up to point out the hypocrisy at work. As Democrat Senator Theodore Randolph asked, "Is not this a flat contradiction; or is the Bible a nonreligious book?"[35] The proposal, as one Democrat paper noted, used the cover of nonsectarianism to "sectarianize the public schools in the interests of Protestantism."[36] Even the majority of Republican Senators seemed uncomfortable with the provision. As Steven K. Green notes, most refrained from publicly defending the clause on Bible-reading, concentrating instead on the less controversial ban on state funding of religious institutions.[37] Though the amendment fell only four votes short of the required two-thirds majority, the Bible-reading clause was arguably as much a hindrance as an advantage to its passage. By then, the ambiguity in the term "sectarian" seemed undeniable. Until Congress set out a precise definition of the term, the *Daily Graphic* in New York argued, the school amendment was best left alone.[38]

The School Question in Europe

For both sides in the debate on Bible-reading, the international dimension was a constant point of reference. From the advent of the common school system, American educationalists had taken a strong interest in European approaches. As early as 1836, the Ohio legislature asked Calvin E. Stowe, then professor of sacred literature at Lane Theological Seminary in Cincinnati, to prepare a report on the educational systems of Europe. A decade later, Horace Mann published his own detailed survey of mass education in various European states.[39] The decades after the Civil War witnessed a flowering of these connections. Educational experts crisscrossed the Atlantic, producing detailed reports on the strengths and weaknesses of various national school systems, and weighing up their applicability at home. Another opportunity for international comparison came at the great international expositions of the era. Alongside the displays of cultural and industrial products, educational exhibits provided a forum to showcase national achievements and engage in dialogue with foreign pedagogues.

These international linkages were encouraged, in part at least, by a growing sense of national rivalry. Education was widely understood as one of the keys to national strength. In the words of Francis Adams, one of the many foreigners who came to America to examine its school system, "international comparisons are now forced upon all countries by international competition."[40] Success or failure in mass education helped to explain the rise and fall of nation-states. In 1871, Henry Wilson, one of the leading voices in the Republican Party, called for the creation of a national public school system. Under Reconstruction, the federal government had been actively reshaping social and political institutions in the defeated South. The next phase of Reconstruction, Wilson argued, should be a transfer of control over education from the states to Washington, DC. In making this case, Wilson drew on the recent Franco-Prussian war. Far earlier than its rival, Prussia saw that it "needed an educated people to cope with surrounding powers." While France vacillated, Prussia took the initiative, creating a rigorous, centralized, and comprehensive education system that worked to bind its citizens to the nation-state. The outcome was now clear: Prussia was triumphant, while France lay "humbled, bleeding," a once glorious nation reduced to a "second-rate power."[41]

Two rival impulses jostled with each other in relation to this international dimension. On the one hand, Americans who looked abroad saw strong grounds to reaffirm their nation's exceptional character. Only the great beacon of democracy and of liberty could have invented the common school; having done so, it had established a model which all other nations were desperately trying to emulate. This perception was not merely the product of national boastfulness. A stream of foreign visitors conveyed the same message. In 1870/71, the Connecticut School Board reported an address by an English minister, Reverend William M. Taylor, to an educational convention at Hartford. The schools of New England, Taylor told his audience, were a shining light for educational reformers everywhere. "The fame of them has gone abroad," Taylor told the audience, "they are talked about, and written about in my own country."[42] French interest in the American system was if anything even higher. In 1876, as part of the Centennial Exposition in Philadelphia, the French government commissioned Ferdinand Buisson along with five colleagues to report on the organization, teaching methods, and pedagogic outcomes of the free school system. Buisson was a future national director of primary education who would become a leading figure in the drive to secularize the French system. When the 677-page report was published two years later, it was celebrated as the most comprehensive and detailed survey yet produced. The Secretary of the Connecticut Board of Education summarized Buisson's findings. To an extent unparalleled elsewhere, the United States had made "public instruction the supreme guarantee of its liberties, the condition of its prosperity, the safeguard of its institutions." The foreign observer could not help but be impressed by the enthusiasm of Americans for their free schools and their unshakeable belief that mass instruction lay at the basis of national greatness.[43]

Underlying such exchanges and comparisons was a sense of confronting common challenges, and one of the most pressing was what was commonly termed the "religious difficulty." American commentators often expressed the view that their nation was not alone in struggling to reconcile the demand for mass education with the fact of growing religious diversity. As debate raged in 1869, England was preparing for what seemed an analogous confrontation. In that year, a National Education League was established to lobby for a national system of schools based on the principles of compulsory attendance and local funding. In addition, the League called for religious and secular teaching to be made distinct, with the former provided by churches at their own cost.[44] The American press took an intense interest in the battle between English secularists and their clerical opponents. As in America, the League's proposals had been assailed, the *New York Times* noted, by both Protestants and Catholics.[45] The following year, the press reported the outcome. The Elementary Education Act (1870) created Great Britain's first taxpayer-funded primary education system. It allowed schools the choice to offer religious teaching or not, and included a "conscience clause" for parents who objected to the form of such teaching. But few American commentators thought that the religious issue was settled, either in Great Britain or at home. As the *North American Review* concluded, this was the latest phase in "that irrepressible conflict between medieval authority and modern civilization on the great battle-field of education, which is being waged over the whole of Europe, and of which America has not seen the last."[46]

As the Bible Wars raged at home, various parties drew on the international dimension to further their case. In Cincinnati, defenders of the Bible routinely cited the example of Prussia, drawing on the report prepared decades earlier by Calvin Stowe. In Stowe's assessment, the Bible was at the heart of the Prussian classroom. At each level, the Bible was deployed to impress moral lessons, to aid students to decipher the natural world, and to explore the lessons of history. Far from simply reciting excerpts, students were encouraged to ask questions of the teacher and to discuss the moral and practical implications of each text. And all of this was accomplished, in Stowe's view, without the slightest hint of what he called "sectarian particularities." Every teacher with whom he discussed the subject, Stowe reported, was indignant at the notion that the Bible injected sectarian bias or division into the classroom. Such an allegation, Stowe reported with approval, was "spurned with contempt" by this body of committed and sincere Christian teachers.[47] Such was Stowe's enthusiasm for the Prussian system that he recommended Ohio adopt it in its entirety. This would involve a considerable escalation of resources and effort in what was still a fledgling society. But Stowe was unfazed. "If it can be done in Prussia," he asserted, "I know it can be done in Ohio."[48]

The example of Europe was just as prominent in the court battles that followed the 1869 Cincinnati decision to ban the Bible. In his submission to the Cincinnati Superior Court in favor of Bible-reading, William M. Ramsey drew on the work of both Stowe and Mann to prove that a combination of religious and secular instruction, even in schools which mixed Protestants, Catholics, and Jews, could be managed successfully. In Prussia, he told the Court, Protestant and Catholic children received explicitly religious instruction separately, and all sects strove to ensure the harmony and success of the system.[49] Another member of the legal team seeking to overturn the 1869 vote, George Sage, appealed to a spirit of national pride. The American common school, Sage argued, served as a model for European nations which now understood the importance of mass education to national success. But just at the moment when "all the world has set its approval" upon the American approach, the city of Cincinnati was proposing to strip the common school of one of its greatest strengths, the power of the Bible to train students in morals. None of the European imitators of the common school would even think, Sage told the Court, of adopting this "crude idea of secularizing education"; all knew from experience that religious and secular education could happily coexist.[50] America's much vaunted lead in education was on the point of being thrown away by a reckless clique of secularists.

Leading Catholics, in turn, looked to the nations of continental Europe to make a very different case. The experience there proved the practicality as well as the justice of state support for denominational schools. In this regard, the despotic powers of Europe had put republican America to shame. In an exchange with the *Independent* on the question of dividing the school fund, Isaac Hecker, the son of German immigrants and founder of the Paulist fathers, described the plight of poor American Catholics forced to contribute through their taxes to a school system which did not recognize their faith and which was saturated with Protestant sectarianism. Catholics in authoritarian Prussia and Austria, however, faced no such discrimination. Surely, Hecker asked, the great republic could frame educational policies that were as equitable as those of the monarchies of Austria and Prussia? All that Catholics asked, he concluded, was the access to state funding that was enjoyed by the subjects of the despotisms of Europe.[51] This strategy of using the European example to prick an inflated belief in national superiority was followed by other Catholic leaders. In 1876, the Bishop of Rochester, Bernard J. McQuaid debated Francis Abbot before the Free Religious Association in Boston. McQuaid was a fervent advocate of Catholic education, working assiduously throughout his long tenure in Rochester to build up a system of parochial schools. McQuaid provocatively argued that on the question of schooling, the rights of religious minorities were better respected in Europe than at home. Americans liked to vaunt the superiority of their democracy over Old World despotisms. But they should remember, McQuaid argued, that the despotism of Prussia or Austria "never goes so far as to interfere with the religious convictions of Catholic, Jew, or Evangelical." These authoritarian regimes had managed to accommodate freedom of conscience in their state-run schools, and Americans should heed the lesson. "The wisdom and good sense of the world," he reminded his audience, "are not concentrated in the American people."[52]

Secularists, however, deployed the international dimension with greater effectiveness than their opponents. On the one hand, in a strategy which was familiar from the Sunday mail battle of the Jacksonian era, secularists pounced on any allusion to Europe as proof that their opponents wished to enact a state church. For one of the lawyers defending the Cincinnati Board, Stanley Mathews, the fact that all the foreign examples cited by proponents of Bible-reading came from regimes with established churches "is sufficient to show the source of the opinion, and to turn the example into a warning."[53] Secularists also turned the example of states like Prussia and France against their opponents by arguing that it revealed their hypocrisy. The key point here was that none of these systems imposed one version of the Bible on students from different faiths. Mathews cited a report on continental schools by the Englishman Mathew Arnold. In France, Catholic, Protestant, and Jewish boys all received instruction from ministers of their creed; as a result, there were no complaints of proselytism. A similar balance between different faiths was the rule in the German states. Mathews was not advocating the adoption of such a system in Ohio. But he could not resist contrasting this fair-minded approach with his opponents' belief that only the Protestant Bible should be read in the classroom. This was a policy, Mathews argued, which "excludes the Catholic and insults the Jew," and which compared unfavorably with the more balanced approach adopted in continental Europe.[54]

Secularists also cited the example of Prussia to show that Bible-reading in schools was no guarantee of either popular piety or elevated morals. The incidence of crime and vice was higher in Prussia than in the United States, and its elites were notoriously tainted by religious skepticism. Such observations were confirmed by foreign visitors. In 1873, for example, a Professor Heikel from Finland addressed the Ohio State Teachers

Association. In the midst of a typically effusive account of the school system that he had spent months observing, Heikel turned to the question of Bible-reading. In both Prussia and his native Finland, Heikel told the Ohio teachers, teachers spent hours each week forcing their students to memorize episodes of biblical history and to mouth long passages from Scripture. In contrast to this, the presence of religion in American classrooms was light. But what American schools did offer was an unmatched level of discipline and order. The outcome of each approach was clear. The United States far exceeded these European states both in its popular attachment to religion and in its level of public morality.[55]

Finally, secularists took heart from the evidence that enlightened international opinion was moving in their direction. In the decade after the close of the Civil War, the efforts of various European governments to secularize their education systems were widely reported, and many commentators saw the influence of the American model at work. In Cincinnati, the superintendent of schools described the poor state of education in Great Britain before the passage of the 1870 Education Act. The key problem was sectarian control. Citing Mathew Arnold, the superintendent described a school system weakened by denominational jealousy. As the many English observers of the American approach were coming to understand, achievement of a "great, harmonious, and efficient system" would remain a distant goal "until the State has entirely cut loose from the church, and resolved to act independently of all sects" in its approach to education.[56] As school boards moved to follow Cincinnati's lead after 1869, these references to Europe multiplied. In an 1870 sermon to his Broadway congregation, Joseph P. Thompson, one of the founding editors of the *Independent*, declared his support for removing the King James Bible from schools on the grounds that more and more parents saw it as a sectarian text. He then drew on the example of England to show that this was the path of enlightened nations everywhere. England was finally moving toward a system that would be both unsectarian and secular, though the reforms proposed to date showed that it was sadly "not yet free from the embarrassments of the religious question."[57] Thompson then cited a survey by a Belgian pedagogue, Émile de Laveleye. In an exhaustive study of various national systems of popular instruction, Laveleye ranked America ahead of all others as the only one founded on "sound and enduring principles." Chief among these, Thompson reported, was that it gave "secular instruction without any connection with religion."[58]

As ever, it was Prussia that attracted most attention. At precisely the moment when advocates of the Bible in schools were pointing to the Prussian example, the forces unleashed by Chancellor Otto von Bismarck's *Kulturkampf* appeared to be pushing the nation toward a more secular system. In 1871, the *New York Times* explained the *Kulturkampf* as a government attack on hostile religious forces, and particularly the Catholic Church. But in the eyes of the American press, liberal forces in Bismarck's Germany were just as intent on removing Protestant control of the education system. In this task, their inspiration was the great republic. What Bismarck and his fellow reformers wished to achieve was "a system of popular schools which shall be as free from influence of Church or State as our own." While it might take several years for such a program to be enacted, its final victory, the "complete secularization of all public institutions," was assured.[59] The following year, the press reported the first steps toward this goal. The *Times* informed its readers that Bismarck was now pushing for what it called a "downright secularism," or the strict separation of church and school.[60] Such a policy was aimed at combating the power of the Catholic Church in the wake of the 1869 ecumenical council, but Protestant churches were caught up in it as well. The *New York Herald* similarly reported that "the secularist movement in Germany gains ground daily," and that both Protestants and Catholics were feeling its effects.[61]

Bible-Reading and the Puritan Legacy

Alongside the international dimension was a vigorous contest over history. In the case of Bible-reading, the battle concerned the founders in the colonial rather than the Revolutionary era. Looming over the school question was the ambiguous and increasingly divisive figure of the Puritan. For defenders of religious instruction, the common school with the Bible at its heart was one of the Puritans' most enduring legacies. In an address to the Ohio State Teachers Association, Michigan teacher David Putnam traced the origins of the American common school directly to the first settlers in Massachusetts Bay. "Hardly," he declared, "had the first rude cabins been erected, or the first acres been cleared of the primitive forests, when our fathers began to provide for the instruction of their children." This impulse was soon codified into law. As early as 1647, Putnam reminded his audience, a law in the colony of Massachusetts stipulated that every town which reached a population of fifty householders was obliged to provide for the instruction of its children. In this way, the hardy Puritans laid the "deep and strong foundations" on which the "magnificent structure of our modern school system has been built."[62] The Puritans cherished education because they revered the Bible. As a contributor to the *Massachusetts Teacher* argued, the men who established the common school "believed in the Bible and loved it." They desired all children to read and study it themselves, and from this simple ambition came the modern common school. The Bible in schools would be safe, the author concluded, as long as the descendants of the Puritans cherished their memory.[63]

The problem with linking Bible-reading to the Puritans was that more and more Americans were coming to a darker vision of these colonial settlers. The South, as we have seen, had long decried the air of religious fanaticism which pervaded New England and which had envenomed, in southern eyes, the national debate over slavery before the Civil War. Now, anti-Puritan sentiment flowered in other sections as well. In works of history, newspapers, and Congressional debates, the Puritans were increasingly depicted as religious fanatics who, having fled persecution in England, made their Massachusetts Bay colony a home of intolerance.

Hostility to the Puritans flared in relation to a range of issues. One was the commemoration of their most famous adversary, Roger Williams. On January 11, 1872, Congressman Benjamin Eames informed the House that his state, Rhode Island, had selected Williams as its contribution to the National Statuary Hall in the Capitol Building. Established in 1864, the Hall gathered marble and bronze statues of distinguished men and women from each state in the union. In his speech, Eames recounted the key moments in Williams' life. A Puritan himself, Williams had quickly fallen foul of the intolerant regime established in colonial Massachusetts. For the crime of espousing heterodox religious views, and particularly for insisting that the jurisdiction of the state extended only to civil and not to religious matters, Williams was in 1635 convicted of sedition and heresy by the General Court, and banished from the Massachusetts Bay colony. In exile, Eames reminded the House, Williams founded the colony of Rhode Island as a haven of religious liberty. This was Williams' gift to the nation. He was the "great advocate and defender of soul liberty," a man who more than any other deserved to be recognized as the inspirer of the eminently American principle that church and state "should be entirely and absolutely separate."[64] Religious liberty had its origin not in the Puritans, but in their staunchest opponent.

All of this was too much for Eames' fellow Republican, Nathaniel Banks of Massachusetts. Banks began by disputing the picture of Williams as a victim of religious persecution. Instead, he described a troublemaker who stubbornly refused to accept the rule of law and whose open defiance of the authorities threatened to destabilize a still fragile and isolated settlement. Furthermore, Banks argued, it was unfair to see the Puritans as the enemies of religious liberty. Their commitment to this principle was sincere, but always balanced by the needs of state. As pragmatists, the Puritans believed in freedom to the extent that it could be reconciled with "practical government."[65] Banks' impassioned defense of the New England founders in turn drew a series of rebukes from the representatives of neighboring states. Democrat Samuel Cox of New York issued a particularly scathing assessment. The Puritans, Cox told the House, were despots of the worst kind, erecting a system of government without "one element of democratic, religious or civil liberty." The nation should be forever thankful that the Revolution had cleansed the nation of this Puritan stain.[66] In 1872, a marble statue of Roger Williams by the prominent sculptor Franklin Simmons took its place in the Statuary Hall.

Another forum for debating the character and legacy of the Puritans was Forefathers' Day (December 22). First held in 1769, Forefathers' Day commemorated the landing of the Pilgrims at Plymouth on December 21, 1620. The strongly Puritan Massachusetts Bay Colony came about eight years later. But few nineteenth-century commentators saw any meaningful distinction between the Pilgrims and Puritans, and Forefathers' Day became an invitation to denounce the zealots who had banished Roger Williams.[67] The temptation was particularly strong in the mid-Western states. One Cleveland newspaper attacked the practice of celebrating the Puritans each December 22. Their modern-day descendants should remember, the paper argued, that these men and women whose memory they so venerated were "bred in the school of persecution" and had begun, almost as soon as they disembarked, "to persecute all who would not subscribe to their iron-clad creed."[68] The *Cincinnati Enquirer* took the opportunity to debunk the myth that the Puritans believed in religious liberty. Though eulogized as a saint in the New England states, the paper argued, it should be remembered that the Puritan "came to America to found religious liberty not for all the world, but only for himself."[69]

This debate about the legacy of the Puritans shaped the case against Bible-reading in different ways. Some sought to discredit the claim that

Bible-reading was an act of homage to the Puritan forebears. As William W. Patton argued, the Puritans were firmly of the view that the Bible be expounded rather than merely read. As such, they would have been shocked at the "naked Bible-reading" practiced in American schools. The "last authority" that should be appealed to by defenders of Bible-reading, then, was these "pious forefathers" who used Scripture in schools not as a reading book but as a textbook.[70] But more often, the secularist argument drew on a set of negative images of the Puritans as persecutors. The historical record, they argued, was clear and dismal. The Puritans had no conception of civil liberty, requiring all voters to belong to an orthodox congregation. Nor could they tolerate dissent, banning Catholics, exiling theological opponents and most shockingly, launching a harsh crackdown on Quakers that included imprisonment, floggings, and from 1659 to 1661, four public hangings. How, then, could their views on religious education carry any weight? Writing in the *Independent*, W.T. Clarke argued that, in deciding whether or not to keep the Bible in schools, there should be no recourse to the discredited Puritan legacy. We should never pay heed, he wrote, to the opinions of "the men who flogged Baptists and hung Quakers."[71] Samuel T. Spear took a more constitutional stance. The Puritan school, he argued, was the embodiment of a "legally-preferred religion." As such, it was incompatible with the modern-day understanding of civil government and should be quietly discarded.[72]

WILLIAM TORREY HARRIS AND MORAL EDUCATION

For a decade after the Cincinnati Board's bombshell in 1869, defenders and opponents of Bible-reading had battled in local districts, debating halls and legislatures, and the columns of the press. Neither side, however, could claim a clear victory. In school districts with relatively homogenous Protestant populations, the use of the King James Bible continued largely as before. In Pennsylvania, the Bible was read in 12,756 of 18,607 public schools in 1877–1878. Furthermore, there was little sign of a trend away from the practice, for this figure represented a decrease of only 152 from the previous year.[73] In New York State, 56% of cities in an 1889 survey reported daily Bible-reading, while in 20% the practice was banned.[74] In New York City, an 1877 by law mandated the reading of Scripture during morning exercises. Furthermore, the absence of the Bible did not render a school wholly secular. Many school readers remained imbued with Protestant references and imagery, celebrating the triumphs of the Reformation and its leaders, and adding a strong dose of anti-Catholic venom.[75]

Nevertheless, it would be a mistake to underestimate the shift that had occurred. Various school boards in New York State—among them Troy, Rochester, Albany, and Buffalo—as well as the cities of Chicago, New Haven, and Atlanta followed Cincinnati's lead in banning the Bible. In 1890, the Wisconsin Supreme Court decreed that Bible-reading was inherently sectarian and therefore unconstitutional. Even in states such as Pennsylvania where Bible-reading remained relatively common, local compromises were sometimes hammered out to assuage Catholic sensibilities. In 1871, the *Pennsylvania School Journal* reported a dispute in Plains County, where a School Board had rejected Catholic demands for the King James Bible to be excluded. Criticizing the decision, the journal noted that the Board should have opted for a compromise, with Bible-reading reserved to the close of the day rather than the opening, thereby allowing students to avoid it if they wished. This was the solution adopted, according to the journal, in many local districts.[76] Even when morning readings were the rule, there were signs that the use of the Bible was seen as little more than perfunctory. As R. Laurence Moore argues, even its most committed proponents no longer saw Bible-reading as a means of imparting Divine truths to students. Instead, it was justified on pragmatic grounds as a form of moral training.[77] Finally, the trend in school readers was away from Protestant triumphalism. The revised McGuffey reader of 1879 contained fewer Biblical references, for example, than the previous 1857 version.[78]

The strength and limitations of the push for secular schools were apparent in the career of William Torrey Harris. If Horace Mann was the dominant figure in shaping the antebellum school system, Harris assumed that mantle in the Gilded Age and Progressive eras. In St. Louis, he oversaw one of the fastest growing and most extensive public school networks in the nation, seizing the opportunity to implement a number of innovative and influential reforms. Chief among these was the introduction of the kindergarten in 1873, considered a radical experiment at the time, but later adopted by cities across the nation. By the mid-1870s, Harris enjoyed a national reputation as a leading educational theorist, a man whose views on the management and organization of schools carried immense weight both with his fellow educators and with the broader public. As such, he was the natural choice to serve as National Commissioner of Education from 1889 to 1906.[79]

Harris was an avowed secularist in regard to schools as well as to the state. But he was singular in showing very little anti-Catholic animosity. Perhaps as a result of his experience in St. Louis, a city with a large German-born population, Harris was convinced that the Catholic laity were by and large committed to a separation of church and state, and suspected that much of the clergy were of the same view. Even in his opposition to parochial schools, Harris refrained from attacking the church. In an 1876 article for the *Atlantic Monthly*, Harris was adamant that the state should not encourage in any way a denominational or parochial school system which might become a rival to the common schools. But rather than drawing on religious prejudice, Harris staked this argument solely to a vision of social cohesion. The common school was crucial in cultivating the mutual respect and cooperation which were the basis of social harmony. Only in the common schools, he argued, did children learn "to know, love, and respect each other."[80] Religious schools, whether Protestant or Catholic, bred instead narrow-mindedness and bigotry.

Harris saw the necessity of moral training, but argued that it occurred naturally in a well-organized school. What, after all, was morality, and how was it best acquired? In a statement of educational philosophy which he helped to draft in his position as National Education Commissioner, Harris responded to the first question by stating that the "essence of moral behavior is self-control."[81] As to the best manner of acquiring this self-control, Harris favored habit over instruction. Morality, he wrote, "consists in practice rather than in theory," and the key was "not to learn correct doctrines on the subject of virtue and vice" but to acquire instead "correct habits."[82] Merely by attending school, by conforming to the rules and expectations of the classroom, and by imitating the example of their teachers, pupils would develop the self-control that was the hallmark of a virtuous citizen. Regulated interactions with fellow students worked to the same effect. Precisely because it occurred almost without the student being aware of it, this cultivation of what Harris termed "moral acts of self-control" was far more effective than the perfunctory reading of the Bible. Compared to the good behavior and firm self-discipline demanded of pupils every day in a well-run school, Bible exercises were sadly inefficient.

There was one class of students, however, who still required a firm religious hand. These belonged to a race that Harris deemed to be primitive, Native Americans. In 1895, Harris addressed the men and women who gathered annually at Lake Mohonk, New York, to discuss Indian affairs and debate appropriate government policies. For Harris, Native Americans were still firmly locked in the "lower stadia of civilization," the tribal phase. Education, Harris argued, was the necessary destructive agent which would free Indians from their tribal relations and allow them to progress upward toward the apex of civilization occupied by whites. Central to this education was a thorough Christianization. "The Christian idea of the family, of society, of the State, and of the church," Harris argued, "must become theirs by adoption."[83] Harris was not strictly arguing for Bible instruction. But many other white reformers were. Lamenting the trend toward what he regarded as godlessness in the common schools of Pennsylvania, Edward Magill, the President of Swarthmore College, warned against any temptation to adopt a similar approach in Indian education. An instruction that neglected the moral and spiritual elements, he argued, would never lift the Indian out of a state of savagery.[84] Again and again through the 1880s, speakers at Lake Mohonk warned against any temptation to transplant the secular theory of education to the tribal school. Posing the question "What is an ideal Indian school," Dr. William Hayes Ward listed religious instruction as one of its essential features. Ward was the editor of the *Independent*, a journal which opposed Bible-reading in white schools. Religious instruction was no longer, he conceded, the ideal in public schools. Yet, "it is and must be for the Indian." There could be no overlap in this regard between the two sorts of schools. "I do not think," he told those present, "that the parallel holds at all between the public school in the civilized community and the Indian school."[85]

The question of Indian education shows once again the racial bias within the argument for a strict separation of church and state. Only white Americans had that critical quality which enabled religious control to be safely lifted, the capacity for self-government. Indigenous peoples, mired in their primitive state, required still a firm religious tutelage. This explains why a particularly egregious example of a religious establishment in the nineteenth century, the alliance between the federal government and missionaries to the Indian tribes, attracted so little opposition. As early as 1819, Congress created the "Civilization Fund" to support mission schools among various tribes. Under President Grant's "Peace Policy" which aimed to assimilate the tribes, missionaries from various denominations served on the government's Board of Indian Commissioners. In contrast to policies that affected white Americans, such as Sabbath laws or Bible-reading, this blurring of religion and government raised only a muted protest. There was a consensus among whites that the essential work of civilizing the tribes required their conversion to Christianity, and that it was in the government's interest to support the process. Yet even here, the secularizing trends in the broader society were beginning to have an impact. When Harris made his speech in 1895, the propriety of government funding for mission schools was under challenge. In 1889, Commissioner of Indian Affairs, Thomas J. Morgan, proposed a system of government schools, and a decade later, state funding of mission schools came to an end. But secularization in the sphere of Indian education had clear limits. Indigenous students were required, for example, to attend church and Sunday School, and received nonsectarian instruction.[86]

Education and the Meaning of Secularism

One definite outcome of the Bible Wars was that more and more Americans now identified themselves as "secularists." The term was not new and had long been contested. When it first entered American public life before the Civil War, the religious press immediately labeled it a rebadged form of atheism. In 1853, the *Christian Examiner* informed its readers of a growing movement in England led by the reformer George Jacob Holyoake. This movement, which called itself secularist, claimed to represent a third way between positive belief and outright atheism. Secularists, the paper reported, were noncommittal as to the possibility of salvation and the existence of an afterlife, opting instead to accept only those truths which could be validated by experience and which contributed to improving the lived experience of men and women. But readers, the journal warned, should not be fooled. By denying the validity of the "positive, demonstrable and unanswerable evidences" of the truth of Christianity, these secularists were among the "dangerous phalanx of infidels and atheists" which seemed to be gaining ground among the working classes of England.[87]

Largely as a result of agitation on the school question, the term "secularist" acquired a different and much more acceptable connotation after the Civil War. Samuel T. Spear identified himself as one of the growing numbers of Protestants who were embracing the term. These Protestants, he argued, were "*secularists* in respect to the ends and functions of civil government" as well as "the purposes, and hence the management, of the public schools." What did these secularists believe? Their guiding doctrine, Spear contended, was that the state should have nothing to do with spiritual matters. Government should not actively hinder religion, but nor could it be drawn into favoring any particular expression of belief, or even belief over non-belief. In relation to the claims of religion, Spear argued, the only constitutionally valid approach was what he called "masterly inactivity."[88]

For both Spear and his opponents, the school question had bolstered the ranks of these secularists. In 1876, the *New York Evangelist* saw a battle between three forces: conservatives, Catholics, and secularists. The last party wished all "vestiges of religious instruction to be swept out of all the schools."[89] Another defender of the Bible to see a growing mass of secularists was one of the veterans of the Cincinnati battle, the Unitarian Reverend Amory D. Mayo. As a member of the Board of Education, Mayo had fought against the proposal to ban religious instruction, and in the years after 1869, he emerged as one of the most vocal advocates of keeping the King James Bible in the common school. In 1873, Mayo denounced the "growing party of 'secularism' in public education." Its aim, he wrote, was to remove all traces of faith from the nation's classrooms, to "deodorize," as he put it, "the school atmosphere of religious infection."[90] Who were these secularists? Mayo saw them as little more than a dressed-up party of atheists trying to foist their radical European ideals onto a susceptible American public. The secular movement, as he argued in a lecture on Sabbath laws, stemmed from the "materialistic and atheistic philosophers and political agitators of Europe." But even Mayo was forced to concede that a great many sincere and intelligent Protestants now embraced the term. What Mayo regarded as "secular sophistry" was now well on the way to becoming a legitimate American doctrine.[91]

The term secularist would never shed entirely its association with atheism. But through the Bible Wars, the press began to define a secularist as a person who believed that religious instruction was a private and not a public responsibility. Secularists were not, as one paper argued, "atheistical fanatics." They simply held that the state had no right to educate its citizens in anything other than temporal matters, and that the work of religious training should be left to the home or the religious school.[92] Such people could now be found even in the halls of Congress.[93] In May 1878, Republican Senator Stanley Matthews of Ohio made the following statement of belief. He was a firm believer in

God and had no doubt that children should be exposed to the power of faith. But training citizens in religious doctrine was in no way the government's responsibility. "I think the state," Matthews argued, "should attend simply to secular functions and leave all education of a spiritual kind to institutions ordained for that purpose." It was in this sense, he told the Senate, that "I am a secularist."[94]

NOTES

1. *Cincinnati Commercial*, September 7, 1869. The decision did not affect the city's African-American schools, which until 1874 were governed by a separate board.
2. *Cincinnati Enquirer*, September 14, 1869.
3. On the Cincinnati controversy, Ward M. McAfee, *Religion, Race and Reconstruction: The Public School in the Politics of the 1870s* (Albany: State University of New York, 1998), 27–41; Green, *Bible, the School and the Constitution*; and Stephan F. Brumberg, "The Cincinnati Bible War (1869–73) and Its Impact on the Education of the City's Protestants, Catholics and Jews," *American Jewish Archives Journal* 54, no. 2 (2002): 11–46.
4. *Hartford Daily Courant*, November 10, 1869.
5. Henry Martyn Scudder, *The Catholics and the Public Schools* (New York: Mason, Baker & Pratt, 1873), 3.
6. There is a large literature on the historical relationship between religion and schools. In addition to works cited below, see Joan DelFattore, *The Fourth R: Conflicts Over Religion in America's Public Schools* (New Haven: Yale University Press, 2004); Benjamin Justice and Colin Macleod, *Have a Little Faith: Religion, Democracy and the American Public School* (Chicago: University of Chicago Press, 2016). An interesting comparative study is Damon Mayrl, *Secular Conversions: Political Institutions and Religious Education in the United States and Australia, 1800–2000* (Cambridge: Cambridge University Press, 2016)
7. Horace Mann, *Annual Reports on Education* (Boston: Horace B. Fuller, 1868), 730. Emphasis in original.
8. *Milwaukee Sentinel*, December 12, 1871.
9. *Boston Investigator*, September 24, 1873.
10. *Report of the Committee on Schools and Views of the Minority of the Board of Education of the New Haven City School District, Concerning the Discontinuance of Religious Exercises in the Public Schools* (New Haven: Tuttle, Morehouse & Taylor, 1878), 10.
11. William W. Patton, *Purely Secular Public Schools: An Address on the Bible and the Public Schools Delivered in Farwell Hall, Chicago, Sunday, Sept. 24, 1876* (Chicago: Lakeside Publishing, 1876), 1.

12. Naomi W. Cohen, *Jews in Christian America: The Pursuit of Religious Equality* (New York: Oxford University Press, 1992), 85.
13. *Israelite*, October 8, 1869.
14. *Jewish Times* (New York), December 10, 1869.
15. *Jewish Times*, November 12, 1869.
16. Rufus W. Clark, *The Question of the Hour; the Bible and the School Fund* (Boston: Lee and Shepard, 1870), 36.
17. *Report of the Committee on Schools*, 3.
18. Ibid., 4.
19. *Catholic World* 11, no. 61 (1870): 94.
20. Scudder, *Catholics and the Public Schools*, 12.
21. Eugene Lawrence, "The Romish Victory Over the Common Schools," *Harper's Weekly* (1872): 974.
22. *Philadelphia Inquirer*, December 15, 1875. Clipping in Francis Ellingwood Abbot papers, Box 64, Harvard University Archives, Cambridge.
23. Scudder, *Catholics and the Public Schools*, 12.
24. *Philadelphia Inquirer*, December 15, 1875.
25. *Atlantic Monthly*, May 1, 1870.
26. *Nation*, November 18, 1869.
27. John Y. Simon, ed., *The Papers of Ulysses S. Grant*, vol. 26 (Carbondale: Southern Illinois University Press, 2003), 343–44.
28. *Cincinnati Daily Gazette*, December 2, 1875.
29. Simon, ed., *Papers of Ulysses S. Grant*, vol. 26, 388.
30. John Y. Simon, ed., *The Papers of Ulysses S. Grant*, vol. 29 (Carbondale: Southern Illinois University Press, 2008), 46.
31. *Cincinnati Daily Gazette*, January 10, 1876.
32. *Daily Graphic* (New York), December 9, 1875.
33. *Patriot* (Harrisburg, PA), December 9, 1875.
34. *Harper's Weekly*, December 25, 1875.
35. Cited in Green, *Bible, the School and the Constitution*, 219.
36. *Pomeroy's Democrat* (New York), August 19, 1876.
37. Green, *Bible, the School and the Constitution*, 219.
38. *Daily Graphic*, August 8, 1876.
39. Calvin E. Stowe, *Report on Elementary Public Instruction in Europe* (Columbus: S. Medary, 1837); Horace Mann, *Report of an Educational Tour in Germany, and Parts of Great Britain and Ireland* (London: Simpkin, Marshall and Company, 1846).
40. Francis Adams, *The Free School System of the United States* (London: Chapman & Hall, 1875), 5.
41. Henry Wilson, "New Departure of the Republican Party," *Atlantic Monthly* (January 1871): 111.

42. *Annual Report of the Board of Education of the State of Connecticut* (New Haven: Tuttle, Morehouse & Taylor, 1871), 103.
43. *Annual Report of the Board of Education of the State of Connecticut* (New Haven: Tuttle, Morehouse & Taylor, 1879), 56. Buisson's report appeared as *Rapport sur l'instruction primaire à l'Exposition universelle de Philadelphie en 1876* (Paris: Imprimerie nationale, 1878).
44. *The National Education League: Its Objects, Its Gains, Its Wants* (1870), available at: http://www.jstor.org/stable/60201195.
45. *New York Times*, December 4, 1869.
46. Goldwin Smith, "The Ecclesiastical Crisis in England," *North American Review* 110, no. 226 (1870): 166.
47. Stowe, *Report on Elementary Public Instruction in Europe*, 16.
48. Ibid., 44.
49. *Arguments in Favor of the Use of the Bible in the Public Schools* (Cincinnati: Robert Clarke, 1870), 14.
50. Ibid., 153.
51. *Catholic World* 13, no. 74 (1871): 252.
52. *The Public School Question as Understood by a Catholic American Citizen and by a Liberal American Citizen* (Boston: Free Religious Association, 1876), 54.
53. *Arguments against the Use of the Bible in the Public Schools. By J.B. Stallo, George Hoady, and Stanley Matthews, Counsel for the Defendants. In the Case of John D. Minor Versus the Board of Education of the City of Cincinnati in the Superior Court of Cincinnati* (Cincinnati: Robert Clarke, 1870), 140.
54. Ibid., 142.
55. *Proceedings of the Twenty-Fifth Annual Meeting of the Ohio Teachers' Association* (Columbus: Office of the Ohio Education Monthly, 1873?), 72–73.
56. *Common Schools of Cincinnati, Thirty-Ninth Annual Report* (Cincinnati: Times Steam Book, 1868), 58–59.
57. Joseph P. Thompson, *Shall Our Common Schools Be Destroyed? An Argument against Perverting the School-Fund to Sectarian Uses* (New York: E O Jenkins, 1870), 22.
58. Ibid., 26.
59. *New York Times*, September 11, 1871.
60. *New York Times*, March 4, 1872.
61. *New York Herald*, March 9, 1872.
62. *Proceedings of the Twenty-Fifth Annual Meeting*, 39.
63. *Massachusetts Teacher*, March 1, 1870.
64. *Congressional Globe*, vol. 66, part 1 (1871–72), 363.
65. Ibid., 367.

66. Ibid., 370.
67. See Chapter 4, Note 57.
68. *Plain Dealer* (Cleveland), December 23, 1868.
69. *Cincinnati Daily Enquirer*, December 22, 1868. On Forefathers' Day, James W. Baker, *Thanksgiving: The Biography of an American Holiday* (Durham: University of New Hampshire Press, 2009), 63–64.
70. Patton, *Purely Secular Public Schools*, 7.
71. *Independent*, March 2, 1876.
72. Spear, *Religion and the State*, 369–70.
73. *Report of the Commissioner of Education for the Year 1878* (Washington, DC: Government Printing Office, 1880), 204. These figures exclude Philadelphia, which did not measure the practice.
74. Benjamin Justice, *The War That Wasn't: Religious Conflict and Compromise in the Common Schools of New York State, 1865–1900* (Albany: State University of New York, 2005), 181.
75. Ruth Miller Elson, *Guardians of Tradition: American Schoolbooks in the Nineteenth Century* (Lincoln: University of Nebraska Press, 1964).
76. *Pennsylvania School Journal*, vol. 19 (Lancaster: Wylie & Griest, 1870–71), 274.
77. R. Laurence Moore, "Bible Reading and Nonsectarian Schooling: The Failure of Religious Instruction in Nineteenth-Century Public Education," *Journal of American History* 86, no. 4 (2000): 1581–99.
78. McAfee, *Religion, Race and Reconstruction*, 39; John H. Westerhoff III, *McGuffey and His Readers, Piety, Morality and Education in Nineteenth-Century America* (Nashville: Abington, 1979).
79. On Harris, see Merle Curti, *The Social Ideas of American Educators* (Paterson, NJ: Littlefield, Adams, 1965), 310–47; Green, *Bible, School and the Constitution*, 203–6.
80. William T. Harris, "The Division of School Funds for Religious Purposes," *Atlantic Monthly* 38, no. 266 (1876): 176.
81. *Report of the Committee of Fifteen* (Boston, 1895), 41.
82. "Report of Committee on Moral Education to the National Council of Education," Box 2, Folder 35, William Torrey Harris Papers, Manuscript Division, Library of Congress, Washington, DC.
83. *Proceedings of the Thirteenth Annual Meeting of the Lake Mohonk Conference of Friends of the Indian* (Lake Mohonk conference, 1896), 38.
84. *Proceedings of the Fifth Annual Meeting of the Lake Mohonk Conference of Friends of the Indian* (Philadelphia: Sherman and Co., 1887), 61.
85. *Proceedings of the Seventh Annual Meeting of the Lake Mohonk Conference of Friends of the Indian* (Lake Mohonk Conference, 1889), 61.

86. R. Pierce Beaver, *Church, State, and the American Indians* (St. Louis, MO: Concordia Publishing House, 1966); Henry Warner Bowden, *American Indians and Christian Missions* (Chicago: University of Chicago Press, 1981); and Francis Paul Prucha, *American Indian Policy in Crisis: Christian Reformers and the Indian, 1865–1900* (Norman: University of Oklahoma Press, 1976).
87. *Christian Examiner and Religious Miscellany* 55, no. 2 (1853): 286–87.
88. Ibid., 141.
89. *New York Evangelist*, October 26, 1876.
90. *New York Times*, August 1, 1873.
91. *Cincinnati Commercial*, October 2, 1871.
92. *Democrat and Chronicle* (Rochester), May 1, 1876.
93. *Lowell Daily Citizen and News*, December 2, 1879.
94. 7 Cong. Rec. 3813 (1878), May 27, 1878.

CHAPTER 8

"Sunday Clubs for Wealthy People": Taxing the Churches

In 1873, the publication of a set of census figures triggered an intense public debate about the growth of religious power in the republic. Tucked away in the Census Bureau's voluminous analysis of the 1870 survey was a report on the amount of property held by religious corporations. The Bureau claimed this to be the most accurate assessment yet undertaken, and the results were astonishing. Church property was valued at $354,483,581. But just as noteworthy as the raw figure was the trend. With each decade the value of church property had more or less doubled, from $87,328,801 in 1850 and $171,397,932 in 1860. Under the long-standing exemption for property devoted to religious purposes, much of this wealth escaped taxation.

The census statistics drew a flurry of commentary, with several newspapers breaking down the raw data further. The *New York Times* published ranking tables detailing the increase in church property in percentage terms. Particularly telling was the growth relative to church membership. Rapid population growth might of its own accord be expected to bring larger congregations, more church edifices and greater wealth. But as the paper showed, the value of church property was far outstripping any increase in adherents. In the case of the Methodists, church membership had increased by only 4% from 1860 to 1870, yet the value of church property had gone up by 111%. Similarly, Baptist property had nearly doubled in value, though church membership had grown by less than 8%. A similar trend was observed for Congregationalists, Presbyterians, and Episcopalians. Overall, the paper

© The Author(s) 2019
T. Verhoeven, *Secularists, Religion and Government in Nineteenth-Century America*, https://doi.org/10.1007/978-3-030-02877-0_8

calculated that all faiths and denominations had recorded a combined 13% rise in members, but a 108% rise in property value. Such figures, the paper noted, would be of great interest to those "reflecting people," a group it described as "by no means few," who had "pondered over the knotty question of the taxation of church property."[1]

Calls to tax church property were made as early as the Jacksonian era. Labor activists attacked the religious exemption for saddling the poor with heavier taxes. It was, as a group of New York workingmen charged, a "direct and positive robbery of the people" as well as a "connection of Church with State."[2] But as the *Times* predicted, the 1870s witnessed a debate over taxing church property which was unparalleled in its intensity. One measure of this is the frequency of references to the term in published books and journals. On the Google Ngram, the incidence of the phrase "taxation of church property" soars from 1870, and despite some fluctuation, remains high until the end of the century. Newspaper editorialists expressed astonishment that an idea which had once seemed outlandish was beginning to seem like common sense. Until recently, the *Chicago Daily Tribune* reported in 1875, any proposal to tax church property would have "received but little countenance." Now it was "growing into favor."[3] Calls to tax church property were heard in state constitutional conventions and legislatures, tax commissions, the secular press, and even in some pulpits. In 1875, President Ulysses S. Grant threw his support behind the idea. For the first time, churches were forced to defend a privilege which until then had seemed uncontroversial.

This was a product of several factors. One was the growing prominence of organized secularists who made the abolition of the exemption a rallying cry. The fear that Catholics and Mormons were amassing a stockpile of property from which to launch an assault against the republic no doubt swung some public sympathy in favor of the measure. Yet as the *New York Times*' analysis suggests, the growing wealth of Protestant congregations caused just as much concern. The judgment of the Census was indisputable—based on recent trends, the resources enjoyed by church organizations would continue to balloon. Some critics feared the advent in America of what had always seemed a specifically European affliction, *mortmain*, vast church holdings of land which acted like a dead weight on society. Though many scoffed at such fears, in the context of widespread dissatisfaction at the workings of the taxation system and the exemptions granted to powerful corporations, the idea of taxing churches gained a great deal of traction.

The push to end the church exemption was another sign of the growth in secularist ambition after the Civil War. As in the case of removing the Bible from schools, the advocates of taxing churches were seeking to overturn a settled custom. But whereas the reading of the King James Bible was an obvious statement of support for Protestantism, the exemption from taxes was at best an indirect encouragement of religion and not restricted to the evangelical faiths. Working in favor of the campaign, however, were two broader developments. The first was economic collapse. In 1873, a stock-market crash set off the worst depression in the nation's history, leading to wage cuts and mass unemployment. The second was the brazenness with which some churches flaunted their wealth. At the very moment that the urban poor entered a period of utter misery, magnificently decorated and opulent houses of worship sprang up in the nation's cities. The stage was set for a backlash against wealthy congregations which paid no tax.

The Property Tax and Its Exemptions

The framework for the debate was a tax regime that was widely seen to be both inefficient and unfair. One of the leading taxation experts in the nation, David A. Wells, captured the attitude of both specialists and the public alike when he described the American tax system as "antiquated, accidental, unjust, demoralizing and absurd."[4] A series of reports argued that the burden of taxation had never been heavier in peacetime, reaching levels which, in some accounts, exceeded even those endured by citizens of the Old World. According to the commissioners appointed to lead an 1871 inquiry into the assessment and collection of taxes in the state of New York, aggregate taxation had increased across the northern states between 1860 and 1870: in New York from $20,402,276 to $50,328,684; in Massachusetts, from $7,600,000 to $21,921,569; in Ohio, from $11,071,000 to $22,232,877.[5] With the possible exception of Paris, taxpayers in the city of Boston carried a heavier tax burden than "all the governments and communities in the civilized world."[6]

Even worse, the load was not shared equally. The problem lay in the design and administration of the property tax, the main fiscal instrument available to state and local governments. It fell overwhelmingly on property that was tangible and visible, primarily land, buildings, and livestock. But it failed to touch intangible forms of property amassed by corporations, including credits, securities, mortgages, savings, and exchange values. Locally elected assessors did not have the expertise or resources to evaluate the worth of such forms of property; the office of assessor was notoriously corrupt and vulnerable to political manipulation. Making the task harder was the ease with which intangible assets could be transferred to different jurisdictions. As a result, corporate wealth benefited from an informal exemption.

Compounding the problem was the prevalence of formal exemptions. In all states and territories, Federal property was not subject to local or state tax, a situation which, as we shall see, severely hampered the operation of government in Washington, DC. But it created anomalies everywhere. Under New York statutes, a US bond was untaxed, but a city or state bond was taxed. Arousing the most resentment, however, were the exemptions enjoyed by large corporations. Railroads were a particular target. In New Jersey, successive legislatures granted railroad corporations freedom from local taxes as a means of fostering their development. By the early 1870s, this was sapping the revenue of the municipalities through which the lines ran, and which housed large amounts of railroad-owned property. Taxing this property became one of the main demands of the constitutional commission which met in 1873. In the same year, hostility to corporate wealth intensified when a failed sale of railway bonds triggered a chain of events that led to a severe economic downturn. When the wealthy financier Jay Cooke was forced into bankruptcy after failing to find buyers for several million dollars of Northern Pacific Railway bonds, the result was a cascade of bank failures and a disastrous five-year depression.

Church property was also by and large exempt from taxation. As ever in the patchwork American system, regulations varied from state to state. Some Constitutions explicitly guaranteed the exemption. As matters stood in 1870, this was the case in Minnesota and Kansas. Elsewhere the language was less strict. In many jurisdictions (e.g., Ohio, Illinois, and Tennessee), the Constitution merely allowed the legislature to exempt church property or houses of worship from taxation. A third possibility (among others, Massachusetts, Connecticut, and Iowa) was for the Constitution to be entirely silent on the question. In these states, the validity of statutory exemptions granted to religious property rested largely on custom. Whatever its legal basis, however, the upshot was that property used for religious purposes was tax-free in virtually every state in the nation.[7]

The Argument for Taxing Churches

In the midst of this broader debate about taxation, the publication of the 1870 census figures emboldened a series of groups to call for an end to the religious exemption. As in all church-state battles, the anti-exemptionists were a diverse group. The Constitution of the National Liberal League made the "equitable taxation of church property" the second of its specific demands, and state Liberal Leagues were active in organizing petition drives.[8] In Massachusetts, the volume of petitions prompted the creation of a legislative committee in 1874 which held public hearings on the exemption of charitable, religious, and educational institutions, and then appointed a special commission to produce a report. Francis Abbot pleaded the anti-exemptionist case in a submission to that commission.[9] Speaking at the opening of the FRA Convention in Providence, Rhode Island, Octavius Frothingham likened the churches to corporations which exploited the nation's workers. Describing the exemption as a "monstrous burden" on workers, Frothingham called for a campaign against church power, or what he termed the "most stupendous monopoly at present to be found in our society."[10]

But avowedly liberal organizations were only one voice in a growing chorus calling for the taxation of church property. In several states, delegates to constitutional conventions proposed the measure as part of a raft of reforms to the tax system. In many cases, editorialists added their support. As the Ohio convention debated the proposal, the *Cleveland Herald* came out in favor. The exemption of church property worth some fifty million dollars was an injustice to the state's taxpayers. The case for ending this situation, the paper argued, was "so plain, so self-evident, as to need no argument."[11] The Ohio agitation was noted in New Jersey, which had called its own constitutional commission in 1873. When Senator Augustus W. Cutler proposed an amendment which would abolish the exemption, he won the backing of several of the state's leading newspapers. "That it is right to do so," argued the *West Jersey Press*, "cannot be seriously questioned."[12]

The most significant figure to throw his weight behind the idea was President Ulysses S. Grant. In his annual message to Congress in 1875, Grant described the "accumulation of vast amounts of untaxed church property" as an "evil" which, if left unchecked, would bring "great trouble" to the land. Like many commentators, the President saw a disturbing trend at work. Based on the growth since 1850, church property would be worth some $3,000,000,000 by the end of the century. At that point, Grant forecast, there would be a backlash. If taxes were not levied on this property, the result might be "sequestration without constitutional authority and through blood." Grant left open the possibility of exempting cemeteries and, subject to limitations, church edifices. But these exceptions aside, all property should be taxed equally.[13]

As several commentators pointed out, Grant had no jurisdiction over property taxes, which were levied at the state and municipal level. The President, as the *Boston Daily Advertiser* remarked, could be no more effective in shaping state tax policy than in "suppressing the insurrection in Herzogovina."[14] Other critics pointed to another flaw in Grant's approach, his seeming assumption that all property held by religious corporations was in fact exempt. This was the point made by a New York City tax commissioner, George H. Andrews, in a series of letters to the *Times*. In his first, he charged that Grant's message was redundant. In the state of New York, church property was defined as "every building for public worship" as well as the "lots upon which such buildings are situated." An 1852 city regulation limited the exemption further to buildings used exclusively for religious worship. All other property owned by religious corporations, Andrews argued, already paid tax. If the President intended, as he had signaled in his address, to exempt houses of worship, he would be doing no more than replicating the system currently in force in New York City.[15]

What Andrews did not mention was the income generated by buildings that were purportedly reserved for worship only. This was a favorite theme of the Washington Correspondent of the *American Israelite*, who wrote under the name of Sopher. What particularly incensed Sopher was the practice of renting out church buildings for meetings, fairs and lectures, a practice made more lucrative by the fact that the income generated was not taxed. The Congregational Church was an egregious offender. As a venue for popular lecturers, the church took on all the trappings of a theater hall, selling tickets in the vestibule, running advertisements in the press, and providing light entertainment before the main show. It was so imbued with the theater spirit, Sopher noted, that it had even copied the dubious practice of marketing seats as "reserved" or "sold" when they were not reserved or sold at all. When church buildings were used in this way, their exemption from tax became nothing but a fraud against the public.[16] Even more galling, the pastor of the Church then reportedly delivered a sermon attacking the taxing of churches as a form of state-sponsored theft.[17]

In addition to escaping the property tax, churches were often not assessed for street improvements, though they benefited directly from them. The *New York Herald* cited the example of the gas lamps which were erected by the city in front of churches. The cost of installing, maintaining, and operating the lamps for some 400–500 churches amounted, the paper estimated, to $50,000 a year, all at public expense.[18] Such arguments were heard as well in the religious press. The New York *Independent* added to the list of unfair exemptions the $1500 of property which priests and ministers of the Gospel could hold without being taxed. When added to church property, the amount of "priviledged [sic] property" which benefitted from taxpayer-funded infrastructure without "paying a solitary penny for its support" was no less than $75,000,000 in the state of New York. If assessed for state and local taxes, this would raise some $2,000,000.[19] Parsonages were another sore point. Even in states where they were theoretically taxed, some churches found a loophole. The *Israelite's* correspondent, Sopher, gave an example of a New York parsonage which, simply because a prayer meeting was held there once a week, was considered a house of worship and therefore exempt.[20]

Taxation and Church-State Separation

Evoking the streams of untapped revenue enjoyed by churches and the consequent burdening of already aggrieved taxpayers was one way to rally support. Another was to appeal to the separation of church and state. In his submission to the Massachusetts Tax Commission, Francis Abbot announced his intention to refer not to dollars and cents but to constitutional principle. Twenty-three states in the Union, including the state of Massachusetts, banned the taxing of any citizen for the support of a religious congregation to which he or she did not belong. In 1833, the people of Massachusetts had ended direct taxation for the support of religion. Exempting church property, however, was "to tax everybody for its support, whether members or non-members," and as such illegal. In addition to contravening a specific clause of the Massachusetts Constitution, the practice violated the federal Constitution's ban on a religious establishment. Governments were in effect subsidizing churches, in the process offering state sanction to their creeds. Slyly referring to another controversy raging at the time, Abbot declared that such a subsidy would remain unlawful until the day that the Constitution was amended to recognize Christianity as the state religion.[21]

To emphasize the point, anti-exemptionists evoked the uproar which would ensue if the state simply handed churches the amount of money which they did not pay in tax. In Washington, one newspaper attacked a petition in favor of the tax exemption. If a petition asked for direct financial support, it would "not receive a moment's consideration." The vast majority of Americans would not even consider putting their name to such a demand. Yet there was not a "scintilla of difference" between them. The exemption, the paper concluded, was a gift of public money, and as such, amounted to a state establishment of religion, thereby violating the first amendment.[22] Such arguments were heard in state constitutional conventions as well. Jacob Mueller was a refugee from the 1848 failed uprisings in Germany who, after a successful career as a lawyer and insurance director, entered Ohio state politics. In 1871, he was elected a delegate to the Constitutional Convention, where he spoke out strongly for ending the exemption. If churches were to be supported by taxpayers, this should be done "openly and frankly." Doing so would expose the manner in which the practice contravened Article 1, Section 7 of the Ohio Constitution, which declared that no person should be obliged to support a place of worship.[23]

What advocates of taxing churches tried hard to establish was that such a measure would not be a radical change of direction but simply the culmination of a historical sweep toward a greater separation of church and state. The tax exemption, in this conception, belonged with the religious tax in Virginia as a remnant of the colonial era that a modern nation should now discard. As the *Chicago Tribune* argued, society was moving to a consensus on the "true principle" of separation and it was only "a question of time" before tax policy shifted to reflect this. The fact that all churches benefitted from the exemption was no argument in its defense. As the paper argued in a separate article, this only meant that "the State is leagued with every church, instead of with only one."[24] Attacking one Bishop's plea for the exemption to continue, a Wisconsin paper similarly deemed the practice a "relic" of an earlier time with no place in modern America. "The state," the paper argued, "with us is Christian only in a passive sense."[25]

Some liberal Protestants were coming to the same conclusion. In a paper to a meeting of clergymen from the Boston area, Congregational minister Reverend Frederick Baylies Allen weighed up both sides of the argument and came out in favor of ending the exemption. It was a carryover, he argued, of a period of church establishment, when parish and state taxes were collected at the same time. But when, he continued, "we avow it as our settled principle of action that church and state shall be kept scrupulously distinct from one another," the exemption was no longer tenable.[26] Allen hoped too that the cause of true faith might be the ultimate beneficiary. He reminded his audience of the fears held by such prominent churchmen as Lyman Beecher when the state of Connecticut abolished the compulsory religious tax. Beecher initially saw the move as a disaster, predicting that ministers would be starved of support and congregations forced to close. The result, however, had confounded these grim predictions. Forcing churches to stand on their own feet had infused them with energy and with purpose, and the cause of religion had prospered as never before. In New York, the *Independent* rejected the exemption as "an indirect union of Church and State" which harmed the interests of both.[27] Churches, as the *Congregationalist* argued, no longer needed to be "coddled" by the State.[28]

Underlying these religious arguments for taxation was an expectation that such a measure was needed to sort the living from the moribund faiths. As Allen made clear, the "churches which would suffer by this change *would not* for the most part be the living, working, earnest churches, but those that are selfish, cold and dead." It is likely of course that Allen was thinking here of Roman-Catholicism. But he may well have had Protestant faiths in mind too. In this sense, the argument for taxing churches can be seen as part of the never-ending effort to distinguish true and false religion. A vital faith attuned to the wishes of its congregation and nimble enough to meet changing social expectations could expect to thrive even in the absence of the exemption. Those that had stagnated, however, were likely to fall by the wayside.

Defending the Church Exemption

Allen's call to the churches to drop their support for the exemption met a decidedly hostile response. Some may have preferred to ignore the issue entirely. But given the intensifying push for a change in policy, they were forced to mount a defense of the status quo. One response was to dispute the premise that a complete separation of church and state was desirable. Writing in the *North American Review*, Edward Everett Hale criticized writers who carelessly claimed that such a divorce was necessary or even possible. Not only were the two forces closely intertwined, but it was fitting that they be so, for without religion there could be no moral order.[29] Government was, at its most basic level, a "double system": the same citizen voted at an election on Monday and a parish meeting on Tuesday. "Both parts of the system," as Hale put it, were carried forward by the same person. The overlap of church and state was in this sense a daily and lived reality. Other exemptionists maintained that an indirect form of aid differed entirely from direct aid. In his submission to the Massachusetts Tax Commission, the President of Harvard University, Charles Eliot, defended the exemption as an "inducement or encouragement" rather than a subsidy. Seen in this way, it did not contravene any ban on the compulsory support of faith.[30] Some turned to history in support of this constitutional interpretation. Writing in the *North American Review*, Reverend A.W. Pitzer argued that the Founders had seen no hint of a union of church and state in the practice of exemption. "What has been done for a hundred years," he wrote, "ought to be regarded as a fair interpretation of constitutional law."[31]

Where exemptionists felt most confident was on the question of public utility. The reason that governments continued the policy was that churches provided a range of vital services to the community and to the state. For Charles Eliot, both churches and colleges formed and maintained the public virtue which was the basis of social stability. By making men "energetic, honest and sensible," churches made a crucial contribution to the public good.[32] The majority report of the commissioners agreed with Eliot. Removing the exemption would be disastrous for all because, as the Commissioners stated, "the prosperity of any state—its culture, its freedom from crime, its social order—will rest ultimately upon the religion of its subjects."[33] The effects were likely to be felt very quickly. With the churches crippled by taxation, and unable to act as the incubators of virtue, a surge in crime and poverty was sure to result. Whatever revenue was gained from taxing churches would immediately be squandered in boosting police numbers, building prisons, and funding social welfare programs. As one newspaper argued, once church property was taxed, "crime and wickedness would immeasurably increase," and as a result a more "elaborate and costly machinery of government" would be required. Far from alleviating the burden on citizens, the taxing of churches would have the perverse effect of requiring governments to increase taxes.[34] But such an outcome could easily be avoided by maintaining the current policy. As a tool for supporting churches in their vital work of uplifting morality and restraining vice, the exemption was a pragmatic and cost-efficient means of maintaining social order which benefitted everyone. Every church, as Reverend A.W. Pitzer argued, was a "reform school," and property owners should be grateful for their influence. The lessons from abroad were to his mind clear. Attack religion, he warned property owners, and the outcome might be a city in flames, as the Paris Commune so vividly showed.[35]

CHURCHES OR ELITIST CLUBS?

This was a powerful argument which won the support of many commentators and editorialists. But anti-exemptionists had a ready response. Increasingly, they argued, leading congregations in the great cities were becoming exclusive clubs for the wealthy elite. The revenue saved through the tax exemption was not being devoted to helping the poor and needy. Instead, it was allowing a culture of luxury and opulence to flourish, a culture which exposed the hollowness of the churches' claim to be humble servants of the public good.

To prove the argument, anti-exemptionists had only to point to the great churches and cathedrals which were being raised across the North and the mid-West. The post-Civil War era marked the beginning of a heroic phase in church building. One after the other, large neo-Gothic edifices boasting soaring towers, magnificent organs and lavishly decorated interiors appeared in the urban skyline, as different congregations and faiths sought to match the accomplishments of their rivals. Midtown New York was dominated by St. Patrick's Cathedral, which opened in 1879 to the acclaim of even secular commentators. The *New York Times* praised the Catholic cathedral as a "national monument," a physical evocation of the "magnificent and princely worship of our forefathers" which even Presbyterians might appreciate.[36] But Protestants could point with pride to their own splendid and handsome churches. In Boston, the Great Fire of 1872 destroyed a number of historic churches, including Trinity church on Summer Street. Just five years later, Henry Hobson Richardson's ornate edifice on Copley Square was consecrated. Complementing Richardson's elaborate Romanesque style was a sumptuous interior fashioned by some of the leading artists of the day. Four stained glass windows were designed and executed by the pre-Raphaelite Edward Burne-Jones. But he was outdone by John La Farge, who invented a new method of layering glass to create his dazzling windows in the nave.

But it was a church which escaped the 1872 fire that would form the focus of opposition to the tax exemption. The Old South Church on Washington Street was a key architectural link to the conflicts of the Revolutionary era. Its brick meetinghouse was the site of the 1770 meeting protesting the Boston Massacre, as well as the 1773 gathering which led to the Boston Tea Party. Heroic action on the part of citizens and firefighters saved the building from destruction in the 1872 fire, but the congregation decided nevertheless to sell the historic building and its land, and move to the fashionable Back Bay area. The threatened demolition of the historic church sparked the earliest urban conservation campaign in American history. But it was the vast, untaxed profit generated by the sale that drew the ire of the poet, lawyer and future mayor of the city, Josiah Phillips Quincy. In a letter to the *Nation* in 1872, Quincy denounced the tax-free profit from the sale as inimical to the spirit of true religion. The lure of such profits, he wrote, had made the congregation greedy, leading it to abandon the "spirit of equity" for a "headlong hurry to be rich." But more troubling for Quincy was the sight of a wealthy congregation freeloading on the working classes. The tax exemption, he argued, was intended to allow worshippers to furnish themselves with a suitable place of worship. It was not designed "to enable a sect to acquire great wealth by taking it without compensation from the only source of wealth—the labor of the people." Quincy's arguments did not sway the congregation. The land was sold, and the New Old South church, an exuberant Gothic-style edifice with an enormous tower, opened in 1875.

Such cases invigorated the anti-exemptionist cause. The *Chicago Tribune* cited the "fever for large and costly church edifices" as the main force driving the movement. Taxing the churches was the best antidote to needless religious opulence. "We are becoming extravagant," the *North American Gazette* lamented, "in the business of temple-building."[37] Yet extravagant buildings were only part of the problem. In their spirit and operation, congregations appeared to be focused more on pampering a wealthy clientele than serving the needs of the poor. Newspapers published details of pew auctions in wealthy congregations; in one, the Presbyterian Church at the corner of Fifth Avenue and Fifty-Fifth Street in Manhattan, pews were assessed from $300 to $6000, not including a premium as well as the annual rental charge. The total raised was some $600,000.[38] More and more, the *Nation* argued, churches were a "collection of Sunday clubs for wealthy people."[39] At the same time, the poor were shut out. The humble worker, as one newspaper argued, was not welcome in these handsome buildings; he feels "too poorly clad to be at home on the carpets and cushions of our modern churches."[40] The perception that churches were more and more orientated to the wealthy was magnified by the physical move from poorer parts of the city to more fashionable districts. When one congregation abandoned its traditional site in the lower east side of Manhattan for the affluent midtown, the *New York Times* recorded its dismay. "Where its place of worship is now," the paper declared, "the poor will never come." In their scramble for extravagance, the churches had forgotten their mission to the downtrodden.[41]

For critics, the Church which had most shamelessly embraced the mercantile spirit of the corporation was Trinity Church in Manhattan. One of the oldest and most prestigious in the nation, Trinity was also, through its immense property holdings, one of the wealthiest, and as such was soon at the center of the storm over tax exemptions. On January 3, 1878, the *Index* published a story which it hoped would "sweep away all church-exemptions in a sudden and resistless whirlwind of public indignation." It had been informed that Trinity Church Corporation owned city property worth some $70,000,000, on which it paid no tax at all. Like all churches, it defended this exemption on the grounds that it served society as a bulwark of morality. But this claim was a sham. The *Index* had discovered that the Trinity holdings included 764 saloons and 96 brothels, making the corporation the "greatest feeder of vice" in the city. It was time to end this "nauseating hypocrisy," and abolish the exemption once and for all.[42]

These allegations against Trinity drew an immediate riposte from its rector, Morgan Dix. He began by disputing the *Index's* calculation of the value of lots owned by the Corporation; the true figure, he wrote, was closer to $7,000,000. This was still an enormous amount, but Dix went on to state that most was assessed for property tax. Only the church buildings, schools, orphanages, and cemeteries were tax-free. The rest was divided into short-term leases, on which Trinity paid tax, and long-term leases, on which the tenant paid the tax. The former amounted to $46,943 and the latter around $60,000, all of which went to the City treasury. In short, Trinity paid tax "on every foot of ground used for secular purposes." Dix went on to reject the charges of immoral purposes as "reckless" and without foundation. The corporation's short-term leases contained covenants prohibiting the sale of liquor; letters from the Police and Excise commissioners proved that no houses of prostitution were operating in Trinity-owned lots.[43]

The fabled wealth of Trinity Corporation, however, remained a rallying cry for anti-exemptionists across the nation. The time has gone, as one Colorado paper argued, when a religious corporation like Trinity could own vast amounts of property in the largest city in the nation, and not pay its fair share for the municipal services it relied upon.[44] Even defenders of the tax exemption conceded that churches had harmed their cause by so publicly displaying their wealth. Reverend Pitzer suggested that churches be encouraged to build less grandiose places of worship, that the pew system be abolished and that all services be opened free of charge to the public.[45] Edward Everett Hale also thought the churches were partly to blame for the growth of anti-exemptionist sentiment. The entire debate hinged, he argued, on one key question—whether the churches were private or public charities. Once the answer had been clear. Men of faith, through their educational and pastoral role, roles, clearly served a visible and vital social role. Now the public was beginning to have doubts, as churches retreated to a more private and exclusive function.[46]

Anti-Mormonism and Anti-Catholicism

Anti-exemptionists had a further powerful argument at their disposal: that taxing churches would halt the alarming growth of two feared organizations, Mormonism and Catholicism. Several studies have demonstrated the depth of anti-Mormonism in nineteenth-century America.[47] In many aspects, Mormonism figured as the epitome of a fanatical and superstitious faith. Its strange origin story and its bizarre prophets brought to mind the primitive faiths of tribal societies. The power enjoyed by its priests in their strange kingdom of Utah was a brazen transplanting of theocracy to American soil. Most of all, Mormon polygamy was seen as an atrocious deformation of true religion, a cruel and immoral practice dressed up in Scriptural clothes.

Taxing church property was one way to rein in its authority. In 1869, Republican Senator Aaron Cragin introduced a bill which would, among other measures, tax Mormon Church property above $20,000.[48] That bill died in committee, but when the census revealed a vast increase in Mormon property over a decade, Cragin returned to the issue. This time he proposed an amendment to another anti-polygamy bill that would ensure equal and uniform taxation in the territory of Utah. The language of the amendment was on the face of it, unobjectionable. But its true target became clear in his comments. "An immense amount of church property," Cragin reminded the Senate, "is exempt from taxation under the laws of the Territory of Utah."[49] Since his amendment set a precedent for taxing all churches, both inside and outside Utah, it received little support and was withdrawn. Still, anti-exemptionists continued to cite the example of Mormonism, which sinned even more by concentrating its wealth in the hands of its leader, Brigham Young. In an example of the imagined affinity between Mormonism and tribal primitivism, Alvah Hovey, president of Newton Theological Institution in Massachusetts, alleged that their property was placed "directly into the hands of their chief."[50] Excessive wealth was bad enough. But when it could be deployed at will by a hostile leader, it became even more of a menace.

The greatest threat, however, came from Roman-Catholicism. This was a clear lesson from the 1870 census. Amidst the general rise in church wealth, the Catholic Church stood out. From 1860 to 1870, the Church's property had risen in value by 128%, outstripping the Methodist, Presbyterian and Congregational churches. Furthermore, as a percentage of all church property, Catholicism had assumed a greater weight, moving from 10.78% in 1850 to 17.45% in 1870. This was still less than the Methodists, who accounted for almost 20% of all church property. But the trend was clear. The Methodists had virtually stood still in those two decades, increasing their share of the overall figure by less than 3%.[51] The 1880 census, it seemed clear, would show Catholicism as the largest single denomination in terms of the value of its property.

This was an outcome that secularists were determined to prevent. In his submission to the Massachusetts Tax inquiry, Francis Abbot blamed the tax exemption for encouraging the accumulation of property under ecclesiastical control. He then singled out the Catholic Church, which he described as a "cancerous organism in the body politic."[52] The few ministers who spoke in favor of taxing churches were particularly aggressive. Frederick Baylies Allen, as we have seen, came out on balance for taxing churches. The urgency of thwarting the ambitions of Catholicism seemed to tip the scale. This "vast, homogenous, ambitious, unscrupulous corporation," as Allen put it, was making "gigantic strides," and endlessly "absorbing the property of this country." The only effective weapon against it was taxation. "If, as now," he warned, "she pays no taxes, what limit can be placed to her rapacity?"[53]

For proof of what might ensue, anti-exemptionists looked abroad. Several newspapers pointed to the unchecked accumulation of ecclesiastical property in Quebec, noting that a great deal was vested in the church hierarchy.[54] The efforts of successive Mexican governments to tax or appropriate Church lands also drew much attention. But it was Europe that provided the most compelling lesson in the dangers of Catholic ambition. The press reported efforts on the part of European governments to rein in *mortmain*, the weight of property controlled by the Church. In Italy, the government seemed determined to act. A proposal in 1867 to impose a 30% tax on church property attracted considerable attention in the American press.[55] When this measure failed, the government moved to confiscate church property, a process which was being reported in the press at the same time as the debate on taxing property at home was raging. Catholic papers provided detailed descriptions of what was termed the "plunder" of church property.[56] The secular press was more positive. The beneficiaries, the *Chicago Tribune* proclaimed, were poor workers who could work the land; the only parties to suffer were those living in a state of "pious idleness."[57]

Exemptionists ridiculed the idea that the United States might be saddled with *mortmain*. As Charles Eliot declared in his submission to the Massachusetts tax Commission, it was as reasonable for an American to fear this as "for the people of Boston to live in constant dread of being overwhelmed by an eruption of lava from Blue Hill."[58] Nevertheless, some ordinary citizens seemed to believe that such fears were entirely realistic. Following his message to Congress, President Grant received several letters of support from the public. Norman Macleod of Chicago thanked Grant for trying to save America from a European calamity. All church property, he agreed, should be taxed; if not, the specter of Catholic Europe loomed. "look [sic] at France," Macleod wrote, "every fifth acre belongs to the catholic church."[59] The lesson was just as striking for legislators and editorialists. In Ohio, Jacob Mueller cited the European example in his speech in favor of taxing church property. The situation in America, he declared, was now "analogous to the condition of things on the other side of the Atlantic."[60] The *North American Review* considered that the problem at home was not yet as dire, but saw a similar process at work. As the example of Italy showed, ecclesiastical property had the tendency to accumulate with "amazing rapidity," crippling a nation's tax base and forcing governments into dramatic acts of confiscation.[61]

The danger was even more acute since the Protestant churches seemed once again to be mimicking Catholicism's worst tendencies. Surveying the nation's great cities, *Scribner's Monthly* detected a process of Romanization. In Rome, huge and opulent cathedrals towered over a poverty-stricken populace. The people were crushed by taxation, while the all-powerful and wealthy Church contributed nothing to the city's coffers. This was an intolerable situation. Inevitably the government would be roused to attack such property, for else it could not survive. In the judgment of *Scribner's*, Protestant churches were failing to see their part in producing a similar situation at home, particularly the enthusiasm with which they had carried out their "schemes of church aggrandizement" which were "visible on every hand." If state representatives saw millions of dollars being spent on churches which could be built for one-quarter of the amount and which were routinely half-empty, it was not surprising that taxation came to their mind. Protestant churches seemed to be giving into the same greed that marred Catholicism, and the result might well be taxation, the last "corrective of the disposition to grasp at power."[62]

The Failure to Tax Churches

For all their efforts, anti-exemptionists achieved only a handful of victories. The most striking came in the District of Columbia and in California, and they came about thanks to a set of unique circumstances. In the case of the capital, the first was a spiraling debt crisis. The second was the sheer amount of property—notably federal government buildings, but also schools, charitable institutions, and churches—exempt from the property tax. Desperate to boost city revenue, Congress in 1874 passed a bill that failed to list church property among the list of tax exemptions. The lack of debate around the passage of the bill suggests that some Senators simply did not notice the omission. This at least was the claim of Senator Arthur I. Boreman of West Virginia, who the next day moved a motion to reconsider the bill, admitting that he had not read it before the vote.

Other Senators were prepared to defend the legislation. Republican William B. Allison of Ohio began by deflecting the question of principle, suggesting that this was merely a temporary measure to help stabilize the district's finances. But even as he made this case, Allison could not help revealing a sense of frustration that so much property went tax-free. No less than 1/15 of all the property in the district was owned by churches. Furthermore, as a Democrat from Ohio, Allen G. Thurman stressed, much of this was not used for worship at all, but rather consisted of vacant lots which benefitted directly from the program of street improvement currently being carried out by the government. Should such property, William Stewart (Nevada) asked, which seemed to be held for speculative purposes, not make a contribution to the large expense of improving the city? The public, as several Senators suggested, seemed to think so. The Committee which considered the issue had not received one remonstrance against it, the bill had been widely reported in the press, and the District government had issued a favorable resolution.[63]

The taxation of church property won support from newspapers such as the *National Republican* and the *Critic-Record*, with the latter putting public sentiment as nine-tenths in favor.[64] But there was one major problem: enforcement. The majority of churches simply refused to pay. As the House Committee reported, assessed taxes on church property amounted to $42,773, but only $2566 was collected.[65] The response of the district government was swift. In June 1875, it purchased the property at a tax sale, holding it until the assessment was paid, and levying as well an interest bill of 10% per annum. The stalemate, however, continued. When, in 1878, a bill was put forward to repeal the 1874 legislation and refund the small amount of taxes collected, Senator George F. Edmunds of Vermont reacted with fury. Denouncing these "delinquent churches" which had shirked their share of city costs, Edmunds demanded that they be taught to obey the law, in line with Scripture. Edmunds was further incensed by the prospect of the city being unable to fund its schools, a situation he ascribed in part to the failure of churches to pay their taxes. The Senate was being asked, he thundered, to "crucify the schools in order to relieve the church property."[66] Following Edmunds' riposte the bill stalled, but in 1879 President Rutherford B. Hayes signed a law restoring the exemption. With that the capital's brief experiment in taxing churches came to an end.

In California, the power of populist hostility to churches which were seen as havens for the wealthy elite was clearly on display. The 1849 state Constitution decreed taxation to be "equal and uniform," and contained no provision for exemptions. Yet in 1850 the legislature granted exemptions to a large amount of property, including that used for religious purposes. Almost two decades later, in *People vs McCreery* (1867), the state Supreme Court ruled all these provisions, including that enjoyed by churches, to be unconstitutional. The only remedy would be to amend the Constitution.[67] In the meantime, church property came under assessment. The opportunity to reverse this came at the 1878–1879 Constitutional convention. Religious groups organized petition drives asking delegates to exempt "all property used exclusively for Charitable, Educational and Church purposes."[68] But they faced opposition from the Workingmen's Party, which held a third of the 152 delegates, and which was determined to put a radical imprint on the state charter. In the most far-reaching response yet to the inequities of the property tax, the revised California Constitution taxed corporate bonds, stocks, and other forms of intangible property.[69]

Given its determination to spread the property tax burden as widely as possible, the convention was unlikely to treat the holdings of religious corporations with particular leniency. The issue was decided at a closed session of the Committee on Property Exemption. Having agreed to exempt property used for charitable purposes, the committee moved to the question of churches. One of the Committee members, Judge Albert P. Overton, thought an exemption reasonable for plain and popular churches, but not for "large, costly, massive structures which partook more of the character of theatrical performances, where a man paid $3000 a year for a seat."[70] Perhaps with this in mind, the Committee agreed to set a cap of $3000 on exempt property but then, for reasons that are unclear, postponed the discussion.[71] The upshot was that no exemption was granted to religious organizations. For the next two decades, California was the only state in the union to tax the entire value of church property, including houses of worship.

Elsewhere the tax exemption emerged from public debates largely unscathed. This can be explained in several ways. While some liberal churches were prepared to cede their exemption, the vast majority saw the proposal as a deadly threat, and mobilized their supporters accordingly. Wherever threatening legislation was raised, a stream of hostile petitions flooded into the offices of elected representatives. Thousands of churchgoers were no doubt hostile to the idea of a tax on an institution which they supported through voluntary contributions and which played such a positive role in society. Many would have agreed with the *Boston Daily Advertiser* that a proposed bill to tax all church property above the value of $12,000 would "deal a heavier blow at the cause of good morals in Massachusetts than any legislation every yet devised here."[72] When the bill was defeated in the legislature by 116 votes to 64, the paper expressed its relief that good sense had prevailed.[73]

Fundamentally, however, taxing churches was recognized to be an enormous break with precedent that would put the United States at odds with all other advanced nations. This was the factor identified by the Boston politician, writer and lecturer Hamilton Andrews Hill. In a lecture opposing church taxation Hill, the future author of a history of the Old South Church, made the point that "It is for those who advocate a radical change to show conclusively ... that the new will be better than the old has been or is likely to be."[74] Faced with the proposition that the funds raised through taxation would be offset by a general decline in public morals and works of charity, anti-exemptionists were unable to make this case for change. Eventually, California, too, came into line with the rest of the nation. At an election on November 6, 1900, a constitutional amendment to exempt property "used solely and exclusively for religious worship" passed by 115,851 to 102,564.

THE DEMISE OF THE NATIONAL LIBERAL LEAGUE

Adding to the difficulty of sustaining the campaign was the splintering of organized secularism. The issue which led to the demise of the National Liberal League as a unified force was censorship of the mails. In 1873, the anti-vice crusader Anthony Comstock won passage of a law strengthening prohibitions on the mailing of obscene literature. Many freethinkers opposed the Comstock law. Robert G. Ingersoll worried that works of religious controversy might come under the ban. As he wrote in an open letter to the press, he was fearful that it might "include books and pamphlets written against the religion of the day, though containing nothing that can be called obscene or impure."[75] Events would prove these fears to be well-founded. In November 1877, DeRobigne Mortimer Bennett, the editor of the freethought paper the *Truth Seeker*, was arrested for mailing "An Open Letter to Jesus Christ," a series of questions and answers which arraigned Christianity for enshrining persecution and intolerance. Bennett, whom Comstock loathed as a publisher of "Blasphemous & Infidel works," became a hero for freethinkers across the nation.[76] A petition to Congress with some 50,000 names attached, headed by that of Ingersoll, called for the Comstock laws to be repealed, or modified so that they were no longer vehicles for "moral and religious persecution."[77]

Many secularists, however, with Francis Abbot at their head, were horrified to see their movement leading a campaign against a law designed to uphold morality. Regretting Ingersoll's signature on the anti-Comstock petition, Abbot warned of the public hostility that was sure to result. Liberals, he argued, could not afford to be seen to side with publishers of lewd material.[78] The risk appeared even more acute when Bennett was arrested in August 1878 for selling *Cupid's Yokes*, an attack on the institution of marriage. These divisions were laid bare at that year's convention of the NLL in Syracuse, New York. After several sessions filled with insults and angry clashes, a new leadership made up of Bennett's friends and supporters was elected. The incoming President was Elizur Wright, one of the attendees at the 1848 Melodeon Hall anti-Sabbatarian meeting. The bitter feeling continued. In 1879, a subscriber to the *Index* wrote to Abbot in support of his call for modification rather than repeal of the Comstock law. Nevertheless, he was outraged at his lack of solidarity with Bennett, who had by then been convicted and sent to jail. Whatever their differences, he told Abbot, Bennett deserved sympathy as a victim of "sectarian Christian malice."[79]

Many secularists in turn supported Abbot's stance. In a letter to Wright, four of the five members of the Jefferson Liberal League of Rochester formally severed any connection with the NLL. They could no longer abide, they stated, the NLL's obsession with "matters entirely foreign to the object of our organization and distasteful to its members as citizens and gentlemen."[80] The NLL lasted several more years before giving way to a new organization, the *American Secular Union*. Abbot found a home in the *Liberal Union Club* of Boston. Its platform blended familiar secularist principles with a call to "vindicate the good name of liberalism" which had been sadly "tarnished" by its association with "mischievous and demoralizing measures" such as the call for the repeal of laws against immorality.[81]

A number of factors were at work in the disintegration of the NLL. One was the personality clashes that seemed to bedevil liberal movements everywhere. Another was class. As we have seen, class friction often provided a powerful impulse to secularist causes. Opponents of Sabbath laws denounced the elitist churches which in their view paid little heed to the needs or desires of the poor. The case for taxing churches was impelled in part by the resentment of opulent churches which seemed to close their door on the humble. But secularists themselves could not escape the friction caused by class division. As debate over the response to the Comstock laws intensified, the proudly rough-edged Bennett launched a series of bitter attacks on Abbot, painting him as a snobbish elitist. In contrast to the "cultured editor" of the *Index*, he was a man of the people who had never received more than a rudimentary education. The *Index*, he claimed, was kept afloat by its "rich stockholders"; his *Truth Seeker* spoke to the thousands of modest men and women keeping the flag of atheism aloft in small towns across the nation and had no pretensions to be "high-toned." Abbot, he charged, had sold out radical principles for the lure of social respectability. "The cultured editor has the perfect right to be partial to kid gloves, patent-leather boots and twenty-five cent cigars," Bennett wrote. "As for ourselves, we have had no use for either of these."[82] In an already fractious debate, class-based antipathy added even more venom.

Apart from in a handful of jurisdictions, the push to tax churches enjoyed little success. Secularist causes functioned best when they brought together religious and non-religious actors; in the case of the tax exemption, an almost solid bloc of churches rallied for the status quo. Yet the fact that the debate took on such intensity was striking and points to the range of impulses driving the secularist case. Chief among these was popular anger at wealthy churches which resembled the detested corporations of the Gilded Age. The principle of distancing church and state could take many practical applications. It might involve keeping references to God out of the Constitution or ending the practice of Bible-reading in schools. But it might also entail undoing what looked like a cozy arrangement under which churches escaped their share of taxes, leaving the burden to fall on the poor. In a nation beset with economic turmoil and a widening gap between rich and poor, this was a cause that generated a great deal of support.

A final point to make is that, though Comstock had managed to drive a wedge through the freethought movement, this did not signal the demise of popular support for a strict separation of church and state. By the late 1880s, a host of freethought lecturers were crisscrossing the nation, and the popularity of the most renowned of all, Robert Green Ingersoll, was set to reach its zenith. As moral reformers busily set about enacting their vision of a Christian state, a new group of secularist actors emerged. The stage was therefore set for the last great petition war of the nineteenth century, and its focus was the World's Columbian Exposition in Chicago.

NOTES

1. *New York Times*, December 6, 1873.
2. *Report of the Committee of Fifty. In Favor of a Lien Law on Building, Education, and the District System for Presidential Electors, &c., Adopted on the 19th of October, 1829, by a General Meeting of Mechanics and Working Men of the City of New-York* (New York: A Ming, 1829), 23–24.
3. *Chicago Daily Tribune*, May 29, 1875.
4. David A. Wells, "The Reform of Local Taxation," *North American Review* 122, no. 251 (1876): 376. On the taxation system, see C.K. Yearley, *The Money Machines: The Breakdown and Reform of Governmental and Party Finance in the North, 1860–1920* (Albany: State University of New York, 1970); Ajay K. Mehrotra, *Making the Modern American Fiscal State: Law, Politics, and the Rise of Progressive Taxation, 1877–1929* (Cambridge: Cambridge University Press, 2013); and R. Rudy Higgens-Evenson, *The Price of Progress: Public Services, Taxation, and the American Corporate State, 1877 to 1929* (Baltimore: John Hopkins University Press, 2003).
5. *Local Taxation: Being a Report of the Commission Appointed by the Governor of New York to Revise the Laws for the Assessment and Collection of State and Local Taxes* (New York: Harper and Brothers, 1871), 10
6. Ibid., 11.
7. For an overview, see Alpha J. Kynett, *The Religion of the Republic, and Laws of Religious Corporations* (Cincinnati: Cranston & Curts, 1895); Carl Zollmann, "Tax Exemptions of American Church Property," *Michigan Law Review* 14, no. 8 (1916): 646–57.
8. *Index*, July 13, 1876. John Witte Jr., "Tax Exemption of Church Property: Historical Anomaly or Valid Constitutional Practice?" *Southern California Law Review* 64 (1991): 363–416.
9. *Report of the Commissioners Appointed to Inquire into the Expediency of Revising and Amending the Laws Relating to Taxation and Exemption Therefrom. January, 1875* (Boston: Wright & Potter, 1875), 397–403.
10. *Index*, November 19, 1874.
11. Re-printed in *Cincinnati Daily Gazette*, July 24, 1873.
12. *West Jersey Press*, June 4, 1873.
13. *Papers of Ulysses S. Grant*, vol. 26, 388–89.
14. *Boston Daily Advertiser*, December 9, 1875.
15. *New York Times*, December 30, 1875.
16. *American Israelite* (Cincinnati), April 17, 1874.
17. *American Israelite*, November 27, 1874.
18. *New York Herald*, February 27, 1876.

19. Re-printed in *Duluth Minnesotian*, August 23, 1873.
20. *American Israelite*, March 22, 1878.
21. *Report of the Commissioners Appointed to Inquire into the Expediency of Revising and Amending the Laws Relating to Taxation and Exemption Therefrom* (Boston: Wright & Potter, 1875), 397–403.
22. *Critic-Record* (Washington, DC), December 26, 1874.
23. *Official Report of the Proceedings and Debates of the Third Constitutional Convention of Ohio*, vol. 2, part 2 (Cleveland: W.S. Robison, 1873), 2080.
24. *Chicago Daily Tribune*, June 20, 1875; May 31, 1874.
25. *Milwaukee Sentinel*, February 7, 1873.
26. *Boston Daily Advertiser*, February 14, 1874. Allen would become an Episcopalian, and forge a public career as a moral crusader, serving as first President of the New England Society for the Suppression of Vice.
27. Re-printed in *Duluth Minnesotian*, August 23, 1873.
28. *Congregationalist* (Boston), February 19, 1874.
29. Edward Everett Hale, "Shall Church Property Be Taxed?" *North American Review* 133, no. 298 (1881): 255–56.
30. *Report of the Commissioners Appointed to Inquire into the Expediency*, 371.
31. A.W. Pitzer, "The Taxation of Church Property," *North American Review* 131, no. 287 (1880): 367.
32. *Report of the Commissioners*, 371.
33. Ibid., 161.
34. *Daily State Gazette* (NJ), January 5, 1874.
35. Pitzer, "Taxation of Church Property," 370–71.
36. *New York Times*, August 24, 1875.
37. *North American and United States Gazette*, December 22, 1875.
38. *New York Times*, May 23, 1875; *Chicago Tribune*, May 29, 1875.
39. *Nation*, January 13, 1876.
40. *Cleveland Daily Herald*, June 3, 1873.
41. *New York Times*, December 22, 1872.
42. *Index*, January 3, 1878.
43. *New York Times*, April 22, 1878. On the controversy over Trinity, Elizabeth Mensch, "Religion, Revival, and the Ruling Class: A Critical History of Trinity Church," *Buffalo Law Review* 36, no. 3 (1987): 427–571.
44. *Daily Rocky Mountain News*, December 10, 1875.
45. Pitzer, "Taxation of Church Property," 373.
46. Hale, "Shall Church Property Be Taxed?" 260.
47. Fluhman, *A Peculiar People*; Christine Talbot, *A Foreign Kingdom: Mormons and Polygamy in American Political Culture, 1852–1890* (Urbana: University of Illinois Press, 2013).

48. "A bill to provide for the execution of the law against the crime of polygamy in the Territory of Utah, and for other purposes." 41st Congress (1869–70), S. 286.
49. *Congressional Globe*, February 26, 1873. 42nd Congress, 3rd session, 1812.
50. Alvah Hovey, *Religion and the State. Protection or Alliance? Taxation or Exemption* (Boston: Estes and Lauriat, 1874), 108.
51. *New York Times*, December 6, 1873.
52. *Report of the Commissioners*, 402.
53. *Boston Daily Advertiser*, February 14, 1874.
54. *Boston Investigator*, December 31, 1873; *San Francisco Bulletin*, October 12, 1877.
55. *New York Herald*, June 16, 1867; *Commercial Advertiser*, July 18, 1867; *New York Tribune*, August 12, 1867.
56. *Irish American Weekly*, January 24, 1874.
57. *Chicago Daily Tribune*, November 26, 1874.
58. *Report of the Commissioners*, 387.
59. *Papers of Ulysses S. Grant*, vol. 26, 420.
60. *Official Report of the Proceedings and Debates of the Third Constitutional Convention*, 2081.
61. *North American and United States Gazette*, August 23, 1873.
62. "The Taxation of Church Property," *Scribner's Monthly* 7, no. 6 (1874): 756.
63. *Congressional Record* 2 (June 19, 1874), 5171–72.
64. *Critic-Record* (Washington, DC), February 23, 1875.
65. 45th Congress, 2nd Session (April 15, 1878), S. Rpt 255.
66. *Congressional Record*, April 29, 1878, 2914–15.
67. *People of the State of California v. Andrew B. McCreery*, Supreme Court of California, 34 Cal 432 (1868). Claude W. Stimson, "Exemption from the Property Tax in California," *California Law Review* 21, no. 3 (March 1933): 193–220.
68. Constitutional Convention Working Papers, Box 5, Folders 8–12 and Box 6, Folders 1–5, California State Archives. Available at: http://www.sos.ca.gov/archives/collections/constitutions/1879/.
69. Higgens-Evenson, *Price of Progress*, 21–22. On the Convention, Noel Sargent, "The California Constitutional Convention of 1878-9," *California Law Review* 6, no. 1 (1917): 1–22; Harry N. Scheiber, "Race, Radicalism, and Reform: Historical Perspective on the 1879 California Constitution," *Hastings Constitutional Law Quarterly* 17, no. 1 (1989): 35–80.
70. *Oakland Tribune*, October 17, 1878.

71. Constitutional Convention Working Papers, Series 2, Committee Papers, Revenue and Taxation, Committee on Property Exemption, Box 1, Folder 7. Available at: http://www.sos.ca.gov/archives/collections/constitutions/1879/.
72. *Boston Daily Advertiser*, March 30, 1876.
73. Ibid., April 1, 1876.
74. Hamilton Andrews Hill, *The Exemption of Church Property from Taxation* (Boston: A. Williams, 1876), 36.
75. *Boston Journal*, March 18, 1878.
76. Roderick Bradford, *D.M. Bennett: The Truth Seeker* (Amherst, NY: Prometheus Books, 2006), 117. For Comstock's decades-long campaign against freethinkers, Schmidt, *Village Atheists*, 231–45.
77. Rec. March 12, 1878. SEN 45A H10.2. National Archives, Washington, DC.
78. *Index*, May 16, 1878.
79. September 7, 1879. Box 64, Francis Ellingwood Abbot papers, Harvard University Archives, Cambridge.
80. Jefferson Liberal League of Rochester to Wright, December 4, 1878. Folder 15, Elizur Wright papers, Manuscripts Division, Library of Congress, Washington, DC.
81. Box 63, Folder 2, Francis Ellingwood Abbot papers, Harvard University Archives, Cambridge.
82. *Truth-Seeker*, June 8, 1878.

CHAPTER 9

"A Professedly National Secular Show": The Chicago World's Fair and the American Sabbath

In June 1892, Samuel Gompers, the President of the American Federation of Labor (AFL), learnt of a new and unexpected ally. That month he received a letter from the secretary of the National Religious Liberty Association (NRLA), Albion F. Ballenger, commending the AFL for a recent petition drive, and calling on the two bodies to exchange campaign literature.[1] In reply, Gompers wrote that it was "gratifying to know that our work is appreciated," and that the AFL could count on the support of a like-minded organization in its efforts to beat back a "serious encroachment" on republican government.[2]

This was by any measure an odd alliance. The NRLA was an offshoot of a small church, the Seventh-Day Adventists, and was devoted to maintaining a strict separation of church and state. The mission of the AFL, the largest union federation in the nation, was to defend the wages and conditions of its skilled labor membership. But in 1892, church and union found themselves working for a common goal: stopping Congress from shutting the gates of the Chicago World's Fair on the Sunday Sabbath. Whatever their differences, both organizations believed, as Ballenger wrote, in "the American principle of entire separation of Church and State." It would clearly be a mistake, Gompers agreed, for Congress to touch "so serious and delicate a Sectarian question." And both had a formidable weapon at their disposal, the mass petition campaign. Ballenger reported to Gompers that 90% of people solicited for their signature were happy to comply. Gompers was just as ebullient about the AFL's campaign, telling Ballenger that no less than 300,000 citizens were expected to sign its petitions.

Set to open on May 1, 1893, the World's Columbian Exposition, or World's Fair as it was commonly known, was keenly anticipated as one of the great events of the age. As the shining buildings of the famous White City took shape, the public looked forward to reveling in a magnificent showcase of their nation's progress. Yet through the Sunday-closing controversy, the Chicago Fair suddenly became the focus of an intense debate about the public role of religion. Several developments came together at Chicago. One was the ever-present international dimension. The Fair was seen by all as a chance for an ambitious nation to showcase its achievements to the world. Foreign envoys were coming to Chicago, as the Fair's director boasted, to observe our "institutions, customs and privileges, with a view to the adoption of the most advantageous."[3] This gave urgency to the Sunday-closing question. Sabbatarians were desperate to present the redeeming force of the American Sabbath; their opponents, in turn, feared that the nation was on the verge of acquiring an international reputation as the home of narrow-minded dogmatism.

Another long-running effort that reached a culmination at Chicago was the sifting of good from bad religions. Faith had a visible presence at the World's Fair. Running in conjunction with the Fair was the World's Parliament of Religions, a gathering of representatives of ten faiths with a stated aim of promoting dialogue and greater understanding. Yet despite the high-minded aims of the Parliament, for most of its visitors the Fair provided a thrilling lesson in the gulf between primitive and advanced faiths. While the representatives of the world religions (a category that did not include Native American faiths) gathered in one of the stately buildings that made the White City so famous, visitors to the Midway Plaisance, the section of the Fair devoted to popular amusements, were treated to mock displays of cannibalism and human sacrifice.[4] Moving from the White City to the Midway was a journey down the ladder of faiths from the enlightened and rational to the superstitious and fanatical.

For the many Americans who wished the Fair to open on Sundays, however, the specter of fanaticism could be found much closer to home. The anti-Sabbatarian case brought together a range of voices in support of the contention that religion and politics be kept apart. But underneath this core claim was a related project to enshrine a particular model of religiosity. At century's end, and for all their vigor and ambition, the proponents of a Christian nation found themselves branded as the vestiges of an outmoded and intolerant form of faith, the ghostly reminders of a discredited Puritan past. The Sunday-opening controversy became a key moment in enshrining a vision of a republican faith that was reasonable, rational, and aligned with the needs of the masses.

Moral Reform in the 1890s

On one level, evangelicals could by the early 1890s feel satisfied with the cultural authority enjoyed by their faith. The previous decade had witnessed a wave of mass revivals, particularly in inner-city areas. Foreign missions provided a vast new field for evangelical endeavor, with thousands volunteering to spread the twin virtues of Protestantism and democracy to benighted lands abroad. At home, a new breed of liberal ministers, under the banner of the Social Gospel movement, marched their faith into another dark world, that of factories and sweatshops, calling on employers and workers to find common ground in a spirit of Christian charity. More broadly, social commentators saw Protestantism moving in lockstep with free enterprise and democracy to forge a powerful civil religion around which all Americans could unite.[5]

However, for Christian activists, this was not nearly enough. A theologically fuzzy Protestantism might form the core of a shared set of national values. But what they wanted was an explicit affirmation of religious tenets in the laws of the nation as well as a recognition that the fate of their society hung on Divine goodwill. To that end, they embarked on an ambitious campaign of moral legislation. Changes in society would, they hoped, give an impulse to their efforts. Many Americans, particularly in small towns and rural communities, worried that traditional values were under threat. An influx of poor migrants from southern and eastern Europe seemed to bring with it a raft of crime, poverty, and disease. Corruption scandals filled the pages of the dailies, while a new class of rich, the robber barons, flaunted their wealth with an exuberance that was unprecedented. In such a climate, the promise of a return to simple virtues grounded in home-grown Protestant piety won a growing number of followers.

Mass immigration also revived that force which had always enlivened Protestant reformers, anti-Catholicism. In the year that the Chicago Fair opened, William J.H. Traynor assumed the leadership of the main nativist organization, the American Protective Association (APA). Like the Know-Nothings in the antebellum era, the APA issued fiery warnings of the threat to republican liberties posed by the army of Catholic invaders marching under the Vatican's orders. Emboldened by these new arrivals, it predicted, the church hierarchy was set to launch a new campaign against the common school while undermining, through the convent and the confessional, the sanctity of the home. The solution was once again a commitment to the separation of church and state, which in nativist hands became a barrier to Catholic influence while allowing Protestant activism to pass unchecked. Under Traynor's skillful leadership, the APA expanded dramatically, attracting a membership in the hundreds of thousands in support of its call to ban from political office all men and women who were beholden to the "ecclesiastical power."

For those men and women who held their nation to be Christian in nature, the ultimate solution to social problems lay in moral legislation at the national level, and they pushed for a raft of bills against gambling, drinking, and prostitution.[6] Yet translating reform ambition into law proved difficult, as prohibition would show. Buoyed by organizations such as the Woman's Christian Temperance Union (WCTU), reformers lobbied hard for prohibition laws at both state and national level, leading mass petition drives backed by enthusiastic rallies. Breakthroughs occurred at state level. In 1881, Kansas became the first state to enact a constitutional ban on the manufacture and sale of liquor, with North and South Dakota entering the Union as dry states in 1889. Where statewide drives failed, local option laws provided smaller victories. By 1906, more than half the counties in the nation had voted to go dry under such laws.[7]

But the great dream, a national prohibition law, remained as elusive as ever. The 1890s, which began with high prohibitionist hopes, turned out to be a period of frustration. After the Dakotas, it would be eighteen years before another state went dry, and in that time four of seven dry states reversed the policy, while enforcement in Kansas virtually ceased. As Thomas R. Pegram argues, politicians in both parties were wary of taking sides and preferred to avoid the issue.[8] Fundamentally, prohibition faced the same difficulty as in the antebellum era. Commentators agreed that alcohol abuse was a major social problem, and called for moderation. Many townspeople viewed the saloon as a disreputable blight on their community. But outright prohibition struck most as draconian, impossible to enforce, and likely to only foster hypocrisy rather than sobriety.

The prohibition drive also stimulated debate about the right of petitioning. This became apparent in 1888 when Congress was deluged with petitions calling for a ban on alcohol in the District of Columbia. Opponents immediately attacked the campaign. Far from expressing community sentiment, the petitions were churned out through a top-down, centralized, and elite-driven system. "The petition factories of the great northeast and west," as one paper drily noted, "seem to be doing a prosperous business."[9] Others raised the familiar objection to female participation. In 1888, the *Washington Sentinel* reported that petitions calling for prohibition in the District of Columbia were arriving "by the wagon load." Many, it noted, were signed by women and children, and as such should be discounted.[10] Echoing the antislavery debates of the 1830s, some critics further argued that citizens outside the District of Columbia had no right to call for prohibition there. Both criticisms came together in an antiprohibition petition campaign in 1888. Signed only by adult men, with their address in the district listed, the petition set out twelve reasons why Congress should reject prohibition. The first was perhaps the most powerful: "Prohibition does not prohibit." A ban on alcohol would only increase crime and drunkenness, for the "appetite of man cannot be legislated away."[11] Regulation rather than suppression was the only effective path.

THE SABBATH QUESTION

If prohibition was a distant goal, a purified Sabbath seemed even further away. A decade of organizational activity had borne little tangible success. The International Sabbath Association, founded in Philadelphia in 1878, began a petition campaign in 1881 to end the delivery and transportation of mail on the Sabbath. Two years later the NRA endorsed the movement, distributing an anti-Sunday mail tract across the nation. Yet even in that proud stronghold of the Puritan Sabbath, New England, desecration seemed to be spreading. After a long campaign, the Boston Public Library opened on Sunday afternoons and evenings in 1873, and the service quickly proved a hit with the public. As an 1885 Massachusetts report made clear, Sunday mails were not slowing down either. The mailing department of the Boston post office employed sixty-five men on Sunday, or half of the workforce in that division. On the same day, some forty-eight carriers and seventeen clerks worked in the delivery department. A sign next to the general delivery window informed customers that mail could be obtained from mornings to evenings on Sunday by simply ringing the bell. Branch offices across the city were open for shorter periods on Sunday, but anywhere from one to five clerks and four to ten carriers, depending on the size of the office, worked three hours on Sundays.[12]

Most gallingly for Sabbatarians, the two Johnson reports on Sunday mails seemed to have lost none of their authority. This became clear in Congressional hearings organized by Senator Henry W. Blair of New Hampshire.[13] In 1888, as Chair of the Senate Committee on Education and Labor, Blair put forward an ambitious Sunday-Rest Law. To rally support, Sabbatarians formed yet another organization, the American Sabbath Union (ASU), with the backing of a range of Protestant denominations. One of their primary goals, as a leader of the NRA, the Reverend Thomas P. Stevenson admitted, was to overturn the Johnson reports, which remained a formidable obstacle to their efforts. The two reports still bore the approval of the nation's legislature. Even worse, as Stevenson lamented, they were "constantly appealed to by the enemies of all Christian features in our Government."[14] But to Stevenson's disappointment, the victory was not yet at hand. The Blair law died in committee.

Another sign of the challenges facing conservative evangelicals was the enduring popularity of Robert Green Ingersoll. Organized freethought had not recovered from the bitter split over the Comstock laws, and by 1893, old warriors like Francis Abbot had slipped into obscurity. Yet crowds still flocked to hear Ingersoll poke fun at Bible-waving zealots. Freethinkers both at home and abroad looked to him as an inspiration. In 1883, a young woman from Iowa thanked the great orator for his lifelong advocacy of freethought. An atheist in a staunchly Methodist community, she named her son Robert as a mark of her gratitude.[15] English secularists informed him of his growing reputation in their country, urging him to embark on an international lecture tour.[16] Ingersoll made no secret of his view that the best way to spend the Sabbath was in wholesome recreation. As he wrote to one correspondent, "A day of innocent pleasures is a sacred day ... A day spent in hearing an orthodox sermon is a lost day." As ever, his guiding principle was that it "is good to do anything at any time that adds to human happiness."[17] Still scarred by his Calvinist upbringing, Ingersoll called on Americans to break the Sabbatarian grip on the first day.

Sabbatarians and the Fair

For Sabbatarians, the World's Fair was the sort of epochal event that might wrench the nation back on the path to Sabbath observance, and they jumped at the opportunity that presented itself. Even before Congress had authorized an exposition, Sabbatarians were mobilizing to ensure that the gates would be shut on Sunday. The precedents were encouraging. The 1876 Centennial Exposition in Philadelphia had not opened on Sunday, despite a large petition campaign in favor. At the great fairs in Paris, American exhibitors had unanimously agreed to remain shut, braving the ridicule of other nations in the process. The key to maintaining the line at Chicago lay with Congress. Washington had a crucial point of leverage over the Fair in the form of a five million dollar appropriation. Without this money, the ambitious plans of the directors could not be realized. In 1892, as Congress debated the conditions of the grant, Sabbatarians bombarded legislators with petitions, calling on them to ensure that taxpayer money not be used "in destroying or throwing discredit on that American institution so dear to the hearts of the American people—the American Sabbath."[18] The arguments in the petitions ranged from the benefits to body and mind to the rights of conscience of Christian workers. For many petitioners, too, the fear of Divine punishment remained vivid. It was a "recognized fact," as members of the Baptist church in Pewamo, Michigan argued, that the United States was a Christian nation whose prosperity and security depended on the Almighty. Who could be sure that He would not rain down a cholera epidemic on a nation that was so ungrateful as to indulge in a celebration of Sabbath desecration? "We fear," the petitioners told Congress, "a visitation of Divine wrath should we before the assembled world trample His day under foot."[19]

Two other points emerge very strongly from these pro-closing petitions. The first is a sense that a watershed had been reached. Running through them is an anxiety that the Chicago Fair, an event which seemed destined to set the future course of the nation in fields as diverse as architecture, industry, and social reform, might also mark the final demise of the American Sabbath. But as the Michigan petitioners' reference to the "assembled world" suggests, the outward face of the Fair was just as important as the inward. By opening the Fair, the United States, once the proud beacon of Christian virtue, would be signaling to a global audience that it had renounced its leadership role. The stream of visitors expected to arrive in Chicago would go home with the knowledge that America was no longer, in moral terms at least, exceptional. The "eyes of the world," as one Tennessee meeting declared, "will be upon us."[20] The international dimension of church-state battles, which had grown so salient in the decades after the Civil War, thus reached its peak in the World's Fair controversy.

The Drive to Open the Fair on Sundays

As pro-closing petitions poured into Congress, anti-Sabbatarians responded. From 1891 to 1893, 892 petitions in favor of Sunday-opening reached the Senate Select Committee on the World's Fair. Leading this petition drive was a religious minority, the Seventh-Day Adventists. By the end of the century, the Adventists were by far the largest and most active Christian minority consecrating the seventh rather than the first day as the true Sabbath. Their roots lay in the antebellum era. Adventism emerged from the Millerite movement, named after a New York farmer who forecast the Second Coming, or Advent, of Jesus on October 22, 1844. In the aftermath of what became known as the Great Disappointment, a small group of Millerites took a new prophet, Ellen G. White, who claimed to have experienced a series of Divine revelations. The church that emerged in 1863 under the leadership of White, her husband James, and a former sea captain called Joseph Bates brought together Adventism and the Saturday Sabbath. With the restoration of the true Biblical Sabbath, Adventists would at last be prepared for the Second Coming.

Adventists rejected all forms of religious legislation on both theological and secular grounds. As their spokesman, Alonzo T. Jones, told the Committee of Education and Labor during the hearings on the Blair bill, they were as opposed to legislation enforcing the Saturday as the Sunday Sabbath. Laws which enforced doctrine were abhorrent for two reasons. First, they brought a human authority between God and His followers. In addition, any government which set itself to punish the unfaithful was guilty of impiously usurping God's role. For this reason, Jones argued, this "national Sunday bill which is under discussion here today is *antichristian*."[21] The same fault applied to blasphemy laws, efforts to enforce Bible-reading in schools, and temperance laws. Fortunately, Jones continued, the Constitution forbade such anti-Christian legislation. The genius of the Founders was that in framing a Constitution which barred any mingling of the civil and religious, they had forged a government which was entirely civil in nature while infused with eminently Christian principles.

By the early 1890s, the Adventist church boasted the organizational reach to mount a national petition campaign. For a relatively small church, it had an impressive geographic spread. The 1890 census revealed less than 44,000 adherents dispersed across 612 counties.

Many were in the Adventist strongholds which stretched westwards from Maine to Iowa, with a cluster on the west coast as well. But small congregations were found in most regions.[22] The church had as well a commitment to broadcasting its message beyond these followers. In addition to a national newspaper, the *American Sentinel*, the Adventists developed a political lobby in the form of the NRLA. One of its aims was to prevent the passage of moral legislation; to this end, it employed a secretary in Washington, Professor W.H. McKee. Another was "to educate the public mind on the true relations of Church and State."[23] To achieve this, the NRLA distributed a stream of pamphlets and blank petitions. The Sunday-closing controversy would demonstrate the potency of this network. Together the Adventists sent 624 of the pro-opening petitions to the Committee, or some 69% of the total (see Appendix C). The response was strongest in Michigan, home of the Adventist headquarters in Battle Creek, which accounted for 104. But in a reflection of its broad reach, the church gathered petitions in a slew of states, from Kansas to Vermont to Texas (see Appendix D).

This campaign was much more than the protest of a religious minority. In a similar manner to the Primitive Baptist campaign against legislative chaplains in the antebellum era, Adventists sought the support of citizens with no affiliation to their church. The petitions themselves make this intent clear. To begin with, the text of the petition was framed to appeal as broadly as possible. It made no reference to theological debates about the true Sabbath, instead simply rejecting any Sunday-closing measure as "committing the United States government to a union of Religion and State." The layout of the petition further showed the desire to capture a non-Adventist population. Space was left for both the name of the Adventist church but also for "others of the same address." There is much evidence that this strategy worked. A small number of petitions are exclusively Adventist. But in most cases the signers are mixed, with the division between Adventists and non-Adventists made quite clear. Sometimes separate columns indicate the divide; elsewhere canvassers added clarifying notes. In Tina, Missouri, the organizer specified that of the thirty-eight signers, only two were Adventists.[24] In the case of another from the same state, it was two of sixteen. Of the fourteen non-Adventists, the canvasser added, all but three were churchgoers, and most were Freemasons or Oddfellows as well.[25] In several cases, no Adventists at all appear. A petition from Florence, Colorado, listed twenty-six names, all of whom belonged to the Methodist

Episcopal Church.[26] As ever, it is difficult to verify the identity of these signers, and the Adventist canvassers no doubt had a strong motivation to present their campaign as having a broad level of community support. But aside from the strength of Sunday-opening sentiment across the nation, there are other signs that many non-Adventists did indeed add their voices to the campaign. A monster petition from Cook County Chicago contained 2345 names under the heading of citizens.[27] Another with 527 signers came from the Chicago Bar Association.[28] Altogether these 624 petitions contained the names of 10,826 men and women who identified as Adventists and 30,039 as non-Adventists.

In the manner of all secularist campaigns, the push to keep the Fair open gathered a diverse set of bedfellows. Another prominent voice was the German-American Turners. Having entered America in the aftermath of the failed 1848 Revolutions, the Turners won a large membership for their program of physical training, particularly through gymnastics, combined with intellectual cultivation. Turner community centers boasted gymnasiums, libraries, lecture rooms, and, in the case of cities such as Chicago and Indianapolis, dance halls. Alongside these social activities was a firm commitment to political activism in support of what the organization termed "rational opinions and ideas." The Turners endorsed policies which reduced economic inequality and improved laboring conditions, advanced state-funded education, and worked for international peace. Integral to this political philosophy was a commitment to an absolute separation of church and state. Praising this "well-established American principle," the Turners declared their hostility to any "interference on the part of religious organizations in matters of state."[29] This mix of physical education, social recreation, and political activism was enormously successful, with more than 300 Turner societies active across the nation by 1900.

For Sabbatarians, the Turners embodied the old foe, the continental European Sabbath which, with its beer drinking, music, and dancing, had been corrupting the sacred day since the 1840s. In Morristown, Tennessee, the organizer of one Sabbatarian petition had no doubt that the sentiment of "most of the very best people" was for Sunday-closing. Arrayed against this enlightened portion of the community, he claimed, was a mass of city-dwellers, who were "mostly of foreign-birth," and who were guilty of "entertaining European ideas" about the Sabbath.[30] Such attacks did not faze the Turners. The National Executive Committee of the Turnerbund soon drafted a protest against Sunday-closing, and forty-three local associations sent it to the Senate Committee. Beginning with the first amendment, the petition denounced any move on the part of the federal government to close the Fair as foreign to "the very spirit of our political institutions." Central to this spirit was a strict separation of church and state. The petition went on to invoke the Fair's status as an international rather than a national event. Visitors to Chicago were likely to come from nations which entertained very different conceptions of the Sabbath. As a consequence, any attempt to impose a narrow Puritan Sabbath on these thousands of guests would not only expose America to international ridicule, but would in addition show the nation to be a poor host.

These petitions were timed to coincide with the key Congressional debates over whether or not the appropriation for the Fair should be made conditional on Sunday-closing. In July 1892, the Senate took up the issue. Joseph Hawley, a Republican from Connecticut, described a nation and a Sabbath which had reached a critical juncture. Open the Fair on Sunday, he warned, and henceforth "the flood gates are opened."[31] Other Senators spoke out against any Congressional interference on the question. Democrat John Morgan of Alabama showed that the southern aversion to religious legislation was still strong, denouncing blue laws as state-sponsored meddling in matters of faith.[32] Yet others pointed to the hypocrisy of Congress in passing Sabbath legislation. All the members of the chamber, as the Populist Senator William Peffer from Kansas reminded his colleagues, received mail twice on Sundays, and most had little compunction in travelling to and from the capital on that day as well.[33] In the end, the Sabbatarians emerged victorious from this first phase of the battle. After several weeks of debate, first the Senate and then the House voted to insert a Sunday-closing clause in the appropriation bill for the World's Fair.

THE DURBOROW COMMITTEE OF 1893

Exultant at this outcome, Sabbatarians proclaimed a great moral victory. It was not, however, the end of either the controversy or the petition campaign for Sunday-opening. In January 1893, the House Committee on the Exposition, chaired by Allan Durborow of Illinois, opened hearings into the question, and a different set of petitions began arriving. Seventeen were cut from the pages of the *Chicago Herald*, a consistent advocate of Sunday-opening. On one from Missoula Montana, the canvasser noted that he had collected all seventy-six names in less than an hour, and that ninety-nine percent of locals were in favor of Sunday-opening.[34] Another from Great Falls, Montana, listed among its signers a member of the Board of the World's Fair Commission, the Secretary of State of Montana, a State Senator, several bank presidents as well as newspaper editors.[35] Fifty-eight came from the "World's Fair Sunday Opening Association." One, dated January 4, 1893, was signed by the inventor Thomas A. Edison along with most of the employees at his laboratory in West Orange, New Jersey.[36] A petition from Pennsylvania contained a brief note from the agent stating that all but one of those he had encountered were in favor.[37] Yet another petition from St. Louis, Missouri, showed the breadth of support for Sunday-opening. It called for the Fair to open from midday, so as not to disrupt morning church services. The lead signer was the Catholic Archbishop of St. Louis, Peter Kenrick; other prominent men of faith to appear were Vicar General P.P. Brady, as well as Bishop Daniel S. Tuttle of the Episcopal Church.[38]

The Durborow Committee began its hearings on January 10, 1893. With the official opening now just months away, leading voices on both sides took the opportunity to press their case.[39] Sabbatarians began with the familiar contention that theirs was a Christian nation. But this time they had the Supreme Court on their side. In his majority opinion in *Church of the Holy Trinity vs the United States*, delivered on February 29, 1892, Justice David Brewer decreed that "This is a Christian nation." At the hearings, speaker after speaker referred to Brewer's judgment. A pamphlet by an Indiana judge setting out the significance of the Court's decision was distributed to all the Committee members. Here was confirmation, the pamphlet argued, that the republic was governed by Christian rather than Jewish, Muslim, or heathen principles; as a consequence, one of the first duties of any legislator must be to uphold the Sunday Sabbath.[40]

In response, proponents of Sunday-opening drew on a set of arguments which would have been familiar to the defenders of Sunday mails in the Jacksonian era. The Seventh-Day Adventist Alonzo T. Jones accused Congress of overstepping its remit by adjudicating on a theological question and raised the prospect of a cascade of religious laws to come. If Congress, he argued, "can interpret the Bible in one point, it can interpret it on every other point."[41] Several of the speakers were liberal Protestants who voiced their dismay at the political ambition of Sabbatarian ministers. The Unitarian W.H. Thomas warned that what he termed the "old love of power," a love which had forever been the "curse of Christianity," was resurfacing in the push for Sunday-closing. Others attacked the credibility of the Brewer judgment. The Republican Mayor of Chicago, Hempstead Washburne, described the decision as both irrelevant and erroneous. The Fair, he reminded the Committee members, was an international and not a national event; as such, it mattered little if the nation was Christian or not. But Washburne was just as convinced that the Court had erred in its interpretation of the Constitution. The first amendment, he told the Committee, barred any legislative intervention in favor of Christianity, just as it barred any measure in aid of the "Jew, the Hindoo, the Buddhist or the heathen."[42]

Washburne proclaimed this to be the majority view. But his argument was undercut by the fact that, once again, the pro-Sabbath forces had won the petition war. The solution was to claim fraud, again a familiar tactic, but this time backed up by a whistle-blower. A Presbyterian minister from Ohio called H.W. Cross testified that he had witnessed double and even triple signings of pro-closing petitions. Furthermore, Sabbatarians had resorted to their old trick of enrolling innocent Sunday School children. These children, Cross alleged, "were not old enough to know whether the expression 'World's Fair' meant the pretty girls in the next pew, or the Columbian Exposition in Chicago."[43] The paradox of petitioning was once again apparent. Citizens on both sides threw themselves into petition campaigns in order to generate publicity and to sway legislators. But all were conscious of the petition's flaws as a democratic tool, particularly its potential to give a false impression of community sentiment, as well as its susceptibility to manipulation.

The World Fair and the Labor Question

One man stood ready to throw his sizeable organization into the fight for Sunday-opening. Samuel Gompers appeared before the Durborow Committee on its first day of hearings. He could still recall his bitterness, Gompers told the committee, when he had been unable to visit the 1876 Centennial Exposition because it was closed on the one day in the week when he was free to attend. "A pang went through my heart and through my mind," he testified, "at the thought that I was deprived of the opportunity of visiting the handicrafts and the results of human ingenuity." To spare workers in 1893 the same disappointment, the AFL mobilized through petitioning. The records of the Senate Select

Committee contain 150 petitions from a range of AFL-affiliated unions directed at individual members of Congress, requesting their "active support" in the campaign by the "organized wage-workers of the United States" for the repeal of the act closing the Fair on Sundays.[44]

The AFL's intervention raises an issue which, though present in earlier Sabbath battles, now reached a heightened intensity. That issue was class. A number of trends in the decades after the Civil War made what was termed the "labor question" one of the most urgent of the era. Mass industrialization produced a generation of workers for whom the old ideal of artisanal independence was unattainable. Accompanying this transformation from producers to wage earners was an unbridled capitalist system marked by severe and recurring economic crises, mass lay-offs, and violent clashes between strikers and authorities. As workers lost control over wages and conditions, and an industrial elite amassed ever greater fortunes, more and more commentators called for government action to protect workers from exploitation and bring about a greater harmony in class relations.

One response to the plight of urban workers was to broaden their access to what was termed "rational recreation." Already in the antebellum era, opponents of strict Sabbath laws were extolling the benefits of Sunday leisure for urban workers. Amidst the tumult of the Gilded Age, any hesitation on this score was coming to be seen as a dangerous indulgence. Middle-class reformers evoked the nightmare vision of an urban underclass turning to drink, gambling, and prostitution in the absence of more wholesome alternatives. Such arguments were shot through with a haughty disdain for working-class sociability. But in a society riven with anxiety about the demoralization of the urban poor, they could be very powerful. By 1892, scores of public libraries across the nation were opening their doors for at least part of Sunday, and museums were beginning to follow suit. On May 31, 1891, Sunday-opening came to the Metropolitan Museum of Art in New York. As the Board of Trustees reported, the move had led several wealthy supporters to cancel their subscriptions. But the public response had been overwhelming, even if it had taken some time, the trustees reported with a snobbishness that was typical of the reformers of the era, to weed out the disreputable elements. While the initial rush of visitors contained several pickpockets, vandals, and others whose habits were "repulsive and unclean," by the end of the year the Sunday crowd was "respectable, law-abiding and intelligent."[45]

The World's Fair promised to be the most powerful agent of moral uplift that the nation had ever seen. Several of the petitions to Congress evoked the plight of the laboring masses who, forced to work six days a week, would be unable to benefit from the wonders on display. The Fair, the petition of the *Chicago Herald* declared, was "the handmaid of all that operates to advance man in his higher nature," and for this reason should be regarded as a "real promoter of pure religion." The petition of the World's Fair Sunday-Opening Association struck an even more moral note, drawing a picture of fairgoers lost in admiration before the wonders of science, art, and industry, their minds turning to the "great Creator of all things useful and beautiful." Conversely, shutting the gates would only spread immorality, for the thousands of disappointed visitors were likely to find refuge not in a church but in a saloon or a brothel. The nation was witnessing, remarked the satirical magazine *Puck*, the bizarre sight of an "unholy alliance" between the Sabbatarian and the saloonkeeper (Fig. 9.1).

In response, Sabbatarians dusted off a strategy that had failed in the past, but that they were sure now stood a much greater chance of success. Appealing directly to workers, they argued that strict Sabbath laws were their best defense against profit-hungry bosses. There would be no day of rest at all if the Fair directors, masking their greed with talk of uplifting the masses, were allowed to open the gates on Sunday. Workers themselves understood this. "The laboring men of this community," declared the moderator of the United Presbyterian Church in the township of Ellison, Illinois, "do not desire" an open fair; on the contrary, most were opposed, since this "would cause thousands of laboring people to work on the Sabbath."[46] This included those employed in the fairgrounds, but also the greater numbers staffing the trains bringing visitors to the Fair. The number affected, the Illinois Sabbath Association argued, could be as high as 200,000. Any worker that voted for Sunday-opening, then, would be denying a fellow laborer a precious day of rest.

If Sabbatarians were confident that this call for solidarity would find a positive response, a major reason was the broader push on the part of organized labor for Sunday-rest laws. Though overshadowed by the demand for the eight-hour day, a mandated day of rest was a key plank for labor reformers in the Gilded Age. Here was an opportunity for Sabbatarians and unions to find common ground. The best chance seemed to lie not with Gompers' AFL, but with the rival labor organization that it would eventually displace, the Knights of Labor.

Fig. 9.1 *An Unholy Alliance*, Puck (August 24, 1892) (Courtesy of New York Public Library)

In the late 1880s, the Chicago Sabbath Association (CSA) allied with several representatives of the Knights of Labor in support of a bill for Sunday-closing. Drafted by the United Clerks' Assembly, and introduced into the state legislature, the bill mandated the closing of all shops on Sundays, with significant fines for violations. At a public meeting in March 1887, the union called on the "Sabbath-observing people of this city" to come together in order to "set free from Sunday labor those who are now held in bondage to it." The city's Sabbatarians responded favorably to the call, with several members of the CSA speaking in support.

Their overlapping interest was even clearer in a larger meeting at the Central Music Hall on March 3, 1889. With hundreds of men and women listening intently, Presbyterian ministers demanded legislative action to bring to an end all "unnecessary toil and labor" on the Sabbath. Among the speakers to follow was George Rogers who pledged the support of the Knights of Labor Council and assured the audience of its "hearty cooperation." God, he was reported as saying, had ordained men to work, but not seven days a week.[47] As field secretary for the ASU, Wilbur F. Crafts visited several labor organizations in 1888 and 1889 to rally their support for petitions calling on Congress to stop Sunday work. The response, he claimed, was overwhelmingly positive. Among the unions to endorse the petition was the Brotherhood of Locomotive Engineers, whose members often had little choice but to work on Sundays. In 1889, Crafts gave a speech at the Academy of Music in Scranton, Pennsylvania, attended by the leader of the Knights of Labor, Terence V. Powderly. Waving one Sunday-rest petition above his head, its pages marked by the grimy hands of the workers who had signed it, Crafts proclaimed the birth of a new and powerful alliance in defense of the Sabbath.

Another promising sign for a broader alignment of workers and churches was the rise of the Social Gospel movement. By the 1880s, prominent churchmen were speaking out against the excesses of an economic order which seemed to be throwing more and more workers into poverty and despair. One of the most celebrated was the Congregational pastor Washington Gladden. Troubled by the savage inequality he saw around him, Gladden attacked employers who made a show of their Christian faith while rejecting measures which would improve the lives of their workers. On several occasions he intervened in major strikes, defending the rights of unions to organize, and calling on employers to seek common ground with their workers.[48] Labor leaders expressed their appreciation for such efforts on the part of pastors. On August 17, 1892, Samuel Gompers wrote to Reverend H.A. Davis in Logansport, Indiana, to praise a sermon he had given on the labor question. Gompers was particularly moved by his eloquent pleas "on behalf of the down-trodden wealth producers," and hoped that together they could continue the battle for the "emancipation of mankind."[49]

In the end, however, the Sabbatarian effort to win over workers failed. For every minister expressing sympathy for workers, there were several who insisted that the poor should accept their station in life. As conservative pastors offered up sermons justifying poverty as a necessary component of a divinely ordained social order, labor reformers responded with hostility. Gompers may have seen the Reverend Davis as an ally, but he also saw him as an exception. Ministers as a rule had little interest in the poor, he wrote, except to convince them to "to bear a yoke of oppression" or be the "sycophantic slaves of their more favored fellow men."[50] The resentment at the spread of opulent church edifices which seemed purposefully designed to keep out the poor was as biting as ever.

Satirists seized on the Sunday-opening controversy to drive home the point. The magazine *Puck* cheekily suggested that Sunday was already a day of entertainment. One could enjoy the "big Sunday newspaper show," for instance, or the "Sunday Riding and Driving Show." Then there was the "fashionable Sunday worship show." The accompanying image showed haughty and well-dressed attendees being ushered to their pews by a deferential minister. The poor, however, were turned away.[51]

Hostility was just as strong on the part of the organization in which Sabbatarians had placed such high hopes, the Knights of Labor. As its leader Terence V. Powderly affirmed in 1893, the Knights had not resiled from their cardinal principle that men and women should work five days a week, with one day of rest for God and the other for humanity. But they would not support a Sunday-closing movement which, in the present state of affairs, would allow the wealthy to attend the Fair while excluding the poor. Powderly also targeted a weakness that was shared by both the Sabbatarian and Social Gospel movement, their unwillingness to countenance radical reforms to the capitalist system which might truly shift power toward the laboring classes. In an editorial in the Knights' journal, Powderly attacked the prominent Sabbatarian Wilbur F. Crafts, who had proclaimed the alliance between workers and churches in 1889. Rather than "pottering around the country" lecturing workers on religion, Crafts should strike at the root of the problem. Only a government takeover of the railroad industry could bring to an end Sunday trains. Crafts and his fellow ministers would never support this, Powderly noted, for fear of being labeled socialists. But until they did, workers would rightly see them as the handmaidens of the rich and the enemies of the poor.[52] The only conclusion that a worker could draw was that all the agitation for Sunday-closing had little to do with Christianity. Instead, it was yet another manifestation of that clerical lust for power which Powderly labeled "Churchianity."

Sabbatarians expressed both disappointment and alarm. Writing in *Our Day*, Crafts regretted the Knights' stance as a "flat contradiction" of their earlier petitions for Sunday-closing on the nation's railways. An open fair, he argued, was sure to increase the rail traffic on that day. Just as regrettable was the failure of American unions to follow the lead of their British counterparts. There, Crafts noted, unions firmly resisted the Sunday-opening of museums and libraries on the grounds that it would sabotage the campaign for a shorter working week. Crafts ended with a warning to his fellow Sabbatarians. The fact that labor unions and churches were warring was, Crafts continued, a "national calamity," and a serious threat to the Sunday-closing movement. Congress was sure to be swayed much more, he wrote, by the "aggressive labor vote" than the "too meek church vote."[53]

Women and the Sabbath Question

Crafts and his fellow Sabbatarians could always soothe their disappointment at labor's betrayal by pointing to the loyalty of a much larger group of Americans, white Christian women. Whether through street processions, lobbying politicians, or canvassing for signatures, women were vital to the passage of the moral legislation that would cleanse the nation of its sins. The push for a redeemed Sabbath drew on the support and energy of the largest woman's organization in the nation, the WCTU. Founded in 1874, the WCTU quickly expanded its goals from the enforcement and enactment of temperance laws to the stamping out of social vices of all kinds. The surest way to ensure the passage of such laws, in turn, was to grant women, the great moral custodians of the nation, the right to vote. This was an immensely appealing program. Under the leadership of its second President, Frances E. Willard, the WCTU enjoyed a period of extraordinary growth, reaching a peak membership of 154,213 in 1892.[54] By then, Willard had broadened the organization's program to include a Christian government. In 1887, Willard set out her vision before the delegates assembled at the national convention. It was time to acknowledge that the "supreme authority" in the life of individuals and the nation was Christ's law. This was not a call, she added, for a union of church and state, an outcome which all "enlightened Christians" would abhor. But it was a call for the enactment of what Willard termed "Christian politics and laws."[55]

Central to this Christian politics was Sabbath observance. In 1884, Willard established a special department for the protection of the Sabbath which, under the leadership of Josephine C. Bateham and through a host of local auxiliaries, worked tirelessly to beat back the tide of Sabbath desecration. Much of this effort was directed to the enactment or enforcement of laws against Sunday saloons. But state superintendents reported with as much concern the spread of all forms of secular activity, from mails and trains to baseball games. With the same resolve as their Sabbatarian allies, the WCTU fixed on the coming World's Fair as the moment to draw a line in the sand. As early as

1889, the National Convention formally protested any possible opening of the Fair on Sundays.[56] The following year, Bateham set out what was at stake. So far, she declared, "we have been only skirmishing." The great battle was to come at Chicago. A defeat there would be, Bateham warned, "unmeasured calamity." An open fair would put the nation on a secularizing path from which it could never turn back. Just as alarmingly, America would no longer be the torchbearer of Christian virtue to the world. "We are in imminent danger," Bateham concluded, "of setting an example to the world of a nation that having for one hundred years enjoyed the Sabbath has at last outgrown and discarded it."[57]

Yet women were far from unified in support of moral legislation. The Adventist-organized petitions show a strong female involvement. It is impossible to calculate the number of women who signed Adventist petitions. There is no formal gender division, and in many cases, signers simply put their initial rather than their first name or title. But anecdotal evidence points to a sizeable female presence both as canvassers and supporters. In a wholly Adventist petition from San Jose, California, the lead signer is Mrs. Nichols; of the thirty-four other signers, half can be identified on the basis of their first name or title as women.[58] Adventist women were also clearly active in collecting both male and female signatures from outside their church. In Plum River, Illinois, Charlotte Taylor gathered thirty-eight names on her petition, with fifteen identifying as Adventists.[59] In Lawrence County, Arkansas, Mrs. Hannah Beach sent a petition to Senator James H. Berry with the names of seventy-five non-Adventists attached.[60] Nancy F. Wilson sent a petition with the names of eight residents of Mount Pleasant, Missouri, and specified that none were Sabbath-keepers apart from herself.[61]

Alongside such religiously inspired protests was a mobilization on the part of secular-minded women's organizations. In the post-Civil War era, women's clubs flourished across the nation, gathering thousands of mostly middle-class members to a program which initially focused on self-improvement and education, but then turned in the Progressive era to the cause of social reform. Clubwomen undertook research, engaged in public debates and lobbied for remedial legislation on a range of social ills. They soon turned their attention to the World's Fair. By 1890, the Chicago Woman's Club was declaring the coming Fair a "subject of overwhelming interest" to its members, with Sunday-opening a key point of concern.[62] By a large majority, they were in favor. Some envisaged the fate of the poor woman shut out of the Fair on the one day that she might attend. One clubwoman professed herself to be a member of the working-class who would suffer most from Sunday-closing.[63] Not content with passing resolutions, the Clubwomen decided to join the public campaign. In a letter to the Senate Committee, the Secretary attached the Club's resolutions. In addition to the powerful moral uplift promised by an open Fair, the resolutions referred to the global dimension. Echoing the concerns of the Turners and many others, the Chicago Woman's Club saw a nation which was about to make a show of its narrow-mindedness. This was, the Club reminded the Senate Committee, a "*World's* Exposition." For this to be true, it went on, "we must be *cosmopolitan* and not *provincial* in its administration."[64]

ELIZABETH CADY STANTON AND THE OPENING OF THE FAIR

The Sunday-opening controversy gave one woman in particular a platform from which to attack clerical influence and to urge other women to embrace secularist principles. Elizabeth Cady Stanton was a drafter of the 1848 Declaration of Sentiments, the call to arms which electrified the campaign for women's civil and political rights, before founding the National Woman Suffrage Association (NWSA) with Susan B. Anthony. Stanton was also a freethinker who welcomed the advent of the National Liberal League and subscribed to the *Index*. By her own account, her hostility to churches stemmed from a personal crisis during her adolescence. In her memoirs, she recalled the terrifying impression made on her by one of the leaders of the Second Great Awakening, Charles Finney, when he preached at the church she attended in Troy, New York. She could remember clearly the sight of Finney, or the "terrifier of human souls" as she called him, in the pulpit, his arms flailing and eyes rolling, casting anathemas on the depravity of the human heart and evoking in gruesome detail the fiery torments that awaited all sinners.[65] As a result of what she called her gloomy Presbyterian upbringing, Stanton was soon was wracked with fears of eternal damnation. The crisis was relieved when she at last found salvation, though not in the form that Finney would have approved. Through her brother-in-law, Stanton found an escape from spiritual torment in the writings of European phrenologists and materialists such as George Combe and Franz Joseph Gall. From that moment her "religious superstitions," as she put it, "gave way to rational ideas based on scientific facts," and the rightness of her new path was confirmed by a powerful sensation of happiness.[66]

Stanton would go on to make two very powerful arguments concerning religion and the role of women. The first was that Christianity had worked to subjugate rather than liberate women. In an article published in the *North American Review* in 1885, entitled "Has Christianity Benefited Women?", Stanton answered overwhelmingly in the negative.[67] Churchmen liked to argue, she began, that Christianity had elevated women from their degraded position in pagan societies to their current honored rank. History showed the opposite to be true. With the spread of Christianity, women's social influence had in fact diminished. The leaders of the Primitive Church, she argued, systematically denied women any position of influence. Even more damaging was the Augustinian conception of original sin which, more than any other doctrine, cast women in the role of sinful temptresses. For Stanton, any rise in women's status that had occurred over the centuries was the result of two non-religious factors: the democratic customs of the primitive Germanic tribes which exerted such an influence over the Anglo-Saxon races, and the tradition of gallantry which evolved from the French courts of the medieval era. The church, meanwhile, clung to its traditional view of women as inferior and corrupting.

Stanton's historical sketch would be given much greater heft in the hands of Matilda Joslyn Gage. In 1878, Gage launched a stunning attack on churches at an assembly in Rochester to celebrate the thirtieth anniversary of the Seneca Falls convention. In a series of resolutions, she denounced the "lessons of self-sacrifice and obedience" drilled into women by organized Christianity, and which had left them "completely subjugated by priestcraft and superstition."[68] Fifteen years later, in the very year that the World's Fair opened, she published a detailed exposition of her thesis entitled *Woman, Church and State*. In over 500 pages of dense historical analysis, she charted the manner in which the rise of organized Christianity had displaced matriarchal societies and created the political, civil and spiritual subservience under which women labored still. For Gage, the key to this subservience was the "long continued and powerfully repressing influence of church teaching in regard to the created inferiority of women," a teaching which even the powerful forces of nineteenth-century civilization had been unable to dispel.[69] In a manner that was typical of secularists, Gage also drew on anti-Catholic sentiment. Citing a series of graphic exposés written by former priests and nuns, she denounced clerical celibacy and the confessional box as incitements to sexual abuse. But in relation to the status of women, Protestants were just as culpable. The Reformation might have cured the church of many of its abuses, but Luther and the other reformers had not wavered in the slightest from the papacy's hostility toward the female sex.[70]

Freethinkers, as we have seen, often worried that women were innately susceptible to religious influence. Many opposed giving women the vote, for example, out of fear that the churches would be armed with a powerful and pliable electoral force. Stanton rebutted these arguments by asserting that the problem was not biological but pedagogical. Women simply needed to be taught about the secular origins of their government. The "brave heroes of our revolution," as she wrote to Clara Bewick Colby in 1887, were fearful of "priestcraft & religious fanaticism in politics"; for this reason, and with the example of European nations in mind, they had sought to safeguard their republic from ecclesiastical power.[71] Once they understood this history, women would be able to see the religious chains in which they were held, and would then become the fiercest opponents of any push for a Christian government. Gage agreed, citing the example of Frances Wright, who as early as the Jacksonian era had seen the threat to civil and political liberties posed by the Christian party. Women would do well, she argued, to draw inspiration from that "clear-seeing, liberty-loving, Scotch free-thought woman," and throw off the tyranny of church and state which held them in bondage.[72]

The World's Fair was the perfect opportunity to force a breach between women and the moral lobby. In an 1889 article, Stanton made clear her hostility to Blue Laws, which she considered a vehicle for evangelical aggrandizement. The power of the pulpit, she wrote, is "always aggressive and proscriptive," and always aiming at despotic control. "There is no tyranny so insidious," she wrote, "as that in the name of religion." Furthermore, the real enemy of a tranquil Sabbath was churches and their bells. She had once lived, she recalled, within one block of five different churches. "With the meetings, funerals and Lenten seasons, all punctuated and emphasized with those bells," Stanton wrote, "I was nearly distracted."[73] As the controversy escalated, Stanton began issuing a series of articles and pamphlets. In the *North American Review*, she called on women to emulate Lucretia Mott. A member of the Hicksite branch of Quakers, Mott campaigned against the closing of the Philadelphia Exposition in 1876, and once that battle was lost, refused to set foot on the fairgrounds.[74]

In her arguments for Sunday-opening, Stanton found support from her great collaborator, Susan B. Anthony. It was Anthony and not

Stanton who appeared before the Durborow Committee on Sunday-closing. Like Stanton, Anthony paid tribute to Lucretia Mott and her stand against "the bigotry that shut the doors on Sunday." She then reminded the Committee of the past battles over the Sabbath, and how ludicrous they now seemed. She could recall, for instance, the long and bitter fight for Sunday streetcars in Philadelphia. Now, however, Sunday cars were beloved by all. "What Philadelphian," she asked, "what churchman, or minister would propose to stop the street-cars in Philadelphia or any other city on Sunday?"[75] Anthony refrained from the kind of assault on organized Christianity that Stanton reveled in. Nevertheless, she was forthright in her belief that shutting the Fair at the behest of an intolerant minority would be an affront to American democracy. There were thousands of working women, she reminded the Committee, who had patiently saved what little money they had in order to experience the marvels of the fair. For Congress to deny them this chance would be nothing less than a "tyranny."

When Stanton and Anthony set out to bring their fellow suffragists on board, however, the divisions within the movement were laid bare. At the 1892 meeting of what was now the National American Woman Suffrage Association (NAWSA), Stanton put forward a resolution in support of the fair opening. While the majority view seemed favorable to the resolution, several delegates were opposed, and others thought the entire question a distraction from their core purpose of winning the vote.[76] With deadlock likely, Stanton withdrew her resolution. The following year's convention was the first in forty years that Stanton had not attended, but her absence did not prevent the question returning with even greater force. Some of the delegates denounced any push for Sunday-opening as an affront to religious women. As Martha Davis argued, thousands of women in her state of Kansas signed petitions against Sunday-opening, and their view should be respected.[77] Not surprisingly, delegates who were also members of the WCTU were adamant in their opposition. One of these, Alice Pickler, reminded her fellow suffragists that their movement stood no chance of success without the support of religious men and women.[78] But the views of Stanton and Anthony found support as well. The bill which mandated Sunday-closing, Helen Tindall argued, was a landmark in the history of religious legislation, and an attack on freedom of conscience that all delegates should oppose.[79] In the end, the delegates pulled back from any decisive stance. The motion for a resolution was indefinitely postponed.

New England Historians and the Image of the Puritan

In these debates, Sunday-openers were keen to stress that they did not oppose religion itself, but merely what they saw as its exploitation for intolerant ends. The question, then, at least in part, was what constituted a true religion, and as ever secularists gave it clarity by pointing to negative examples. One of the speakers at the Durborow Committee hearings was the novelist Marion Foster Washburne. For Washburne, the temerity of Sabbatarians in demanding the closure of the Fair was startling. Most Americans, she contended, "are simply quiet and tolerant private citizens, who, for the most part, are rather amused that any one should be intolerant."[80] What she was doing here was ascribing to Sunday-closers an outmoded model of religiosity, one based on coercion rather than assent and prejudice rather than charity.

The shorthand for such an illegitimate religion was the Puritan. In popular prints, Sabbatarians were depicted as witch-burners and heresy hunters casting their dark colonial shadow over the White City. The controversy thus brought to a climax the long-running polemic over the legacy of the Puritan settlers. By the last decade of the century, anti-Puritanism had spread from the South and the mid-West to New England itself. Leading the charge were two members of an esteemed Massachusetts family. In 1887, Brooks Adams published the book which established his reputation as a historian, *The Emancipation of Massachusetts*. Adams was unsparing in his denunciation of the Puritan settlement and its leaders. The Puritan clergy were bigots and zealots, driven by a love of worldly power, and relishing the chance to punish any man or woman who dared to challenge their despotic authority. For these men, persecution was not a regrettable necessity, but Heaven-sent opportunity.[81] A similarly damning portrayal came from Charles Francis Adams. But he drew a broader lesson from the sorry story of Puritan intolerance. The ability of the nation to move past its dark opening chapter pointed to an important law of historical progress. All modern societies, Charles Adams argued, were moving together in the same upward direction—not toward an abandonment of religion, but simply "the emancipation of man from superstition and caste."[82] The Puritan stage was a necessary though retrograde phase of social development in the unstoppable march toward greater freedom.

As ever, the Puritans had their defenders. John Gorham Palfrey's five-volume *History of New England* presented Puritan intolerance as a forgivable response to the fragile nature of their settlement. Isolated in a harsh and strange wilderness, and far removed from any support or comfort, the Puritans were desperate to maintain a rigid discipline and cohesiveness. In this situation, they rightly judged that tolerating dissent was an indulgence they could not afford. A similar case was made by Henry Martyn Dexter. In an argument often used by defenders of the Puritans, Dexter warned of the folly of judging men and women of the seventeenth century by the standards of the nineteenth. "We may as well," Dexter wrote, "blame the New England colonists for not using the telegraph and the fast mail train."[83] It was absurd to castigate the Puritans for not embodying the enlightened principles of the nineteenth century.

Such defenses attracted scorn from the anti-Puritan school. Charles Francis Adams dismissed Palfrey and Dexter as members of what he termed the "filio-pietistic" branch of New England historians. Judged solely by the standards of the seventeenth century, the leaders of the Puritan colony stood out as intolerant and cruel, even when set against the excesses of the Spanish Inquisition. Palfrey and Dexter, Adams noted, attacked the medieval church for its ruthless crackdown on heretics. Yet when Puritans engaged in the same practice, they found mitigating factors. For Adams, the two were near-identical. "One may in color be a dark drab," he wrote, "while the other is unmistakably a jetty black."[84] Alongside these attacks on the Puritan was a growing veneration for their most famous victim, Roger Williams. Persecuted by theocrats, Williams more than ever took on the aura of a martyr for civil and religious liberty. In his 1896 work, *The Beginners of a Nation*, historian and novelist Edward Eggleston described Williams as a "secularist in governmental theory" whose commitment to church-state separation was a lesson still for modern Americans.[85]

The Outcome: A Semi-open Fair

In 1893, the lesson appeared even more salient, for Sabbatarians seemed on the verge of a famous victory. On May 1, 1893, the White City was at last unveiled to the public by President Grover Cleveland. Reporters described the mix of joy and awe which swept over the hundreds of thousands of men, women, and children as they thronged to see the beautiful buildings and wondrous inventions on display. But on the first Sunday of the Fair, the picture was very different. Thousands arrived to find the gates locked; only those with urgent business to carry out were allowed into the fairgrounds.

Events, however, would soon turn against the Sunday-closers. On May 16, the Fair directors voted by a margin of thirty-four to two to open the gates on the following Sunday, on the grounds that a large majority of the people were in favor. To satisfy the Sunday-rest movement, they resolved that no employee would be expected to work seven days a week. Nor was this an entirely open Fair. The machinery would not run, and individual exhibitors were free not to open their doors. Yet even a restricted Sunday Fair represented a major blow to the Sabbatarians. Thanks to what it called "dishonest and irreligious schemers," one Christian paper lamented, the great Fair had become a "professedly national secular show."[86] *Puck*, in contrast, was exultant. As early as December 1892 in a drawing entitled "It Will Be Open" (Fig. 9.2), it had anticipated the moment when a mass of respectable visitors streamed through the gates, while a sour-faced Sabbatarian looked on aghast.

Initially, the public response was strong. A Sunday in June attracted 98,300 attendees; according to the *Chicago Tribune*, most seemed to

Fig. 9.2 *It Will Be Open!* Puck (December 14, 1892) (Courtesy of New York Public Library)

belong to the poorer classes.[87] Their numbers, however, soon declined. On Saturday July 8, for example, there were 94,897 admissions, falling to 44,461 the next day, before rising again to 88,797 on Monday, a pattern that was repeated on the following Sundays.[88] For Sabbatarians, the low turnout on Sundays was a welcome sign of mass piety. In a revised edition of his *Sabbath for Man*, Wilbur F. Crafts celebrated what he saw as a boycott on the part of a "ruling majority" in the nation.[89]

For most commentators, however, there was a far more pragmatic set of factors at play. Put simply, Sunday visitors were expected to pay the full price of admission for a diminished experience. With the machinery silent, and several major exhibits closed, there was little to do apart from wander the grounds and study the architecture. All that the attendance figures proved, as the *Nation* argued, was that the public were rightly reluctant to pay "the full price of fifty cents for only about half of the show."[90] The mistake of the Directors was not in opening the Fair, but in refusing to try the experiment of half-price admission.[91]

For this reason, the opening of the fair was celebrated as a decisive repudiation not just of Sabbatarians but also of their vision of law-enforced faith. Robert Ingersoll proclaimed the power of religious orthodoxy to be once and for all broken. No longer were the minister and priest "regarded as the foundation of wisdom."[92] One paper decreed that what it termed "theological legislation" would never be tried again.[93] Both judgments proved to be premature. In the decade after 1893, the NRA and its allies would continue to lobby Congress for their cherished goals, from a national Sunday law to a prohibition amendment to that great dream, the Christianized Constitution. Yet for all their vigor, they made little headway, and the Chicago Fair controversy reveals a key reason why: the entrenched public hostility to anything that smacked of religious fanaticism. Most of the advocates of an open fair agreed that religion had a vital role to play in cultivating and preserving public morality. But they demanded as well that religion be modest, non-coercive and dedicated to the interests of the greatest number possible. Throughout the contest, secularists made the familiar call for the separation of religion and politics. But just as striking is the ongoing strength of their conviction that only a secular state would save religion from the temptation to zealotry which, in the minds of so many, had hung over it since the Puritan era, and which it was time to renounce once and for all.

NOTES

1. Ballenger to Gompers, June 20, 1892, Files of the Office of the President, General Correspondence April 1888–December 1904, The Samuel Gompers era (microfilm).
2. Gompers to Ballenger, June 22, 1892, *American Federation of Labor Records, 1883–1925*, Manuscripts Division, Library of Congress, Washington, DC.
3. Trumbull White and Wm. Igleheart, *The World's Columbian Exposition, Chicago, 1893* (Philadelphia: P.W. Ziegler, 1893), 19–20. On the Sunday-closing controversy, McCrossen, *Holy Day, Holiday*, 70–77; Foster, *Moral Reconstruction*, 101–105.
4. Orsi, *Between Heaven and Earth*, 189; John P. Burris, *Exhibiting Religion: Colonialism and Spectacle at International Expositions, 1851–1893* (Charlottesville: University Press of Virginias, 2001), 123–66. On the Parliament of Religions, Tomoko Masuzawa, *The Invention of World Religions: Or, How European Universalism Was Preserved in the Language of Pluralism* (Chicago: University of Chicago Press, 2005), 265–74.
5. Mark D. McGarvie, *Law and Religion in American History: Public Values and Private Conscience* (Cambridge: Cambridge University Press, 2016), 83–84.
6. Gaines M. Foster identifies 511 moral legislation bills from the 47th (1881–1883) to 56th (1899–1901) Congresses. Of these, only 30 passed. *Moral Reconstruction*, 237.
7. Thomas R. Pegram, *Battling Demon Rum: The Struggle for a Dry America, 1800–1933* (Chicago: Ivan R. Dee, 1998), 111.
8. Ibid., 52. See also Jack S. Blocker, *Retreat from Reform: The Prohibition Movement in the United States, 1890–1913* (Westport, CT: Greenwood Press, 1976).
9. *Washington Bee*, February 4, 1888.
10. Cited in *Wheeling Register*, February 6, 1888.
11. Rec. January 16, 1888. SEN 50A-J6.1 (Committee on the District of Columbia), National Archives, Washington, DC.
12. *Massachusetts. Report on the Statistics of Labor. Boston* (1885), Part II. Sunday Labor, 87. For the sign next to the window, *Woman's Journal*, March 11, 1893.
13. Gordon B. McKinney, *Henry W. Blair's Campaign to Reform America: From the Civil War to the U.S. Senate* (Lexington: University Press of Kentucky, 2013).
14. "Sunday Rest Bill", Senate Misc. Documents 43, 50th Congress, 2nd Session, 36.
15. Jessie Wilson Manning to Ingersoll, April 16, 1883. Papers of R.G. Ingersoll, Manuscripts Division, Library of Congress, Washington, DC.

16. G.J. Holyoake to Ingersoll, June 16, 1888, in ibid.
17. Ingersoll to unknown correspondent, July 20, 1885, in ibid.
18. The Sabbatarian and anti-Sabbatarian petitions in this chapter come from the records of the Senate Select Committee on the World's Fair, SEN 52A-J27.1., National Archives, Washington, DC.
19. Rec. January 17, 1893. SEN 52A-J27.1.
20. Signed May 4, 1892. SEN 52A-J27.1.
21. "Sunday Rest Bill", 22. Italics in original.
22. William M. Newman and Peter L. Halvorson, *Atlas of American Religion: The Denominational Era, 1776–1990* (Walnut Creek, CA: Altamira Press, 2000), 159–61.
23. *American Sentinel*, March 6, 1890.
24. No date. SEN 52A-J27.1.
25. Sprague (MO). Rec. May 2, 1892. SEN 52A-J27.1.
26. Rec. May 2, 1892. SEN 52A-J27.1.
27. Rec. July 6, 1892. SEN 52A-J27.1.
28. Rec. July 11, 1892. SEN 52A-J27.1.
29. Henry Metzner, *A Brief History of the American Turnerbund*, tr. Theodore Stempfel (Pittsburgh: American Turnerbund, 1924), 54.
30. Signed March 9, 1892.
31. *Congressional Record* (Senate), July 11, 1892, 5999.
32. Ibid., 6003.
33. Ibid., 6000. The charge of hypocrisy was also made in reference to prohibition. As one Senator remarked, whiskey was freely available in the Senate restaurant, where it was sold as "cold tea." *Congressional Record*, July 12, 1892, 6101.
34. Rec. January 21, 1893. SEN 52A-J27.1.
35. Rec. January 1893. SEN 52A-J27.1.
36. Signed January 4, 1893. SEN 52A-J27.1.
37. No date. SEN 52A-J27.1. SEN 52A-J27.1.
38. Rec. January 21, 1893. SEN 52A-J27.1
39. The transcript does not appear in either the published or unpublished records of the House Committee hearings. The following analysis relies on an account published by the Seventh Day Adventist church, entitled *The Captivity of the Republic* (International Religious Liberty Association, 1893).
40. *Captivity of the Republic*, 47.
41. Ibid., 38.
42. Ibid., 112.
43. Ibid., 25.
44. Ibid., 115–16.
45. *Annual Report of the Trustees of the Association* (New York: Metropolitan Museum of Art, 1892), 13. See McCrossen, *Holy Day, Holiday*, 65–71.

46. Rec. January 19, 1893. SEN 52A-J27.1.
47. *Chicago Tribune*, March 14, 1887; *Inter Ocean*, March 4, 1889. On the Chicago meetings, and the failed alliance for Sunday-rest laws between the city's Sabbatarians and labor leaders, William A. Mirola, "Shorter Hours and the Protestant Sabbath: Religious Framing and Movement Alliances in Late-Nineteenth-Century Chicago," *Social Science History* 23, no. 3 (1999): 395–433.
48. Christopher H. Evans, *The Social Gospel in American Religion: A History* (New York: New York University Press, 2017).
49. Gompers to H.A. Davis, August 17, 1892. American Federation of Labor records, Manuscripts Division, Library of Congress, Washington, DC.
50. Ibid. On Chicago workers' hostility to churches and their rival vision of true Christianity in the Gilded Age, Heath W. Carter, *Union Made: Working People and the Rise of Social Christianity in Chicago* (New York: Oxford University Press, 2015), 89–96.
51. *Puck*, October 21, 1891.
52. "Powderly on Sunday Rest," *Journal of the Knights of Labor*, March 23, 1893. On religion and the Knights of Labor, Robert E. Weir, *Beyond Labor's Veil: The Culture of the Knights of Labor* (University Park: Pennsylvania State University Press, 1996), Ch. 2.
53. "Editorial Notes," *Our Day*, 11 (Jan–June 1893): 150.
54. Foster, *Moral Reconstruction*, 86.
55. "President's Annual Address," *Minutes of the National Woman's Christian Temperance Union, at the Fourteenth Annual Meeting* (Chicago: Woman's Temperance Publication Association, 1887), 75.
56. *Minutes of the National Woman's Christian Temperance Union, at the Sixteenth Annual Meeting* (Chicago: Woman's Temperance Publication Association, 1889), 24.
57. *Minutes of the National Woman's Christian Temperance Union, at the Seventeenth Annual Meeting* (Chicago: Woman's Temperance Publication Association, 1890), 259.
58. Rec. May 4, 1892. SEN 52A-J27.1.
59. Rec. May 26, 1892. SEN 52A-J27.1.
60. No date. SEN 52A-J27.1.
61. Rec. June 20, 1892. SEN 52A-J27.1.
62. Henriette Greenbaum Frank and Amalie Hofer Jerome, *Annals of the Chicago Woman's Club for the First Forty Years of Its Organization, 1876–1916* (Chicago: Chicago Woman's Club, 1916), 103.
63. Ibid., 106.
64. Signed December 3, 1892. Italics in original. SEN 52A-J27.1.
65. Elizabeth Cady Stanton, *Eighty Years and More (1815–1897): Reminiscences of Elizabeth Cady Stanton* (New York: European Publishing Company, 1898), 41.

66. Ibid., 44.
67. Elizabeth Cady Stanton, "Has Christianity Benefited Women?" *North American Review* 140, no. 342 (1885): 389–99. For Stanton's views on religion, Sue Davis, *The Political Thought of Elizabeth Cady Stanton: Women's Rights and the American Political Traditions* (New York: New York University Press, 2008), 178–195; Kathi Kern, *Mrs Stanton's Bible* (Ithaca, NY: Cornell University Press, 2001); Sehat, *Myth of American Religious Freedom*, 98–108, 133–34, 148–54.
68. Elizabeth Cady Stanton, Susan B. Anthony and Matilda Joslyn Gage, eds., *History of Woman Suffrage*, vol. 3 (Rochester, 1886), 124.
69. Matilda Joslyn Gage, *Woman, Church and State: A Historical Account of the Status of Woman Through the Christian Ages, with Reminiscences of the Matriarchate* (New York: Truth Seeker, 1893), 64.
70. Ibid., 137.
71. Stanton to Clara Bewick Colby, December 25, 1887, in *Selected Papers of Elizabeth Cady Stanton and Susan B. Anthony*, ed. Ann D. Gordon, vol. 5 (New Brunswick, NJ: Rutgers University Press, 2009), 72.
72. Gage, *Woman, Church and State*, 515.
73. *Omaha Daily Bee*, March 17, 1889.
74. Elizabeth Cady Stanton, "Sunday at the World's Fair," *North American Review* 154, no. 423 (1892): 255.
75. *Captivity of the Republic*, 121.
76. Elizabeth Cady Stanton, Susan B. Anthony and Matilda Joslyn Gage, eds, *History of Woman Suffrage*, vol. 4 (Rochester, 1902), 185–86; *Washington Post*, January 22, 1892.
77. *Proceedings of the Twenty-Fifth Annual Convention of the National American Woman Suffrage Association* (Washington, DC, 1893), 97.
78. Ibid., 96.
79. Ibid.
80. Cited in Jones, *Captivity of the Republic*, 50.
81. Brooks Adams, *The Emancipation of Massachusetts* (Boston: Houghton Mifflin, 1887).
82. Charles Francis Adams, *Massachusetts: Its Historians and Its History. An Object Lesson* (Boston: Houghton Mifflin, 1893), 2.
83. Henry Martyn Dexter, *As to Roger Williams and His 'banishment' from the Massachusetts Plantation* (Boston: Congregational Publishing Society, 1876), 106.
84. Adams, *Massachusetts*, 34.
85. Edward Eggleston, *The Beginners of a Nation: A History of the Source and Rise of the Earliest English Settlements in America* (New York: D. Appleton, 1896), 305.
86. *Northern Christian Advocate*, May 31, 1893.

87. *Chicago Daily Tribune*, June 13, 1893.
88. *Springfield Republican*, July 16, 1893. The average paid admissions for the Fair was 119,984. White and Igleheart, *World's Columbian Exposition*, 632.
89. Wilbur F. Crafts, *The Sabbath for Man* (Washington, DC: International Reform Bureau, 1894), 12.
90. *Nation*, July 13, 1893.
91. *Washington Post*, July 5, 1893; *New York Times*, July 29, 1893.
92. *The Works of Robert Green Ingersoll*, vol. 12 (New York: C. P. Farrell, 1900), 373.
93. *Daily Inter Ocean* (IL), June 21, 1893.

CHAPTER 10

Conclusion

In 1912 Sunday mails, which evangelicals had for so long regarded as a curse on the nation, came largely to an end. But while applauding the result, Sabbatarians could hardly take the credit. The impetus came instead from union activism in support of a six-day week combined with Congressional penny-pinching. As the postmaster general reported in 1911, new regulations stipulated that the thousands of postal employees who worked on Sundays had to be given time off during the week as a compensation. Without extra funding to make up for the shortfall, the department chose to minimize the number of staff affected by slashing the Sunday service. Henceforth, the general delivery window would cater only to those collecting urgent mail as well as certain groups, notably traveling salesmen and hotel guests, who could not return the next day. Collection of mail from street boxes would now occur only once. Cutting the service to the bone led to a dramatic fall in the numbers of Sunday workers. Some 20,000 clerks and 15,000 carriers, the report noted with satisfaction, who had previously worked on Sunday were now no longer required to do so.[1]

Nervous about a public backlash, the department conducted a survey of postmasters across the nation.[2] Their responses provide an intriguing snapshot of public attitudes to Sunday mails and the opening of the post office. In a handful of towns, such as Shelton Connecticut, Sunday mails had long been discontinued. But elsewhere, public support remained strong, and the post office was as attractive as ever as a hub of social activity. In Macon, Georgia, the daily average of Sunday callers was 650. In Lewistown, Pennsylvania, the postmaster reported that a Sunday service, which had begun as recently as 1905, was now embraced by the "best people in town". Many were churchgoers, who had no qualms about collecting mail and chatting with friends on the sacred day. A similar observation was made by the postmaster in Canton, Illinois, who judged many of his 600 Sunday customers to be women and children on their way home from church. Young people saw the post office as an ideal place, to use a modern term, to hang out. The postmaster in Keokuk Iowa described a lobby packed with young people who were ostensibly there to collect family mail but who seemed to relish the chance to escape parental supervision. They may have bumped into their parents anyway. Townspeople of all ages had caught, in a term that recurs in the surveys, the "Sunday habit" of strolling to the post office and greeting their friends and neighbors. Some postmasters thought the habit would be hard to break; one even feared a popular riot once the new policy came into effect.

To the postmasters' surprise, there was little sign of the feared backlash. Most of the public came quickly to accept the reduction in Sunday service. The key question is why. The survey reveals some religious pressure on the ground. In Medina, New York, the Baptist minister agitated for change; elsewhere, churches and some business groups welcomed the reduced Sunday service. But in the eyes of the postmasters, public acceptance came for two reasons. First, there was widespread support for the idea that postal employees deserved a day of rest. Secondly, it was not a full closure; in many places, general collection windows remained open for a short period, and the transportation of mail across the nation continued as before. Very few record acceptance of the measure as based on religious scruples or a desire to redeem the nation of the sin of Sabbath-breaking.

The change in the Sabbath question since the Jacksonian era became clearer when, the following year, Congress toughened the measure. Under a clause slipped into the annual appropriations bill, and that went into effect on August 24, 1912, the delivery of mail to the general public ceased on Sundays. Amidst widespread concern, the postmaster general rushed to reassure the public that this was still less than a full closure. The measure applied only to the general window. Locked boxes would still be accessible. Mail destined for hotels, hospital, and clubs could still be collected. Special deliveries were also unaffected. Furthermore, to avoid clogging the network, mail would still be sorted and dispatched along the main transportation routes.[3] Still, critics were not mollified. The postal service, as the *Brooklyn Daily Eagle* argued, was a public institution that should do its utmost to cater to community needs. Who, though, was to blame? Significantly, the paper pointed not to Sabbatarian organizations, even though some, such as the Lord's Day Association, had been petitioning on the question for several years. The chief villain instead was the union movement. The law showed that postal employees were now "so powerful that they can force Congress into making a drastic cut in Sunday mail service."[4] What at first glance might seem a crowning victory of a fearsome moral establishment turns out on close examination to be quite different. Union power rather than religious power had finally brought Sunday mails undone.

This outcome captures in a snapshot the frustration felt by the advocates of a Christian nation at the close of the long nineteenth century. Whether lobbying for a national Sabbath law, a Christian amendment to the preamble of the Constitution, or the retention of the King James Bible in public schools, Protestant evangelicals strove to harness state power in order to build a truly Christian republic. Many historians argue that they largely succeeded, inaugurating a golden age of an informal religious establishment that would only be dismantled in the twentieth century. Yet this consensus approach, where Christian activists dominate and forlorn dissenters are pushed to the margins, fails to account for either the intensity of church-state controversies or, in several cases, their outcome. Over the course of the nineteenth century, those evangelicals who hoped to forge a Christian republic fell well short of their goal.

There are no doubt many reasons for their failure. Broad cultural, intellectual, and social trends—mass immigration, the gradual acceptance of Darwinian science, the rise to dominance of liberal currents within theology—all played their part, and to these we might add an attachment to individual liberty that, on issues such as temperance, frustrated moral reformers. This study has focused on secularist mobilization. The dream of a Christian nation subsided not in an inexorable tide of secularization but because of a groundswell of support for the notion that religion and politics be kept at a distance. This was not a vision either that was fully achieved. At the end of the century, faith and government remained entangled in a myriad of ways. But secularists were successful in checking and in some cases defeating the forces of the moral establishment, in the process offering a vigorous and popular defense of a strict separation of Church and State.

To make sense of this outcome, we need to take a broad perspective. This means, first and foremost, recognizing that secularists were found on a spectrum from the devout to the irreligious. In some studies, the secularist camp is largely identified with freethinkers. But while the late nineteenth century was an era of unheralded success for American freethought, the argument for a secular state was made with just as much force by men and women of faith. Their guiding principle was a dread of state entanglement. When we focus on specific controversies rather than ideological platforms, it becomes immediately clear that we are dealing with a diverse set of actors, most of whom were willing to set aside their differences and unite in a common cause and against a common enemy. This approach also brings into view the many men and women who cannot be tagged as belonging to a particular camp but who were prepared to attend mass meetings, write letters to newspapers and, most powerfully, sign petitions.

There was diversity, too, in the range of arguments at secularists' disposal. One of the intriguing facets of church-state clashes is the manner in which they ballooned into larger debates about history and national mission. Evangelicals believed that their nation above all others was blessed with Divine approval. But secularists deployed national exceptionalism for their own ends. One of America's great and unique virtues, they argued, was its strict separation of Church and State. In seeking to inject theological disputes into the sinews of government, evangelicals were guilty of staining the New World with the jealousies and discords of the Old. Revolutionary history was another contested terrain. As evangelicals set about constructing an image of pious Founders looking anxiously to the Almighty for guidance, secularists responded with their own depiction of a group of men who, if not necessarily irreligious, were so wary of clerical ambition that they sought to inoculate their republic against it. Part of this endeavor was a national origin story scrubbed free of Puritan fanaticism. The Revolution in this secularist narrative was a clean break not just from British mastery but also the legacy of the New England settlers who had first planted theocracy and intolerance on American soil.

Class and race were also woven into the argument for a secular state. Whenever activists sought to enforce Sabbath laws, they ran into a deep vein of working-class resentment at an elitist clergy intent on robbing the poor of their few earthly pleasures. The Social Gospel movement certainly tried to build bridges with the labor movement. But its efforts were constantly undone by conservative preachers urging the poor to accept their lowly position in this life and to pin their hopes on reward in the next. As luxurious church edifices sprang up after the Civil War, the sense of a ministerial class out of touch with the concerns of the masses became ever stronger. At certain times and in certain quarters, too, the claim for a secular state aligned with the cause of white supremacy. The South occupies a distinctive position in the history of political secularism. White southerners congratulated themselves for upholding a pure religion which kept the grubby world of politics at arms-length. But their cry of "no religion in politics" was aimed squarely at northern abolitionists and served above all to defend slavery, while conveniently masking the presence of so many clerical agitators in their own section.

Running through these diverse arguments was an effort to enshrine true religion. The secular state would not expel religion so much as reshape it to fit the needs of a democratic and diverse nation. Again and again, secularists argued that a true religion disdained state enforcement and instead relied on nothing more than its spiritual resources. This was a religion that stayed clear of political quarrels and that could not be charged with the worst crime of all, fanaticism. The virtues of such a faith became clear when contrasted with other, degraded models of religiosity. In her study of the classificatory system of religions that emerged at the end of the nineteenth century, Tomoko Masuzawa argues that the modern discourse on religions was a "discourse of othering." Europeans regarded with a mix of fascination and horror the oppressive and primitive faiths that dominated tribal societies. But as Masuzawa suggests, the self-proclaimed representatives of enlightened religiosity feared the savages lurking at home.[5] For secularists, Mormons and, even more pointedly, Roman Catholics embodied the disturbing resilience of priestcraft and superstition. Yet it was a far more familiar faith that represented the greatest threat. Evangelicals seeking to ban Sunday mails or rewrite the Constitution showed most starkly the deformation of true religion wrought by a thirst for political power.

Petitions and the First Amendment

As powerful as these arguments were, they would not have succeeded without a determined mobilization at the grass roots of American society, and petition campaigns provided the necessary mechanism. Mass petition campaigns cannot give us an unfiltered view into popular opinion. Drafted by committees and circulated through a network of canvassers, petitions are in one sense elite productions. Nor is this their only limitation. In the case of the secularist petitions I have examined, there is no evidence of African-American or indigenous participation, and the involvement even of white women proved controversial for a surprisingly long time. Yet even so, petitions were a vital democratic tool that can tell us a great deal about feelings on the ground. They provided a shared platform through which groups with otherwise little in common could build effective coalitions. Even as it became shorter and more uniform as the century progressed, the petition claim is a revealing insight into secularist arguments. Occasionally, too, these documents give up nuggets of fascinating information. Canvassers sometimes attached covering letters or added explanatory notes, while providing clues as to social identity of signers in the form of occupation lists. The signers themselves jotted down comments or amendments. For these reasons, and despite their limitations, petitions are an indispensable gauge of secularist sentiment, and the surest way to move beyond the focus on courtrooms and the lettered elite which marks so much of the scholarship on church-state relations.

Examining secularist petition campaigns over decades reveals some significant trends. The most obvious is geographic. By the end of the century, the mid-Western states had emphatically emerged as secularist strongholds, displacing the mid-Atlantic states of New York and Pennsylvania. To a degree, this reflected their broader rise not only as economic powerhouses but as laboratories for a host of political and social experiments. After the Civil War, the dynamic and confident cities of the mid-West attracted scores of reformers and radicals, and it is not surprising that secularists found a growing constituency for their ideas. The Adventists made their base in Battle Creek, Michigan; the German Turners drew strength from the large immigrant communities in Chicago, Indianapolis, and Milwaukee. Freethought flourished in the mid-West too. Francis E. Abbot launched the *Index* in Toledo, Ohio; his great adversary D.M. Bennett started the *Truth-Seeker* in Paris, Illinois. A second development is the public visibility of women. As the career of Frances Wright demonstrated, individual women were at the forefront of secularist movements as early as the 1820s. Yet it would take time for large numbers of female names to appear on secularist petitions. When women did join such campaigns, it was not only those who, in the manner of Elizabeth Cady Stanton, identified as freethinkers. Whether as

Spiritualists, Adventists or members of other faith communities, religious women played a strong role.

This study, then, has aimed to be a contribution toward an as yet unwritten history of the role of petitioning in nineteenth-century political culture. The right of petition is enshrined in the first amendment to the national Constitution. But there was much scope for disagreement over its meaning. Defenders of slavery argued that while abolitionists were free to circulate and sign petitions, there was no obligation on Congress to debate or even receive them. The involvement of citizens who were not directly affected by the issue at hand was another point of contention. Was it appropriate, for example, for a resident of Iowa to urge Congress to ban alcohol in the District of Columbia? Then there was the question of gender. The nineteenth century witnessed a clear shift as women petitioning on public issues became first an accepted and then a common practice. Yet as late as the postbellum era, some secularists still questioned the legitimacy of petitions that were signed by women.

As this study has shown, even as petitions exploded in number and in size, there were always persistent doubts about their value. For those who were outgunned in petition wars, a fate which often befell secularists, the sheer number of signers was a poor guide to public opinion. After all, zealots could always tap a pool of committed supporters who would sign without demurring. And how could anyone be sure that a petition signer had any real commitment to, or even knowledge of, the cause in question? As some critics reasoned, many added their names for no other reason than politeness, sometimes without even bothering to read the text. In 1887, the *New York Herald* reported an anecdote which showed where such thoughtlessness might end. Having signed in a hurry, one man was surprised to discover that he was urging Congress to take active steps to spread cholera throughout the nation.[6]

These criticisms multiplied as the nation entered the era of what the *Boston Daily Advertiser* called "machine made" petitions. By the late nineteenth century large, centralized organizations were pushing petitions into communities across the nation, reaping thousands of signatures and clogging Congress with protests. The right of petition was still, as the paper noted, sacred. But it was fast losing its value as petitions plainly lost even the appearance of spontaneity.[7] Yet such hostile commentary did little to slow the pace of petitioning in communities across the nation. In this regard, the church-state controversies examined in this book are only a part of a wider story. Whether campaigning for suffrage, protective tariffs or the eight-hour day, a range of activists deployed the petition for a number of reasons: to forge internal bonds, to attract new members, to generate publicity and debate, and finally, by amassing thousands of signatures, to show off their democratic muscle.

The Legacy of Nineteenth-Century Secularists

In the case of secularist petitioners, the arguments that they put forth would continue to reverberate well into the twentieth century. The decades after 1900 offered a mixed picture in terms of church-state relations. In 1919, moral crusaders achieved perhaps their greatest victory with the ratification of the eighteenth amendment which banned the sale, manufacture, and transportation of alcohol. It might be tempting to read this victory backward as the culminating triumph of the nineteenth-century moral establishment. But prohibition owed as much to twentieth as nineteenth-century developments. The implementation of a federal income tax reduced government dependence on what had long been a major revenue stream, alcohol excise. White supremacism in the South, which had always worked against moral legislation, now became an ally. Southern progressives slowly embraced prohibition for several reasons, but one of the most decisive was their fear that liquor would fuel violent resistance on the part of disenfranchised African-American men to the Jim Crow system. The advent of World War I tilted the landscape further in favor of prohibition. Wartime patriotism turned the nation against the large beer brewers which had their roots in German immigrant communities. A sharp emphasis on national efficiency spurred the government to launch campaigns against a series of social evils that undercut individual performance. These included venereal disease as well as a related vice, drinking.

In addition, the prohibition forces now boasted an organization, the Anti-Saloon League (ASL), which was nimble enough to take advantage of the opportunity that presented itself. Unlike previous prohibition parties, the ASL downplayed religious arguments in favor of a more pragmatic approach.[8] Wary of the stigma of fanaticism that had hampered prohibition efforts since the days of the Maine Law, the ASL targeted the liquor traffic while largely avoiding the question of personal consumption. In the context of a wartime drive for efficiency, the ASL cleverly painted the saloon as unpatriotic rather than sinful. By corrupting young men and women, the saloon and its backers were akin to enemy agents.

The repeal of the eighteenth amendment did not shatter the dream of a Christian nation. As Kevin M. Kruse shows, in the 1930s wealthy industrialists promoted Christian libertarianism, a heady mix of faith and free enterprise, as a means of opposing the New Deal.[9] The menace of Godless Communism prompted another push for an assertion of the nation's Christian character. In 1956, a joint resolution of Congress named "In God We Trust" as the nation's motto, and the next year it appeared for the first time on paper currency. Yet there was also much evidence that public life was moving further in a secular direction. The 1925 Scopes trial showed the cultural shift that was underway. When a Tennessee teacher was charged under a statute banning the teaching of evolution, the ensuing trial shone a spotlight on the literal interpretation of the Bible that was so dear to Christian fundamentalists. Scarred by the public ridicule that followed, many fundamentalists withdrew from political controversy for decades. The liberal theology that had emerged after the Civil War, with its commitment to a broad-based and nonsectarian faith, set the tone for mainline Protestantism. Most dramatically, from the 1940s courts began handing down decisions that significantly furthered the secularist cause.

Two Supreme Court decisions in particular sparked a bitter controversy that would show the enduring resonance of the nineteenth-century arguments for a secular state. On the question of religion in schools, the situation across the nation remained a patchwork. By 1941, twelve states as well as the District of Columbia mandated Bible-reading in public schools, eleven prohibited it, and elsewhere it was either permitted or optional. In two decisions, the Supreme Court moved decisively to strike down compulsory Bible-reading and prayer in the nation's schools. In *Engel v Vitale* (1962), the Court determined that a New York state law requiring prayer at the beginning of each school day violated the establishment clause of the first amendment. The following year, in *Abington v Schempp*, the Court struck down a Pennsylvania statute mandating that ten verses of the Holy Bible be read without comment at the opening of each school day. The result was public uproar. Amidst a wave of attacks on the Court for imposing a godless classroom on the nation's children, New York Republican Frank Becker revived the old dream of a Christian amendment to the Constitution. The proposed Becker Amendment, as it became known, stipulated that the religious clauses of the first amendment did not prohibit "the offering, reading from, or listening to prayers or Biblical Scriptures" in any public school, on condition that such exercises be conducted on a voluntary basis.[10] Once again, the nation was witnessing an attempt to rewrite the Constitution in support of a privileged place for Christianity.

The Becker Amendment sparked another intense petition war. Yet alongside the petitions are a set of documents that provide an even more detailed insight into public feeling. In 1964, the House of Representatives Judiciary Committee received thousands of letters both for and against the amendment.[11] It is instructive to compare the anti-amendment letters with nineteenth-century secularist petitions. One difference is a greater prominence for avowed atheists. Overall, though, the arguments put by the correspondents would have been familiar to their predecessors. For most, the cause of true religion was a primary concern. To their mind, the recourse to enforced prayer or Bible-reading in schools was the mark of a lifeless rather than a vibrant faith. What was being proposed, as one writer argued, was a "state sanctioned veneer of religiosity," a strategy that would only succeed in producing an "illusion of piety." For devotion to be true and deep, it had to be offered willingly. Many cited the Founders in support. These were men, one wrote, who felt impelled to preserve their nation from this "dreaded Church-State combination." A few even cited the 1873 Ohio Supreme Court ruling in favor of the Cincinnati School Board and its decision to exclude the Bible. Others expressed their fear of a deeper plot against their liberties. Using identical language to petitioners in the Jacksonian era, several labeled the Becker Amendment as an "entering wedge" that would pave the way for further coercive measures. The language of anti-Catholicism appeared frequently, with references to inquisitions and persecutions. Seventh-Day Adventists wrote letters, as did Baptists and, in large numbers, Jewish organizations. Alongside this groundswell of opposition, many of the most prominent clergymen in the nation expressed their abhorrence at the proposed amendment, with the National Council of Churches issuing a strong protest. Eventually the Becker Amendment died in committee.

The arguments in 1964, then, drew on nineteenth-century models, and the outcome was familiar as well. Once again, a Constitutional amendment designed to assert the Christian character of the nation had sparked a popular, diverse, and ultimately successful secularist mobilization. Across the nineteenth century, Protestant reformers fought hard for the tenets of their faith to be enshrined in law and in public policy, and set about persuading Americans that theirs was a Christian nation. But a diverse set of campaigners responded in turn, articulating a rival vision of a largely secular state, and in the process delineating a model of religiosity that accorded with a democratic and diverse republic. In the fierce and never-ending tussle over the relationship between religion and government, secularists put their stamp firmly on the nineteenth century.

NOTES

1. "Post Office Department Annual Reports for the Fiscal Year Ended June 30, 1911." H. Doc 118, 62nd Congress, 2nd Session, 91–92.
2. The surveys are collected at "Reports Relating to Sunday Service and the Need for Additional Personnel, 1911–12," RG28 (Records of the Post Office Department), National Archives, Washington, DC.
3. "Post Office Department Annual Reports for the Fiscal Year Ended June 30, 1912." H. Doc 931, 62nd Congress, 3rd Session (1913), 13–14; *New York Times*, August 28, 1912.
4. *Brooklyn Daily Eagle*, August 28, 1912.
5. Masuzawa, *Invention of World Religions*, 19–20.
6. *New York Herald*, December 3, 1887.
7. *Boston Daily Advertiser*, July 8, 1890.
8. Pegram, *Battling Demon Rum*, 112–14.
9. Kevin M. Kruse, *One Nation Under God: How Corporate America Invented Christian America* (New York: Basic Books, 2015).
10. On the Becker Amendment, Steven K. Green, "Evangelicals and the Becker Amendment: A Lesson in Church-State Moderation," *Journal of Church and State* 33, no. 3 (1991): 541–67.
11. The letters are gathered in "Prayer and Bible-Reading in Public Schools, Correspondence Against the Protection of," RG233 (House of Representatives, Judiciary Committee), 88th Congress, Boxes 280–98, National Archives, Washington, DC. For a brief analysis, John Herbert Laubach, *School Prayers: Congress, the Courts and the Public* (Washington, DC: Public Affairs Press, 1969), 85–92.

Appendices

Appendix A: Geographic Distribution of Pro-Sunday Mail Petitions, 1828–1831

	No. of petitions	% of total	No. of signatures	% of total	Population as % of total
New England					
Connecticut	1	0.39	104	0.36	2.74
Maine	5	1.95	322	1.11	3.68
Massachusetts	2	0.78	605	2.08	5.62
New Hampshire	11	4.3	522	1.79	2.48
Vermont	2	0.78	491	1.69	2.58
Total	*21*	*8.2*	*2044*	*7.03*	
Mid-Atlantic					
Delaware	2	0.78	26	0.09	0.71
New Jersey	10	3.9	1268	4.35	2.95
New York	43	16.8	4832	16.58	17.67
Pennsylvania	118	46.1	15848	54.39	12.42
Total	*173*	*67.58*	*21974*	*75.41*	
South					
Kentucky	13	5.1	925	3.17	4.77
Maryland	1	0.39	24	0.08	2.68
North Carolina	1	0.39	0	0	4.36
Virginia	4	1.56	606	2.08	4.95
Total	*19*	*7.42*	*1555*	*5.33*	

	No. of petitions	% of total	No. of signatures	% of total	Population as % of total
Northwest					
Indiana	5	1.95	159	0.55	3.16
Ohio	34	13.28	2888	9.91	8.64
Total	*39*	*15.23*	*3047*	*10.46*	
Unknown	4	1.56	518	1.78	
Combined Total	*256*		*29138*		

Petition and signature counts based on examination of records of the House and Senate Committees on the Post Office, National Archives (Washington, DC), 20th and 21st Congresses.

No petitions from Rhode Island, Alabama, District of Columbia, Georgia, Louisiana, Missouri, Mississippi, South Carolina, Tennessee, Illinois.

Population figures based on total number of residents excluding slaves in 1830. State population figures drawn from Richard Sutch and Susan B. Carter (eds.), *Historical Statistics of the United States Earliest Times to the Present*, Vol. 1, Part A Population (Cambridge: Cambridge University Press, 2006).

Appendix B: Regional Breakdown of Anti-Christian Amendment Petitions (1872), as Percentage of Numbers and of Signers

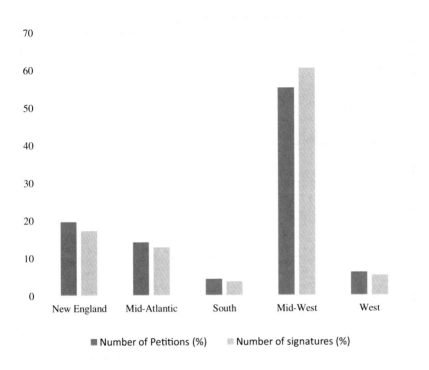

Drawn from Senate Judiciary Committee, 42A-H.11, National Archives (Washington, DC).

No petitions from Alabama, Arkansas, Georgia, Mississippi, North Carolina, South Carolina.

Appendix C: Number of Pro-Sunday Opening Petitions, Chicago World's Fair, 1891–1893

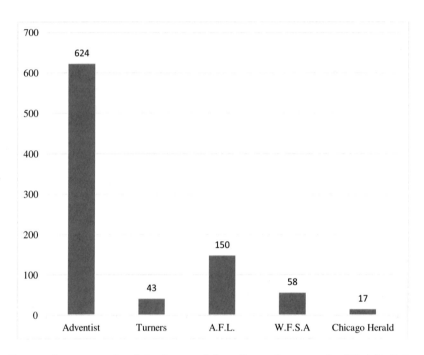

Drawn from records of the Senate Select Committee on the World's Fair, SEN 52A-J27.1., National Archives (Washington, DC).

A.F.L. (American Federation of Labor).

W.F.S.A. (World's Fair Sunday Opening Association).

Appendix D: Regional Breakdown of Pro-Sunday Opening Petitions, Chicago World's Fair, 1891–1893

	Adventist	Turners	A.F.L.	W.F.S.A	Chicago Herald
New England					
Connecticut	4	1	1	1	0
Maine	1	0	0	0	0
Massachusetts	13	0	2	0	0
New Hampshire	5	0	0	0	0
Rhode Island	3	0	0	0	0
Vermont	17	0	0	0	0
Total	*43*	*1*	*3*	*1*	*0*
Mid-Atlantic					
New Jersey	6	4	0	0	0
New York	22	11	0	2	0
Pennsylvania	12	2	26	2	0
Total	*40*	*17*	*26*	*4*	*0*
South					
Arkansas	13	1	0	0	0
Florida	1	0	1	0	0
Georgia	1	0	0	0	0
Kentucky	1	0	0	0	0
Louisiana	1	0	0	0	0
Maryland	2	0	0	0	0
Tennessee	6	2	3	0	0
Texas	21	0	2	1	0
West Virginia	5	0	1	0	0
Virginia	2	0	0	0	0
Total	*53*	*3*	*7*	*1*	*0*
Mid-West					
Illinois	38	3	30	2	0
Indiana	22	1	0	1	0
Iowa	20	0	18	1	0
Kansas	22	9	2	4	0
Michigan	104	0	12	6	0
Minnesota	36	0	7	0	0
Missouri	28	0	10	2	1
North Dakota	1	1	0	1	0
South Dakota	23	0	0	4	0
Nebraska	36	0	6	5	0
Ohio	28	3	12	5	0
Wisconsin	49	3	4	3	0
Total	*407*	*20*	*101*	*34*	*1*

	Adventist	Turners	A.F.L.	W.F.S.A	Chicago Herald
West					
California	9	2	0	0	0
Colorado	14	0	1	0	0
Idaho	0	0	1	3	0
Montana	3	0	6	4	13
Oregon	34	0	0	7	0
Washington	19	0	5	2	2
Total	*79*	*2*	*13*	*16*	*15*
Unknown	*2*	*0*	*0*	*2*	*1*
Combined Total	*624*	*43*	*150*	*58*	*17*

No petitions from Delaware, Alabama, District of Columbia, Mississippi, North Carolina, South Carolina, Nevada, Wyoming.

Drawn from records of the Senate Select Committee on the World's Fair, SEN 52A-J27.1., National Archives (Washington, DC).

A.F.L. (American Federation of Labor).

W.F.S.A. (World's Fair Sunday Opening Association).

Select Bibliography

Main Archival Sources

American Antiquarian Society, Worcester, MA.
    Cheever Family Papers.
Andover-Harvard Theological Library, Harvard Divinity School.
    Francis Ellingwood Abbot Papers.
California State Archives, Sacramento, CA.
    Constitutional Convention Working Papers, 1878–79, available on-line.
Harvard University Archives, Cambridge, MA.
    Papers of Francis Ellingwood Abbot.
Houghton Library, Harvard University, Cambridge, MA.
    James Parton correspondence and other papers.
Huntington Library, San Marino, CA.
    William J. Potter Papers.
Library of Congress, Manuscripts Division, Washington, DC.
    American Federation of Labor Records.
    Elizur Wright Papers.
    Robert Green Ingersoll Papers.
    William Torrey Harris Papers.
National Archives, Washington, DC.
Record Group 28 Records of the Post Office Department.
    Reports relating to Sunday service and the need for additional personnel, 1911–12.
    Record Group 46 Records of the U.S. Senate.

Committee on the District of Columbia, Church Taxation (SEN 43A-H.6); Prohibition (SEN 50A-J6.1).
Committee on the Post Office and Post Roads, Sunday mail (SEN 21A-G15.1).
Committee on the Judiciary, God in Constitution (SEN 40A-H10.1; SEN 42A-H11); Comstock law (SEN 45A-H10.2).
Select Committee on World's Columbian Exposition, Sunday opening (SEN 52A-J27.1).
Record Group 233 Records of the U.S. House of Representative.
Committee on the District of Columbia, Church Taxation (HR43A-H5.4).
Committee on the Judiciary, Chaplains to Congress (HR29A-G8.2; HR31A-G9.4; HR 32A-G10.2; HR33A-G10.2); Prayer and Bible-Reading in Public Schools, Correspondence against the protection of (HR88-J5).
Committee on the Post Office and Post Roads, Sunday mail (HR20A-G14.2; HR 21A-G15.3; HR 22A-G16.4; HR 62A-H24.2).
Pennsylvania State Archives, Harrisburg, PA.
Record Group 14 Department of Internal Affairs.
Series 15, Annual census reports of railroads.
Virginia State Library, Richmond, VI.
Legislative Petitions, Digital Collections.

Congressional Publications

Congressional Globe

Congressional Record

U.S. Department of the Post-Office. *Letter from the Postmaster-General Transmitting a Statement of the Post Routes Within the United States, on Which the Mail Is Transported on Sunday.* 21st Congress, 1st session, 1830. H. Doc. 73.

U.S. Department of the Post-Office. *Post Office Department Annual Reports for the Fiscal Year Ended June 30, 1911.* 62nd Congress, 2nd session, 1911. H. Doc. 118.

U.S. Department of the Post-Office. *Post Office Department Annual Reports for the Fiscal Year Ended June 30, 1912.* 62nd Congress, 3rd session, 1913. H. Doc 931.

U.S. House Committee on the Judiciary. *Acknowledgment of God and the Christian Religion in the Constitution.* 43rd Congress, 1st session, 1874. H. Rpt. 143.

U.S. House Committee on the Judiciary. *Chaplains.* 31st Congress, 1st session, 1850. H. Rpt. 171.

U.S. House Committee on the Judiciary. *Chaplains in Congress and in the Army and Navy.* 33rd Congress, 1st session, 1854. H. Rpt. 124.

U.S. House Committee on the Judiciary. *National Chaplains.* 34th Congress, 1st session, 1856. H. Rpt. 63.

U.S. House. Committee on Post-Office and Post Roads. *Sunday Mail.* 21st Congress, 1st session, 1830. H. Rpt. 271.

U.S. Sen. Committee on the District of Columbia. *Letter from the Commissioners of the District of Columbia, in Answer to Senate Resolutions of January 8, 1879, and May 23, 1879, Accompanying Reports of the Auditor and the Collector of the District. May 27, 1879.* 46th Congress, 1st session, 1879. S. Misc. Doc. 35.

U.S. Sen. Committee on the District of Columbia. *Memorial of the Churches of the District of Columbia, Praying the Passage of a Joint Resolution Declaring the Act of June 17, 1870, to Be Still in Force, and for the Passage of a Bill to Relieve the Churches of the District of Columbia from Taxation.* 46th Congress, 1st session, 1879. S. Misc. Doc. 37.

U.S. Sen. Committee on the District of Columbia. *Petition of Clergymen of Various Denominations in the District of Columbia, Praying Exemption of Churches and Church Property from Taxation.* 43rd Congress, 2nd session, 1874. S. Misc. Doc. 14.

U.S. Sen. Committee on the District of Columbia. *Report on the Bill (H.R. 3690) to Relieve the Churches of the District of Columbia.* 45th Congress, 2nd session, 1878. S. Rpt. 255.

U.S. House. Committee on the District of Columbia. *Tax on Ecclesiastical Property.* 43rd Congress, 1st session, 1874. H. Misc. Doc. 279.

U.S. Sen. Committee on Education and Labor. *Notes of a Hearing on the Bill (S. 2983) Entitled "A Bill to Secure to the People the Enjoyment of the First Day of the Week, Commonly Known as the Lord's Day".* 50th Congress, 2nd session, 1889. S. Misc. Doc. 43.

U.S. Sen. Committee on the Judiciary. *Abolition of Office of Chaplain.* 32nd Congress, 2nd session, 1853. S. Rpt. 376.

U.S. Sen. Committee on Post-Office and Post Roads. *Mails on the Sabbath.* 20th Congress, 2nd session, 1829. S. Doc. 46.

U.S. Senate. *Memorial of the Kehukee Primitive Baptist Association in North Carolina, Praying the Repeal of All Laws Authorizing the Appointment of Chaplains to Congress, the Army, Navy, and Other Public Stations, and that Congress Will Legislate No Further on the Subject of Religion.* 30th Congress, 2nd session, 1848. S. Misc. Doc. 2.

U.S. Sen. *Preamble and Resolutions, Adopted at a Meeting of the Citizens of New York, Against the Passage of Any Law Prohibiting the Transportation and Opening of the Mail on the Sabbath.* 20th Congress, 2nd session, 1829. S. Doc. 64.

Select Newspapers and Periodicals

American Israelite
Atlantic Monthly
Banner of Liberty
Banner of Light
Boston Daily Advertiser
Boston Evening Transcript
Boston Investigator
Brooklyn Daily Eagle
Catholic World
Chicago Tribune
Cincinnati Commercial
Cincinnati Daily Gazette
Cincinnati Enquirer
Congregationalist
Critic-Record
Daily Cleveland Herald
Daily Crescent
Daily National Intelligencer
Daily Picayune
Democrat and Chronicle
Democratic Press
Free Enquirer
Harper's New Monthly Magazine
Harper's Weekly
Hartford Daily Courant
Independent
Index
Inter Ocean
Jewish Times
Journal of Commerce
Liberator
Mechanics' Free Press
Milwaukee Sentinel
Nation
New Englander and Yale Review
New Orleans Advocate
New York Evangelist
New York Herald
New York Times

New York Tribune
North American and United States Gazette
Occident and American Jewish Advocate
Old Guard
Philadelphia Inquirer
Public Ledger
Puck
Sabbath Recorder
Signs of the Times
Sunday Dispatch
Times-Picayune
Truth-Seeker
United States Democratic Review
United States Gazette
Washington Post

Select Primary Sources

An Account of Memorials Presented to Congress During Its Last Session by Numerous Friends of Their Country and Its Institutions: Praying That the Mails May Not Be Transported, Nor Post-Offices Kept Open, on the Sabbath. New York: T.R. Marvin, 1829.

Adams, Brooks. *The Emancipation of Massachusetts*. Boston: Houghton Mifflin, 1887.

Adams, Charles Francis. *Massachusetts: Its Historians and Its History: An Object Lesson.* Boston: Houghton Mifflin, 1893.

Adams, Francis. *The Free School System of the United States.* London: Chapman and Hall, 1875.

Agnew, John Holmes. *A Manual on the Christian Sabbath.* Philadelphia: Presbyterian Board of Publication, 1852.

Annual Report of the Board of Education of the State of Connecticut. New Haven: Tuttle, Morehouse & Taylor, 1871, 1879.

Arguments in Favor of the Use of the Bible in the Public Schools. Cincinnati: Robert Clarke, 1870.

Atwater, Lyman H. "Civil Government and Religion." *Princeton Review* 5, no. 18 (1876): 195–236.

Bancroft, George. *An Oration Delivered Before the Democracy of Springfield and Neighbouring Towns, July 4, 1836.* Springfield: George and Charles Merriam, 1836.

Beebe, Gilbert J. *Maine Liquor Law Debate, at Clinton, New-Jersey, Wednesday, October 9, 1852, Between Rev. Mr. Mcneir, Pastor of Presbyterian Church,*

Clinton, N.J. and G.J. Beebe. Middletown, NY: Printed at the Banner Office, 1853.

Beecher, Lyman. *Lectures on Political Atheism and Kindred Subjects.* Boston: J.P. Jewett, 1852.

The Bible in the Public Schools: Proceedings and Addresses at the Mass Meeting, Pike's Music Hall, Cincinnati, Tuesday Evening, September 28, 1869. Cincinnati: Gazette, 1869.

Brooks, Phillips. *Lectures on Preaching, Delivered before the Divinity School of Yale College in January and February, 1877.* New York: E.P. Dutton, 1877.

Buisson, Ferdinand. *Rapport sur l'instruction primaire à l'exposition universelle de Philadelphie en 1876.* Paris: Imprimerie Nationale, 1878.

Burrowes, Thomas Henry, ed. *Pennsylvania School Journal.* Vol. 19. Lancaster, PA: Wylie & Griest, 1870–1871.

Bushnell, Horace. *Building Eras in Religion.* New York: C. Scribner's Sons, 1881.

———. *Reverses Needed.* Hartford: L.E. Hunt, 1861.

Cathcart, William. *The Lord's Day Not the Sabbath of the Jews.* Philadelphia: C. Sherman's & Son, 1859.

Cheever, George B. *God against Slavery: And the Freedom and Duty of the Pulpit to Rebuke It, as a Sin Against God.* Cincinnati: American Reform Tract and Book Society, 1857.

Clark, Rufus W. *The Question of the Hour: The Bible and the School Fund.* Boston: Lee and Shepard, 1870.

Common Schools of Cincinnati, Thirty-Ninth Annual Report. Cincinnati: Time Steam Book, 1868.

"The Conspiracy of Fanaticism." *The United States Democratic Review* 26, no. 143 (1850): 385–400.

Crafts, Wilbur F. *The Sabbath for Man, a Study of the Origin, Obligation, History, Advantages and Present State of Sabbath Observance.* Washington, DC: The International Reform Bureau, 1894.

Crosby, Howard. *The Christian Preacher: Yale Lectures for 1879–80.* New York: A. D. F. Randolph, 1879.

de Tocqueville, Alexis. *Democracy in America.* 2 vols. New York: Vintage, 1990.

Dexter, Henry Martyn. *As to Roger Williams, and His 'Banishment' from the Massachusetts Plantation.* Boston: Congregational Publishing Society, 1876.

Diman, J. L. "Religion in America, 1776–1876." *North American Review* 122, no. 250 (1876): 1–47.

Dwight, Timothy. *Theology Explained & Defended, in a Series of Sermons.* Vol. 3, New York: G&C Carvill, 1828.

Eggleston, Edward. *The Beginners of a Nation: A History of the Source and Rise of the Earliest English Settlements in America.* New York: D. Appleton, 1896.

Ely, Richard T. *Taxation in American States and Cities.* New York: T. Y. Crowell, 1888.
Emmons, William. *Authentic Biography of Colonel Richard M. Johnson, of Kentucky.* New York: H. Mason, 1833.
Equal Rights in Religion: Report of the Centennial Congress of Liberals, and Organization of the National Liberal League, at Philadelphia, on the Fourth of July, 1876. Boston: Published by the National Liberal League, 1876.
An Exposé of the Rise and Proceedings of the American Bible Society, During the Thirteen Years of Its Existence. New York, 1830.
Farrand, Max, ed. *The Records of the Federal Convention of 1787.* 4 vols. New Haven: Yale University Press, 1966.
Fisher, William Logan. *History of the Institution of the Sabbath Day.* Philadelphia: T.B. Pugh, 1859.
Fitch, Charles E. *Church and State: An Address, Delivered at the Annual Meeting of the School Commissioners and Superintendents of the State of New York, at Rochester, NY, December 29, 1875.* Rochester, NY: Democrat and Chronicle, 1876.
Frank, Henriette Greenbaum, and Amalie Hofer Jerome. *Annals of the Chicago Woman's Club for the First Forty Years of Its Organization, 1876–1916.* Chicago: Chicago Woman's Club, 1916.
Gage, Matilda Joslyn. *Woman, Church and State: A Historical Account of the Status of Woman Through the Christian Ages, with Reminiscences of the Matriarchate.* New York: Truth Seeker, 1893.
Gordon, Ann D., ed. *Selected Papers of Elizabeth Cady Stanton and Susan B. Anthony.* Vol. 5. New Brunswick, NJ: Rutgers University Press, 2009.
Hale, Edward Everett. "Shall Church Property Be Taxed?" *North American Review* 133, no. 298 (1881): 255–56.
Harris, William T. "The Division of School Funds for Religious Purposes." *Atlantic Monthly* 38, no. 226 (1876): 171–184.
———. *Report of the Committee of Fifteen on Elementary Education.* Boston: National Education Association of the United States, 1895.
Hill, Hamilton Andrews. *The Exemption of Church Property from Taxation: A Paper Read Before the American Statistical Association, May 5, 1876.* Boston: A. Williams, 1876.
Hills, Thomas. *Report of the Commissioners Appointed to Inquire into the Expediency of Revising and Amending the Laws Relating to Taxation and Exemption Therefrom.* Boston: Wright & Potter, 1875.
Holyoake, George Jacob. *The Principles of Secularism Illustrated.* London: Austin & Co., 1871.
Hovey, Alvah. *Religion and the State: Protection or Alliance? Taxation or Exemption.* Boston: Estes and Lauriat, 1874.
Hurlbut, Elisha P. *A Secular View of Religion in the State, and the Bible in the Public Schools.* Albany, 1870.

Hutchinson, William T., and William M. E. Rachal, eds. *The Papers of James Madison*. Vol. 1. Chicago: University of Chicago Press, 1962.
Farrell, C. P., ed. *The Works of Robert G. Ingersoll*. 12 vols. New York: Dresden Publishing, 1900.
Jones, Alonzo T. *The Captivity of the Republic*. Silver Spring, MD: International Religious Liberty Association, 1893.
Journal of the Common Council, of the City of Philadelphia. Philadelphia: Inquirer, 1836–1920.
Kilgore, Damon Y. *The Bible in Public Schools*. Philadelphia: Liberal League of Philadelphia, 1875.
Kingsbury, Harmon. *The Sabbath: A Brief History of Laws, Petitions, Remonstrances and Reports, with Facts, and Arguments, Relating to the Christian Sabbath*. New York: Robert Carter, 1840.
Klingberg, Frank J., and Frank W. Klingberg, eds. *The Correspondence between Henry Stephens Randall and Hugh Blair Grigsby, 1856–61*. Berkeley: University of California Press, 1952.
Lawrence, Joshua. *A Patriotic Discourse: Delivered by the Rev. Joshua Lawrence, at the Old Church in Tarborough, North Carolina, on Sunday, the 4th of July, 1830*. Tarborough, NC: Free Press, 1830.
Lee, John Hancock. *The Origins and Progress of the American Party in Politics*. Philadelphia: Elliot and Gihon, 1855.
Local Taxation: Being a Report of the Commission Appointed by the Governor of New York, Under the Authority of the Legislature, to Revise the Laws for the Assessment and Collection of State and Local Taxes. New York: Harper & Brothers, 1871.
Lovejoy, J. C. *Speech of Rev. J.C. Lovejoy, Before the Committee of the Legislature of Mass: On the Petition of Thomas H. Perkins, and Others, for the Repeal of the Liquor Law, March 15th, 1853*. Boston: R.C. Nichols and H.W. Muzzey, 1853.
M'Guire, E. C. *The Religious Opinions and Character of Washington*. New York: Harper and Brothers, 1836.
Mann, Horace. *Annual Reports on Education*. Boston: Horace B. Fuller, 1868.
———. *Report of an Educational Tour in Germany, and Parts of Great Britain and Ireland*. London: Simpkin, Marshall, 1846.
Massachusetts Bureau of Statistics of Labor. *Report on the Statistics of Labor*. Boston, 1885.
Mayo, A. D., ed. *The Bible in the Public Schools, Addresses of Rev. A.D. Mayo and Rev. Thos. Vickers, of Cincinnati*. New York: J.W. Schermerhorn & Co., 1870.
———. *Religion in the Common Schools: Three Lectures Delivered in the City of Cincinnati, in October 1869*. Cincinnati: R. Clarke, 1869.
McQuaid, Bernard J., and Francis Ellingwood Abbot. *The Public School Question as Understood by a Catholic American Citizen and by a Liberal American Citizen*. Boston: Free Religious Association, 1876.

Minor, John D. *Arguments Against the Use of the Bible in the Public Schools. By J.B. Stallo, George Hoady, and Stanley Matthews, Counsel for the Defendants. In the Case of John D. Minor Versus the Board of Education of the City of Cincinnati in the Superior Court of Cincinnati.* Cincinnati: Robert Clarke, 1870.

Morris, Benjamin Franklin. *A Discourse on the Christian Character and Influence of Washington.* Rising Sun, IN: Office of the Indiana Blade, 1846.

"National Sins and Their Retribution." *New Englander and Yale Review* 14, no. 56 (1856): 527–42.

New Haven City School District. *Report of the Committee on Schools and Views of the Minority of the Board of Education of the New Haven City School District, Concerning the Discontinuance of Religious Exercises in the Public Schools.* New Haven: Tuttle, Morehouse & Taylor, 1878.

New York State. *Annual Report of the State Superintendent.* 50 vols. Albany: State Printer, 1854–1904.

Parton, James. *Life of Thomas Jefferson, Third President of the United States.* Boston: J.R. Osgood, 1874.

Patton, William W. *Purely Secular Public Schools: An Address on the Bible and the Public Schools Delivered in Farwell Hall, Chicago, Sunday, September 24, 1876.* Chicago: Lakeside Publishing, 1876.

Phelps, Amos A. *The Sabbath.* New York: M.W. Dodd, 1844.

Phelps, Austin. *The Theory of Preaching: Lectures on Homiletics.* New York: C. Scribner's Sons, 1882.

Pitzer, A. W. "The Taxation of Church Property." *North American Review* 131, no. 287 (1880): 362–74.

"Politics and the Pulpit." *New Englander and Yale Review* 12, no. 46 (1854): 254–75.

"The President's Speech at Des Moines." *Catholic World* 22, no. 130 (1876): 433–43.

Proceedings at the First Annual Meeting of the Free Religious Association, Held in Boston, May 28–29, 1868. Boston: Adams & Co., 1868.

Proceedings of the Annual Meetings of the Lake Mohonk Conference of Friends of the Indian. 17 vols. New York: Lake Mohonk Conference, 1887–1904.

Proceedings of the Anti-Sabbath Convention, Held in the Melodeon, March 23rd and 24th. Boston: Anti-Sabbath Convention, 1848.

Proceedings of the National Convention to Secure the Religious Amendment of the Constitution of the United States, Held in Cincinnati, January 31 and February 1, 1872. Philadelphia: James B. Rodgers, 1872.

Proceedings of the National Convention to Secure the Religious Amendment of the Constitution of the United States, Held in Pittsburg, February 4 & 5, 1874. Philadelphia: Christian Statesman Association, 1874.

Quincy, J. P. "An Abuse of Tax-Exemption." *Old and New* 9, no. 3 (1874): 358–60.

———. *Tax-Exemption No Excuse for Spoliation: Considerations in Opposition to the Petition.* Boston: Old South Church, 1874.

Randall, Henry Stephens. *The Life of Thomas Jefferson.* Vol. 3, New York: Derby & Jackson, 1858.

Report of the Committee of Fifty: In Favor of a Lien Law on Building, Education, and the District System for Presidential Electors, &C. New York: A. Ming, 1829.

Rutland, Robert A., ed. *The Papers of George Mason.* Vol. 2. Chapel Hill: University of North Carolina Press, 1970.

Rutland, Robert A., et al., ed. *The Papers of James Madison.* Vol. 8. Chicago: University of Chicago Press, 1973.

Schaff, Philip. *America: A Sketch of the Political, Social, and Religious Character of the United States of North America, in Two Lectures, Delivered at Berlin.* New York: C. Scribner's Sons, 1855.

———. *Church and State in the United States, or, the American Idea of Religious Liberty and Its Practical Effects: With Official Documents.* New York: C. Scribner's Sons, 1889.

Scudder, Henry Martyn. *The Catholics and the Public Schools.* New York: Mason, Baker & Pratt, 1873.

Simon, John Y., ed. *The Papers of Ulysses S. Grant.* 32 vols. Carbondale: Southern Illinois University Press, 1967.

Smith, Goldwin. "The Ecclesiastical Crisis in England." *North American Review* 110, no. 226 (1870): 151–208.

Spear, Samuel T. *Religion and the State, or, the Bible and the Public Schools.* New York: Dodd, Mead, 1876.

"The Sphere of the Pulpit." *New Englander and Yale Review* 15, no. 1 (1857): 135–53.

Stanton, Elizabeth Cady. *Eighty Years and More (1815–1897): Reminiscences of Elizabeth Cady Stanton.* New York: European Publishing Company, 1898.

———. "Has Christianity Benefited Woman?" *North American Review* 140, no. 342 (1885): 389–99.

———. "Let the Blue Laws Rest." *Omaha Daily Bee*, March 17, 1889.

———. "Sunday at the World's Fair." *North American Review* 154, no. 423 (1892): 255.

Stanton, Elizabeth Cady, Susan B. Anthony, and Matilda Joslyn Gage, eds. *History of Woman Suffrage.* 6 vols. New York: Fowler & Wells, 1881–1922.

Story, Joseph. *Commentaries on the Constitution of the United States.* Vol. 3, Boston: Hilliard, Gray, 1833.

Stowe, Calvin E. *Report on Elementary Public Instruction in Europe.* Columbus: S. Medary, 1837.

Strong, Josiah. *Our Country: Its Possible Future and Its Present Crisis.* New York: Baker and Taylor, 1891.

Thompson, Joseph P. *Church and State in the United States.* Boston: J.R. Osgood, 1873.

―――. *Shall Our Common Schools Be Destroyed? An Argument Against Perverting the School-Fund to Sectarian Uses.* New York: E.O. Jenkins, 1870.

Upton, Harriet Taylor. *Proceedings of the Twenty-Fifth Annual Convention of the National American Woman Suffrage Association.* Washington, DC: The Association, 1893.

Vinet, Alexandre Rodolphe, and Thomas H. Skinner. *Homiletics: Or, the Theory of Preaching.* New York: Ivison & Phinney, 1854.

Washington, H. A., ed. *The Writings of Thomas Jefferson.* Vol. 8. Washington, DC: Taylor & Maury, 1854.

Weems, M. L. *The Life of George Washington: With Curious Anecdotes, Equally Honourable to Himself and Exemplary to His Young Countrymen.* Philadelphia: Mathew Carey, 1809.

Wells, David A. "The Reform of Local Taxation." *North American Review* 122, no. 251 (1876): 357–403.

Woman's Christian Temperance Union. *Minutes of the National Woman's Christian Temperance Union Annual Meeting.* 13 vols. Chicago, IL: Woman's Temperance Publication Association, 1882–1894.

Wright, Frances. *Course of Popular Lectures as Delivered by Frances Wright with Three Addresses on Various Public Occasions.* New York: Office of the Free Enquirer, 1829.

Select Secondary Sources

Albanese, Catherine L. *America, Religions and Religion.* 5th ed. Belmont, CA: Cengage, 2013.

Alley, Reuben E. *A History of Baptists in Virginia.* Richmond: Virginia Baptist General Board, 1973.

Anidjar, Gil. "Secularism." *Critical Inquiry* 33, no. 1 (2006): 52–77.

Asad, Talal. *Formations of the Secular: Christianity, Islam, Modernity.* Stanford, CA: Stanford University Press, 2003.

Bailey, Raymond C. *Popular Influence Upon Public Policy: Petitioning in Eighteenth-Century Virginia.* Westport, CT: Greenwood Press, 1979.

Beaver, R. Pierce. *Church, State, and the American Indians.* St. Louis, MO: Concordia Pub. House, 1966.

Belz, Herman, Ronald Hoffman, and Peter J. Albert, eds. *To Form a More Perfect Union: The Critical Ideas of the Constitution.* Charlottesville: University Press of Virginia, 1992.

Bittker, Boris I., Scott C. Idelman, and Frank S. Ravitch. *Religion and the State in American Law.* New York: Cambridge University Press, 2015.

Blocker, Jack S. *Retreat from Reform: The Prohibition Movement in the United States, 1890–1913*. Westport, CT: Greenwood Press, 1976.
Boyer, Paul. *Urban Masses and Moral Order in America*. Cambridge, MA: Harvard University Press, 1978.
Bradford, Roderick. *D.M. Bennett: The Truth Seeker*. Amherst, NY: Prometheus Books, 2006.
Braude, Ann. *Radical Spirits: Spiritualism and Women's Rights in Nineteenth-Century America*. 2nd ed. Bloomington: Indiana University Press, 2001.
Brumberg, Stephan F. "The Cincinnati Bible War (1869–73) and Its Impact on the Education of the City's Protestants, Catholics and Jews." *American Jewish Archives Journal* 54, no. 2 (2002): 11–46.
Buckley, Thomas E. *Establishing Religious Freedom: Jefferson's Statute in Virginia*. Richmond: University of Virginia Press, 2013.
Butler, Jon. *Awash in a Sea of Faith: Christianizing the American People*. Cambridge, MA: Harvard University Press, 1990.
Cady, Linell E., and Elizabeth Shakman Hurd, eds. *Comparative Secularisms in a Global Age*. New York: Palgrave Macmillan, 2010.
Cady, Linell E., and Tracy Fessenden, eds. *Religion, the Secular and the Politics of Sexual Difference*. New York: Columbia University Press, 2013.
Carpenter, Daniel P. "Recruitment by Petition: American Antislavery, French Protestantism, English Suppression." *Perspectives on Politics* 14, no. 3 (2016): 700–23.
Carwardine, Richard J. *Evangelicals and Politics in Antebellum America*. New Haven, CT: Yale University Press, 1993.
Cohen, Naomi W. *Jews in Christian America: The Pursuit of Religious Equality*. New York: Oxford University Press, 1992.
Conkin, Paul K. *The Uneasy Center: Reformed Christianity in Antebellum America*. Chapel Hill: University of North Carolina Press, 1995.
Cox, Harold E. "'Daily Except Sunday': Blue Laws and the Operation of Philadelphia's Horsecars." *Business History Review* 39, no. 2 (1965): 228–42.
Curry, Thomas J. *The First Freedoms: Church and State in America to the Passage of the First Amendment*. New York: Oxford University Press, 1986.
Davis, Sue. *The Political Thought of Elizabeth Cady Stanton: Women's Rights and the American Political Traditions*. New York: New York University Press, 2008.
Dawson, Jan C. *The Unusable Past: America's Puritan Tradition, 1830 to 1930*. Chico, CA: Scholar's Press, 1984.
DelFattore, Joan. *The Fourth R: Conflicts Over Religion in America's Public Schools*. New Haven, CT: Yale University Press, 2004.
Dorrien, Gary. *The Making of American Liberal Theology: Imagining Progressive Religion, 1805–1900*. Louisville, KY: Westminster John Knox Press, 2001.
Drakeman, Donald L. *Church, State and Original Intent*. New York: Cambridge University Press, 2010.

Dreisbach, Daniel L. *Thomas Jefferson and the Wall of Separation between Church and State.* New York: New York University Press, 2002.
Elson, Ruth Miller. *Guardians of Tradition: American Schoolbooks in the Nineteenth Century.* Lincoln: University of Nebraska Press, 1964.
Evans, Christopher H. *The Social Gospel in American Religion: A History.* New York: New York University Press, 2017.
Fea, John. *Was America Founded as a Christian Nation? A Historical Introduction.* Louisville, KY: Westminster John Knox Press, 2011.
Feldman, Noah. *Divided by God: America's Church–State Problem—And What We Should Do About It.* New York: Macmillan, 2005.
Fessenden, Tracy. *Culture and Redemption: Religion, the Secular, and American Literature.* Princeton, NJ: Princeton University Press, 2007.
Fluhman, J. Spencer. *A Peculiar People: Anti-Mormonism and the Making of Religion in Nineteenth-Century America.* Chapel Hill: University of North Carolina Press, 2012.
Foster, Gaines M. *Moral Reconstruction: Christian Lobbyists and the Federal Legislation of Morality, 1865–1920.* Chapel Hill: University of North Carolina Press, 2002.
Fox-Genovese, Elizabeth, and Eugene D. Genovese. *The Mind of the Master Class: History and Faith in the Southern Slaveholder's Worldview.* Cambridge: Cambridge University Press, 2005.
Fredrickson, George M. *The Inner Civil War: Northern Intellectuals and the Crisis of the Union.* New York: Harper and Row, 1965.
Gjerde, Jon, and S. Deborah Kang, *Catholicism and the Shaping of Nineteenth-Century America.* New York: Cambridge University Press, 2012.
Gordon, Sarah Barringer. *The Mormon Question: Polygamy and Constitutional Conflict in Nineteenth-Century America.* Chapel Hill: University of North Carolina Press, 2002.
Green, Steven K. *Inventing a Christian America: The Myth of the Religious Founding.* New York: Oxford University Press, 2015.
———. *The Bible, the School and the Constitution: The Clash That Shaped Modern Church–State Doctrine.* New York: Oxford University Press, 2012.
———. *The Second Disestablishment: Church and State in Nineteenth-Century America.* New York: Oxford University Press, 2010.
Gunn, T. Jeremy, and John Witte, eds. *No Establishment of Religion: America's Original Contribution to Religious Liberty.* New York: Oxford University Press, 2012.
Hamburger, Philip. *Separation of Church and State.* Cambridge, MA: Harvard University Press, 2002.
Handy, Robert T. *A Christian America: Protestant Hopes and Historical Realities.* 2nd ed. New York: Oxford University Press, 1984.
———. *Undermined Establishment: Church–State Relations in America, 1820–1920.* Princeton, NJ: Princeton University Press, 1991.

Haselby, Sam. *The Origins of American Religious Nationalism*. New York: Oxford University Press, 2015.
Hatch, Nathan O. *The Democratization of American Christianity*. New Haven, CT: Yale University Press, 1989.
Hershberger, Mary. "Mobilizing Women, Anticipating Abolition: The Struggle Against Indian Removal in the 1830s." *Journal of American History* 86, no. 1 (1999): 15–40.
Hoffman, Ronald, and Peter J. Albert, eds. *Religion in a Revolutionary Age*. Charlottesville: University Press of Virginia, 1994.
Howe, Daniel Walker. "The Evangelical Movement and Political Culture in the North During the Second Party System." *Journal of American History* 77, no. 4 (1991): 1216–39.
Hutchison, William R. *Religious Pluralism in America: The Contentious History of a Founding Ideal*. New Haven, CT: Yale University Press, 2003.
Isaac, Rhys. *The Transformation of Virginia: 1740–1790*. Chapel Hill: University of North Carolina Press, 1982.
Jacoby, Susan. *Freethinkers: A History of American Secularism*. New York: H. Holt, 2004.
———. *The Great Agnostic: Robert Ingersoll and American Freethought*. New Haven, CT: Yale University Press, 2013.
Jentz, John Barkley. "Artisans, Evangelicals and the City: A Social History of Abolition and Labor Reform in Jacksonian New York." PhD Dissertation, City University of New York, 1977.
John, Richard R. "Taking Sabbatarianism Seriously: The Postal System, the Sabbath, and the Transformation of American Political Culture." *Journal of the Early Republic* 10, no. 4 (1990): 517–67.
Jordan, Ryan P. *Church, State and Race: The Discourse of American Religious Liberty, 1750–1900*. Lanham, MD: University Press of America, 2012.
Justice, Benjamin. *The War That Wasn't: Religious Conflict and Compromise in the Common Schools of New York State, 1865–1900*. Albany: State University of New York, 2005.
Kabala, James S. *Church–State Relations in the Early American Republic, 1787–1846*. Brookfield, VT: Pickering & Chatto, 2013.
Kahn, Jonathon S., and Vincent W. Lloyd, eds. *Race and Secularism in America*. New York: Columbia University Press, 2016.
Kammen, Michael. *A Season of Youth: The American Revolution and the Historical Imagination*. Ithaca, NY: Cornell University Press, 1978.
Kirkley, Evelyn A. *Rational Mothers and Infidel Gentlemen: Gender and American Atheism, 1865–1915*. Syracuse, NY: Syracuse University Press, 2000.
Kruse, Kevin M. *One Nation Under God: How Corporate America Invented Christian America*. New York: Basic Books, 2015.
Lambert, Frank. *Religion in American Politics: A Short History*. Princeton, NJ: Princeton University Press, 2008.

Laurie, Bruce. *Working People of Philadelphia: 1800–1850*. Philadelphia: Temple University Press, 1980.
Lazerow, Jama. *Religion and the Working Class in Antebellum America*. Washington, DC: Smithsonian Press, 1995.
Lengel, Edward G. *Inventing George Washington: America's Founder, in Myth and Memory*. New York: Harper, 2011.
Mahmood, Saba. *Religious Difference in a Secular Age: A Minority Report*. Princeton, NJ: Princeton University Press, 2016.
Masuzawa, Tomoko. *The Invention of World Religions: Or, How European Universalism Was Preserved in the Language of Pluralism*. Chicago: University of Chicago Press, 2005.
Mathis, James R. *The Making of the Primitive Baptists: A Cultural and Intellectual History of the Antimission Movement, 1800–1840*. New York: Routledge, 2004.
McAfee, Ward M. *Religion, Race and Reconstruction: The Public School in the Politics of the 1870s*. Albany: State University of New York, 1998.
McCrossen, Alexis. *Holy Day, Holiday: The American Sunday*. Ithaca, NY: Cornell University Press, 2000.
McGarry, Molly. *Ghosts of Futures Past: Spiritualism and the Cultural Politics of Nineteenth-Century America*. Berkeley: University of California Press, 2008.
McGarvie, Mark. *One Nation Under Law: America's Early National Struggle to Separate Church and State*. DeKalb: Northern Illinois University Press, 2004.
———. *Law and Religion in American History: Public Values and Private Conscience*. New York: Cambridge University Press, 2016.
McKivigan, John R., and Mitchell Snay, eds. *Religion and the Antebellum Debates over Slavery*. Athens: University of Georgia Press, 1998.
McLoughlin, William G. *New England Dissent, 1630–1833: The Baptists and the Separation of Church and State*. Vol. 2, Cambridge: Harvard University Press, 1971.
Mensch, Elizabeth. "Religion, Revival, and the Ruling Class: A Critical History of Trinity Church." *Buffalo Law Review* 36, no. 3 (1987): 427–571.
Miller, Randall M., Harry S. Stout, and Charles Regan Wilson, eds. *Religion and the American Civil War*. New York: Oxford University Press, 1998.
Mirola, William A. "Shorter Hours and the Protestant Sabbath: Religious Framing and Movement Alliances in Late-Nineteenth-Century Chicago." *Social Science History* 23, no. 3 (1999): 395–433.
Modern, John Lardas. *Secularism in Antebellum America*. Chicago: University of Chicago Press, 2015.
Moore, R. Laurence. "Bible Reading and Nonsectarian Schooling: The Failure of Religious Instruction in Nineteenth-Century Public Education." *Journal of American History* 86, no. 4 (2000): 1581–99.

Moore, Joseph S. *Founding Sins: How a Group of Antislavery Radicals Fought to Put Christ Into the Constitution.* New York: Oxford University Press, 2016.

Mountford, Roxanne. *The Gendered Pulpit: Preaching in American Protestant Spaces.* Carbondale: Southern Illinois University Press, 2003.

Najar, Monica. *Evangelizing the South: A Social History of Church and State in Early America.* New York: Oxford University Press, 2008.

Newman, William M., and Peter L. Halvorson. *Atlas of American Religion: The Denominational Era, 1776–1990.* Walnut Creek, CA: Altamira Press, 2000.

Noll, Mark A. *America's God: From Jonathan Edwards to Abraham Lincoln.* New York: Oxford University Press, 2002.

———. *The Civil War as a Theological Crisis.* Chapel Hill: University of North Carolina Press, 2006.

Noll, Mark A., ed. *Religion and American Politics: From the Colonial Period to the 1980s.* New York: Oxford University Press, 1990.

Orsi, Robert A. *Between Heaven and Earth: The Religious Worlds People Make and the Scholars Who Study Them.* Princeton, NJ: Princeton University Press, 2004.

Pegram, Thomas R. *Battling Demon Rum: The Struggle for a Dry America, 1800–1933.* Chicago: Ivan R. Dee, 1998.

Peterson, Merrill D. *The Jefferson Image in the American Mind.* Charlottesville: University of Virginia Press, 1960.

Peterson, Merrill D., and Robert C. Vaughan, eds. *The Virginia Statute for Religious Freedom: Its Evolution and Consequences in American History.* Cambridge: Cambridge University Press, 1988.

Porterfield, Amanda. *Conceived in Doubt: Religion and Politics in the New American Nation.* Chicago: University of Chicago Press, 2012.

Portnoy, Alisse Theodore. *Their Right to Speak: Women's Activism in the Indian and Slave Debates.* Cambridge, MA: Harvard University Press, 2005.

Prucha, Francis Paul. *American Indian Policy in Crisis: Christian Reformers and the Indian, 1865–1900.* Norman: University of Oklahoma Press, 1976.

Rable, George C. *God's Almost Chosen Peoples: A Religious History of the American Civil War.* Chapel Hill: University of North Carolina Press, 2010.

Rohrer, James R. "Sunday Mails and the Church–State Theme in Jacksonian America." *Journal of the Early Republic* 7, no. 1 (1987): 53–74.

Schlereth, Eric R. *An Age of Infidels: The Politics of Religious Controversy in the Early United States.* Philadelphia: University of Pennsylvania Press, 2013.

Schmidt, Leigh Eric. *Village Atheists: How America's Unbelievers Made Their Way in a Godly Nation.* Princeton, NJ: Princeton University Press, 2016.

Schultz, Ronald. *The Republic of Labor: Philadelphia Artisans and the Politics of Class, 1720–1830.* New York: Oxford University Press, 1993.

Scott, Sean A. *A Visitation of God: Northern Civilians Interpret the Civil War.* New York: Oxford University Press, 2011.

Sehat, David. *The Myth of American Religious Freedom*. Oxford: Oxford University Press, 2011.
Smith, Christian, ed. *The Secular Revolution: Power, Interests and Conflict in the Secularization of American Public Life*. Berkeley: University of California Press, 2003.
Smith, Gary Scott. *The Seeds of Secularization: Calvinism, Culture and Pluralism in America, 1870–1915*. St. Paul, MN: Christian University Press, 1985.
Snay, Mitchell. *Gospel of Disunion: Religion and Separatism in the Antebellum South*. New York: Cambridge University Press, 1993.
Stimson, Claude W. "Exemption from the Property Tax in California." *California Law Review* 21, no. 3 (1933): 193–220.
Stout, Harry S. *Upon the Altar of the Nation: A Moral History of the American Civil War*. New York: Viking, 2006.
Sullivan, Winnifred Fallers. *The Impossibility of Religious Freedom*. Princeton, NJ: Princeton University Press, 2005.
———. *A Ministry of Presence: Chaplaincy, Spiritual Care and the Law*. Chicago: University of Chicago Press, 2014.
Sullivan, Winnifred Fallers, and Lori G. Beaman, eds. *Varieties of Religious Establishment*. London: Ashgate, 2013.
Taylor, Charles. *A Secular Age*. Cambridge, MA: Belknap Press, 2007.
Turner, James. *Without God, Without Creed: The Origins of Unbelief in America*. Baltimore: Johns Hopkins University Press, 1985.
Volk, Kyle G. *Moral Minorities and the Making of American Democracy*. New York: Oxford University Press, 2014.
Weir, Robert E. *Beyond Labor's Veil: The Culture of the Knights of Labor*. University Park: Pennsylvania State University Press, 1996.
Wesley, Timothy L. *The Politics of Faith During the Civil War*. Baton Rouge: Louisiana State University Press, 2013.
West, John G. *The Politics of Revelation and Reason: Religion and Civic Life in the New Nation*. Lawrence: University Press of Kansas, 1996.
Westerhoff, John H. *McGuffey and His Readers: Piety, Morality and Education in Nineteenth-Century America*. Nashville, TN: Abingdon Press, 1979.
Wilentz, Sean. *Chants Democratic: New York City and the Rise of the American Working Class, 1788–1850*. Oxford: Oxford University Press, 1984.
Witte Jr., John. "Review: That Serpentine Wall of Separation." *Michigan Law Review* 101, no. 6 (2003): 1869–905.
———. "Tax Exemption of Church Property: Historical Anomaly or Valid Constitutional Practice?" *Southern California Law Review* 64, no. 2 (1991): 363–416.
Wyatt-Brown, Bertram. "Prelude to Abolitionism: Sabbatarian Politics and the Rise of the Second Party System." *Journal of American History* 58, no. 2 (1971): 316–41.

Zaeske, Susan. *Signatures of Citizenship: Petitioning, Antislavery and Women's Political Identity.* Chapel Hill: University of North Carolina Press, 2003.

Zagarri, Rosemarie. *Revolutionary Backlash: Women and Politics in the Early American Republic.* Philadelphia: University of Pennsylvania Press, 2007.

Zollmann, Carl. "Tax Exemptions of American Church Property." *Michigan Law Review* 14, no. 8 (1916): 646–57.

Index

A

Abbot, Francis Ellingwood, 126–127, 131, 136–138, 163, 182–183, 185, 187–188, 195, 212
Abolitionism, 115, 127
   and preachers, 12, 99–100, 113, 115, 127, 245
   and Sabbath, 73–75
Adams, Brooks, 231
Adams, Charles Francis, 231–232
Adams, Francis, 160
Adams, John Quincy, 46, 74
African-Americans, 246
   and petitioning, 246
   and political preaching, 109
Agnew, John Holmes, 79
Akin, James, 53
Alcott, Bronson, 75
Allen, Reverend Frederick Baylies, 188–189, 195
American and Foreign Sabbath Union, 74
American Baptist Almanac, 69
American Baptist Magazine, 42
American Federation of Labor (AFL), 207, 219, 221
American Israelite, 186
American Protective Association (APA), 209
American Revolution, 24
American Sabbath Union (ASU), 212, 223
American Secular Union, 201
American Temperance Society, 63
American Tract Society, 63
Anglicans, 20, 28, 47, 118, 140
Anthony, Susan B., 227, 229–230
Anti-amendment campaign, 126–131
Anti-Catholicism, 6, 106
   international dimension, 56, 85
   and nativism, 8, 66–67, 82–83, 210
   and separation of church and state, 8, 171, 172, 202, 228
Anti-prohibition, 211
Anti-Sabbatarianism
   amongst workers, 85–88, 220
   and civil liberty, 46, 87
   and Constitution, 1, 2, 36, 38, 45–48, 55, 76–77, 82, 100
   conventions, 74, 77, 125, 201
   fears of conspiracy, 48–53
   opening of World's Fair, 208–221

and petitioning, 1, 12, 36–46,
    48–50, 51, 52, 66, 69, 75,
    76–77, 79, 82, 213,
    214–221
  Sunday mails, 10–11, 34–58,
    62, 68–70, 73, 78, 82, 85,
    104, 129, 164, 212,
    218, 241
  Sunday travel, 12, 71, 73,
    78–82, 84
  theological arguments, 36, 47,
    81, 110, 214–216, 218, 244
  and true religion, 81
  and women, 39–40, 53, 66, 216,
    225–227, 230
Anti-Saloon League (ASL), 248–249
Anti-suffragism
  and secularism, 125–126

B
Bacon, Leonard, 98
Badger, George, 67, 70
Bancroft, George C., 108
Banner of Liberty, 68–69
Banner of Light, 126, 128, 141
Baptists
  and informal establishment, 42, 68
  persecution of, 26, 42, 168
  and religious tax in Virginia, 19, 27,
    29, 33, 40
  and Sabbath laws, 34, 42–43, 57,
    68, 76, 87, 242
Bateham, Josephine C., 225
Bates, Joseph, 214
Becker, Frank, 249
Beebe, Gilbert Judson (Jr), 68–70
Beecher, Catharine, 40
Beecher, Lyman, 34–35, 75, 189
Beecher, Reverend Henry Ward,
    96–97, 98, 100–102, 107,
    112, 114

Benevolent Empire, 63–66, 87
Bennett, DeRobigne Morton,
    200–202
Bennett, James Gordon, 100
Berg, Reverend Joseph, 85
Bible Wars, 151–175
  and anti-Catholicism, 6, 155–157,
    158–159
  in Cincinnati, 11, 12, 151–163,
    166–169
  and European models, 12, 161–165
  majority rights argument, 154
  petitioning, 153
  and Puritan legacy, 7–14, 166–169
Blaine, James G., 157–159
Blair, Henry William, 214
Brooks, Phillips, 115
Brown, Obadiah, 55
Buisson, Ferdinand, 161
Bushnell, Horace, 124–125

C
California, 129, 226
  taxation of church property,
    198–200
Calvinism, 44, 67, 127, 136, 212
Catholics/Catholic Church
  in Britain, 26, 56
  and church property, 184, 190, 191,
    194–196
  hostility to common schools, 156
  immigration, 52, 83, 87, 154
  and religious instruction, 166
  and Sabbath laws, 36, 82, 83, 85,
    87, 218
Chaplains (Legislative), 11
  Congressional reports in favor,
    70
  defense of, 68, 137
  history of, 64, 138
  opposition to, 65–70, 75

petitions against, 65–66, 68–70
Chaplains (Legislative), 63–70
Chardon Street Convention, 74
Cheever, George Barrell, 97–100, 107
Cherokee Removal, 57
Chicago Sabbath Association (CSA), 222
Chicago Woman's Club, 226
Christian amendment, 243, 249
  arguments in favour, 12
  Congressional report against, 145
  and national exceptionalism, 145
  and National Liberal League, 127
  opposition to, 129–138, 141, 142
  origin of campaign, 128
  petitions against, 126–130, 131
  petitions for, 125
Christian amendment, 121–145
Christian party in politics, 49, 57, 128, 131, 142
Church property, 185–186, 187, 195. *See also* Taxation of Church property
  and census, 185, 195
Cincinnati, 11, 12, 42, 65, 125, 129, 151, 152, 160, 162–165, 168, 174
Civil War, 12, 111–112
Clark, Rufus W., 154
Clergy (Protestant)
  and abolitionism, 95–100
  attacks on, 4, 103–111, 136
  petition of three thousand, 98, 103
  politicking, 115
  preaching manuals, 99, 114
  public role of, 102–103
Colby, Clara Berwick, 229
Comstock, Anthony, 200, 202
Comstock laws, 200–201, 212
Conspiracy, fear of, 48–52
Constitution

and anti-Sabbatarians, 1, 36, 38, 66, 74, 81, 104
and legislative chaplains, 68, 71
function of, 141
Crafts, Wilbur F., 223, 224, 234
Crosby, Howard, 115

D
Darwinism, 243
Democratic Party, 38, 74, 101
Disestablishment
  and evangelicals, 2–4
  in early national era, 23, 29
  in Ireland, 140
  in Massachusetts, 63
District of Columbia, 104, 128–129, 160, 197, 211
Douglas, Stephen A., 103–105
Douglass, Frederick, 100
Durborow, Allan, 217–218, 219, 230, 231

E
Edison, Thomas A., 218
Education
  and Bible-reading, 7–8, 11, 12, 126, 152–175, 185, 202, 214, 243
  common school system, 152–155, 155–157, 161, 167, 170–173, 210
  in Europe, 160–166
  and morality, 164–166, 171
  for Native Americans, 171–172
  and secularism, 4, 7, 154, 157, 164–165, 169–175
  United States as model of, 161, 165
Eliot, Charles, 190, 196
Ely, Ezra Stiles, 49
Emerson, Ralph Waldo, 75

England, 47, 50, 56, 139, 161–162, 162–165, 167, 173, 211
Evangelicals
  on Founding Fathers, 12, 102
  and Second Great Awakening, 33, 67
  and voluntary system, 21, 26, 27, 29, 33, 95, 98
Ezekiel, Jacob, 77

F
Federalism, 11, 46
First Amendment, 1, 2, 7, 9, 10–11, 47–48, 65–66, 135, 158, 188, 217, 219
First Great Awakening, 20
First Vatican Council, 6, 140–142
Fisher, William Logan, 81–82
Founding Fathers
  and religion, 134–145
France, 160, 164, 196
Franklin, Benjamin, 133–134
Free Religious Association (FRA), 126, 163
Freethinkers, 3, 4, 8, 244
  and Christian amendment, 122–123, 138
  debate over female suffrage, 227, 130–131
  divisions within, 43, 129–130
  National Liberal League (NLL), 200
  and Sunday mails, 42–43
  women supporters, 40, 212, 227, 229
Frothingham, Octavius, 185
Fugitive Slave Law, 12, 95–96, 97, 103
Furness, William, 81

G
Gage, Matilda Joslyn, 228
Gag rule, 23, 104
Garrison, William Lloyd, 74–76, 77, 99–100
Gender
  and petitions, 38–39, 53, 125, 216, 224–226, 230
  and preaching, 97–100, 107, 114, 227
  and religion, 105
General Union for Promoting the Observance of the Christian Sabbath (GUPOCS), 35
Germany, 163, 164, 188
Gladden, Washington, 223
Gompers, Samuel, 207, 219, 221, 223
Grant, Ulysses S., 172
  anti-Catholicism of, 159
  Des Moines speech, 157–158
  and religious instruction, 172–173
  and Sabbath, 125
  and taxation of church property, 185–186, 196
Green, Steven K., 107, 159

H
Hale, David, 97
Hale, Edward Everett, 189, 194
Harris, William Torrey, 169–173
Hecker, Isaac, 163
Heighton, William, 43–44, 53
Henry, Alexander, 12, 79, 87
Henry, Patrick, 22
Herndon, William, 136–137
Holyoake, George Jacob, 173
Houston, Sam, 103
Hovey, Alvah, 195

I

Index, 126–131, 136, 143, 193, 201–202, 227, 246
Ingersoll, Robert Green, 127, 212, 234
  and Comstock laws, 201
  popularity of, 2, 128, 202, 212
Inquisition, 24, 52, 85, 232, 250
International Sabbath Association, 211
Islam, 105, 218

J

Jackson, Andrew, 38, 48, 53, 110
Jefferson, Thomas, 2, 46
  debates over piety, 134–136
  and Virginia disestablishment, 19–20, 28
  Wall of Separation metaphor, 136
Jews and Jewish perspective, 82, 154, 250
  on Bible-reading in schools, 7, 8, 153–155, 164–165
  and church taxation, 65
  on Sabbath laws, 48, 76–77, 82, 218–220
Johnson, Richard M.
  attacks on, 53, 55, 74
  and Cherokee removal, 57
  legacy of, 56, 145
  reports on Sunday mails, 53–58, 136, 212
Jones, Alonzo T., 214, 218

K

Kansas-Nebraska Act, 5, 98, 99, 103–104, 109
Knights of Labor, 221–222, 224
Know-Nothing Party, 83, 209
Ku Klux Klan, 114
Kulturkampf, 166

L

Labor movement
  attitude to clergy, 5, 183
  petition campaigns, 207, 221
  and Sabbath laws, 43, 87–88, 208, 219–225
Lawrence, Joshua, 68
Leeser, Isaac, 77
Leland, John, 42
Liberal protestantism, 5, 8, 188, 218
Liberal Union Club, 201
Lilienthal, Max, 154
Lincoln, Abraham
  and Christian amendment, 124
  debate over piety, 136–138

M

Madison, James
  and first amendment, 28
  memorial against religious assessments, 11, 19, 22–25, 26–28, 29, 33, 45
  views on religious liberty, 21–23, 29–30
Maine Law, 71–72, 248
  opposition to, 72, 81
Mann, Horace, 152, 160, 162, 170
Masculinity
  and political preaching, 97–100, 106, 114
Mason, George, 22, 25, 104
Massachusetts, 42, 72, 83, 128, 166–167, 211, 231
  and Church taxation, 184, 185, 187–189, 190, 196–197, 200
  and common schools, 152, 167
  disestablishment in, 23, 28, 34, 64
  and Sunday laws, 50, 212
Mathews, Stanley, 164
Mayo, Amory D., 174
McAllister, David, 13–14

Methodist Church, 3, 33, 79, 113, 181, 195, 212, 215
Mexican-American War, 95
Mormons, 3, 9, 182, 195, 245
mortmain, 182, 196
Mott, Lucretia, 77, 229

N
National American Woman Suffrage Association (NAWSA), 230
National Council of Churches, 250
National Education League, 161
National exceptionalism
 and evangelicals, 37, 164, 212
 and historical writing, 3
 and secularists, 23, 131, 162, 244
National Liberal League (NLL), 127, 185
 and Christian amendment, 123
 divisions within, 200–202
 emergence of, 227
 leadership of, 127
National Reform Association (NRA), 124–127, 130, 131, 134, 137, 140, 141, 144, 211–212, 234
National Religious Liberty Association (NLRA), 207
Native Americans, 40, 56, 171, 172, 208
Nativism, 7–9, 83, 106, 209
 and separation of church and state, 83
New York (city), 135, 137, 139, 141, 143, 156, 158, 159, 220
 anti-Sabbatarianism, 38, 49–51
 church edifices, 191, 192
 debate over political preaching, 96–97
 freethinkers, 43
 school fund, 152, 156
 taxation of church property, 186

New York (state), 35, 36, 38, 40, 43, 44, 49, 64, 72, 168, 182–184, 187, 201, 227, 242, 246, 249
Norton, Charles Eliot, 140

O
Occident and American Jewish Advocate, 77
Ohio, 34, 65, 77, 124, 128, 151, 158, 160, 162, 164–166, 183–185, 188, 197, 219, 246, 250. *See also* Cincinnati
 anti-Sabbatarianism, 39, 41, 46, 52

P
Paine, Thomas, 129, 134, 137
Palfrey, John Gorham, 231–232
Paris Commune, 144, 191
Parker, Theodore, 75, 77–78
Patton, Reverend William Weston, 153, 169
Pennsylvania, 27, 30, 39, 41, 45, 46–47, 52, 64, 69, 70, 73, 76, 83, 101, 125, 169, 172, 185, 218, 223, 242, 246, 249
Petitions and Petition campaigns
 against Kansas-Nebraska Act, 103–104
 in colonial era, 9, 11, 21–22, 24–27
 and Comstock laws, 202
 evolution of, 9–11, 22–23
 format of, 9–10
 and fraud, 51, 53, 219
 and legislative chaplains, 11, 64–66, 66–68, 130
 organization of, 9–10, 65, 69–70
 and prohibition laws, 72, 210–211
 and public opinion, 23, 48–50, 66, 155

and religious instruction, 126,
  152–153, 163
and religious tax in Virginia, 1785,
  11
role of women in, 39–40, 40, 53,
  66, 211, 225, 247
and Sabbath laws, 1, 13, 34–53, 65,
  68–69, 75, 77–78, 79, 82, 211,
  212, 214–221
and taxation of church property,
  185
Pettit, John, 64
  attacks on legislative chaplains,
    64–65, 68
Philadelphia, 35, 38, 42–43, 44, 48,
  50, 74, 125, 126, 139, 213, 229
  Bible wars, 157, 160
  immigration, 83
  nativism, 83, 85
  streetcars, 12, 78–79, 83, 86–88,
    125, 230
  Sunday mail, 38–39, 42, 43, 48,
    211
Political preaching
  after Civil War, 111–115
  and anti-Catholicism, 26, 105–106
  attacks on, 97–101
  defense of, 103, 110, 115
  during Civil War, 107
  and Puritan legacy, 107–109
  and separation of church and state,
    100, 102–103
  southern hostility to, 5, 12
Potter, William J., 98, 100, 126–127
Powderly, Terence V., 223, 224
Presbyterians, 20, 26, 35, 44, 49, 51,
  71, 73, 79, 83, 127, 136, 138,
  143, 181, 192–193, 195, 219,
  221–223, 227
Primitive Baptists
  campaign against chaplains, 11,
    66–67, 68–70

doctrine, 67
opposition to temperance laws, 72
and Sunday mails, 68–69
Prohibition, 9, 71–72, 210–211, 234,
  248–249
Puritans
  commemoration of, 107–108, 167
  defense of, 110, 168, 231–232
  hostility to, 9, 110–111, 167, 209,
    231–232, 244

Q
Quakers, 22, 26, 27, 81–82, 169, 229

R
Reconstruction, 113–114, 160
Religion
  and class, 5, 43–44, 85–88, 192,
    201–202, 209, 220–221, 224,
    227, 234, 245
  true versus false, 7–9, 45, 67, 75,
    105–107, 188–189, 192, 231,
    245
Religious establishment, 3, 13, 65,
  187–188, 243
  in colonial era, 47, 48
  informal, 7, 42, 57
  understandings of, 46
Religious Freedom Amendment, 21,
  28
Republican Party, 111, 114, 158, 160
Ruggles, Samuel G., 81

S
Sabbatarianism
  after Civil War, 207–234
  arguments in favour, 35, 45, 47, 49,
    78, 82, 86
  before Civil War, 63–88

and Church/State controversy, 34, 47–48, 48, 83, 85
and Continental Sabbath, 37
and democracy, 40, 48, 71, 81
and national exceptionalism, 37
theological debate, 36, 47, 76
and workers' rights, 36, 44, 85–88
Sabbath Recorder, 76
Schaff, Dr Philip, 64, 122
Scopes trial, 249
Scudder, Reverend Henry Martyn, 152, 156–157
Seaver, Horace, 126, 153
Second Great Awakening, 3, 4, 67, 227
secularism
    and anti-Catholicism, 6, 8–9, 52, 82–85, 106, 158, 159, 169, 194–197
    and anti-Mormonism, 9, 182, 194–197
    and civil liberty, 22–24, 26, 29, 45, 68, 108, 168
    definition of, 1–2, 3–5
    and education, 7, 12, 152–175
    and race, 4, 56–57, 171, 243, 244, 246
    and religious liberty, 6, 21–23, 26–30, 50, 53, 56, 68, 76, 82, 107–108
    and Sabbath laws, 1–2, 13, 33–57, 72–88, 99–100, 125–126, 172–174, 201, 244
    scholarship on, 2–6, 11–14, 158, 245–246
    and taxation of church property, 12–13, 181–202
    and true religion, 5, 7–9, 23, 29, 33, 35, 44–45, 67–68, 81, 87, 114, 136, 192, 194, 245
Sehat, David, 3, 57
Separate Baptists, 20

Seventh-Day Adventists, 2, 36, 207, 214, 218
Seventh-Day Baptists, 36, 76, 86
Signs of the Times, 68
Smith, Gerrit, 99–100
Smouse, Charles W., 1–2, 3, 7
Social Gospel movement, 209, 223, 224, 244
Southern states, 41, 74, 109, 110
    and political preaching, 4–5, 12, 109–110
    understanding of true religion, 114, 245
    violence in, 113
    white supremacism in, 5, 56, 245, 248
Spear, Samuel Thayer, 169, 173
Spiritualism, 8, 128–129, 130, 247
Stanton, Elizabeth Cady, 227–230, 246
Stevenson, Thomas.P., 125, 212
Story, Joseph, 2–3
Stowe, Calvin E., 160, 162
Streetcars
    development of, 78–81
    and Sabbath laws, 12, 79–81, 85–88, 125
Strong, Josiah, 2
Strong, William, 125
Sunday mails, 4, 33–58
    campaigns against, 11
    campaigns for, 11, 48–53, 68–70, 76, 104, 128
    popularity of, 38, 241–242
    reports on, 53–58, 74
    restriction on, 233
    survey of, 241–242
Sunday travel, 12, 71, 73, 78–82, 85, 125
Supreme Court, 125, 199, 218
    and religion in schools, 249–250
    and wall of separation, 135

T

Tammany Hall, 38, 50, 55
Tappan, Arthur, 35, 41, 51, 97
Tappan, Lewis, 35, 51
Taxation (exemptions), 183–187
Taxation of Church property
   and anti-Catholicism, 182, 194–197
   and anti-Mormonism, 182, 194–197
   arguments against, 191–192, 199
   arguments for, 185–187
   in California, 183, 199–200
   in District of Columbia, 197–199
   in Old World, 183
   response to religious wealth, 184
   state constitutions, 182–183, 198
Temperance movement, 3, 11, 71–72, 83, 210, 225. *See also* American Temperance Society
Thompson, Joseph P., 165
Tocqueville, Alexis de, 37–38, 102, 112
Traynor, William J.H., 209
Treaty of Tripoli, 137
Trinity Church (Manhattan), 193–194
Truth Seeker, 200, 202

U

Unitarians, 81, 98, 126, 143, 174, 218
Universalism, 44, 56

V

Vinet, Alexandre, 95
Virginia, 69–70, 104
   colonial establishment in, 42, 188
   disestablishment in, 19–30, 34
   petitions against religious tax, 11, 21, 26–28
   Sabbath law controversies, 38, 48, 76

W

Wall of Separation, 136
Washburne, Hempstead, 219
Washburne, Marion Foster, 231
Washington, George
   debates over piety, 131–138
   and religious tax in Virginia, 21, 25
Washington, Henry A., 135–136
Weems, Mason, 132
Wells, David A., 183
Westcott, Thompson, 79, 82, 85
Whig Party, 67, 96, 100
White, Ellen G., 214
Willard, Frances E., 225–226
Williams, Roger
   commemoration of, 167–168, 232
   life and career, 167
Wise, Isaac Mayer, 154
Women
   and anti-amendment movement, 130–131
   and Bible wars, 155
   and petitioning, 39–40, 43, 50, 66, 210
   and religion, 105–106, 111, 131, 228–229
   and Sabbath laws, 50, 66, 225–227
   and secularism, 226–229
Women's Christian Temperance Union (WCTU), 210, 225
   and Sabbath observance, 226, 230
Workingmen's Party, 199
World War I, 248
World's Columbian Exposition (Chicago, 1893)
   arguments and petitions against Sunday-opening, 209, 212–214, 218, 226, 233
   arguments and petitions in favor of Sunday-opening, 207, 222–234
   and class, 208, 220–225

debate within women's suffrage movement, 227–230
and national exceptionalism, 209, 214
legacy of Puritans, 209, 231–232
and religion, 208–209, 215, 221, 224

Wright, Elizur, 77, 201
Wright, Frances, 43, 229
Wright Henry C., 77–78